AF652377

Principles of War

Principles of War

Cpt. Prem Singh

Prashant Publishing House
DELHI - 110094 (INDIA)

PRASHANT PUBLISHING HOUSE
C-34, 28 Foota Road, Gali No. 3
West Karawal Nagar, Delhi-110094
Phone : 9810396373, 22963970

Principles of War

© *Publisher*

First Published : 2008

ISBN : 978-81-906344-2-7

[All rights reserved. No part of this publication may be reproduced, stored in a retrieval system or transmitted, in any form or by any means, mechanical, photocopying, recording or otherwise, without prior written permission of the publisher]

PRINTED IN INDIA

Published by Mr. R. K. Jha M/s. Prashant Publishing House, Delhi and Printed at H.S. Offset Press, Delhi.

Preface

Military history today has a much wider scope than previous generations of scholars granted it. More than simply the story of armed conflict, of campaigns and battles, it is the story of how societies form their institutions for their collective security and how those institutions operate in peace and war. It is the story of soldiers and the subculture of which they are a part. It includes the entire range of economic, social, legal, political, technological, and cultural issues that arise from the state's need to organize violence to preserve its existence and accomplish its national goals. Military history cannot be viewed as a separate, quaint, subset of the wider history of a society. It is an integral part of a society; and the essence of a military, the armed citizen, is a reflection of that society.

The present book tries to explore all these topics and problems in an easy and comprehensive manner, undersigned is confident enough that readers will enjoy and grasp the matter of the text. Your valuable suggestions are welcome.

—*Editor*

CONTENTS

1

INTRODUCTION

Since ancient times, military theory tried to define the principles of war, a set of guidelines, both for war strategy and for battle tactics. They are also a useful tool for us in studying and analyzing past wars.

There are somewhat different versions of the principles of war, changing in time and from country to country, and between various theoreticians, but generally speaking, there is little practical difference between the version of Sun Tzu, who lived about 2500 years ago, and the most updated official version of the US Army.

This leads to the further definition of those principles as the timeless principles of war. It's amazing that the principles which were so true in the age of the sword and arrow are still so true in the age of computerized guided weapons.

In a more generalized interpretation, these principles are also true for prewar military force buildup, and even for civilian business and project management.

CONCENTRATION OF EFFORT

"Concentrate your forces and their fire" probably the most important principle. What decides the outcome of wars and battles is usually not the amount of forces you have, but the amount of forces you have where it counts, where the battle is decided.

The commander should concentrate his forces, and their fire, and by doing so achieve a decisive local superiority, that will overwhelm the enemy there, break the balance, and allow a breakthrough to victory. The whole idea of the German Blitzkrieg tactic was to concentrate massive armored forces, and massive close air support, to create an unstoppable rapidly moving "armor fist" that could smash through anything and cause havoc and chaos in the enemy's side, regardless of the enemy's total force.

The naval equivalent of this principle is simply "Don't divide the fleet", which is true both in attack, as was so destructively demonstrated by the German "wolf pack" submarine warfare tactic, and by the convoys tactic which negated it.

Modern air war is where this principle is most evident. When they penetrate enemy airspace to attack, scattered aircraft are easy prey to defenders. But when an entire Air Force takes off and charges as one coordinated force, it's usually an unstoppable overwhelming force.

OBJECTIVE

"Stick to the mission, persist". Military action should have a clearly defined and achievable objective, and all efforts should always be directed to achieving that objective, even despite difficulties and diversions caused by the enemy or other reasons.

A classic example of the devastating results of ignoring this principle is the Battle of Britain. The German Luftwaffe was getting close to achieving its objective of eliminating the British fighter force. An achievement that was essential for making an invasion of England possible. But then, in an emotional response to a bombardment of a German city, Adolf Hitler ordered the Luftwaffe to shift its effort to bombing London.

The result was that the British fighter command was able to recover its strength, win the Battle of Britain, expel the Luftwaffe, and secure Britain as the remaining base of the western front.

FLEXIBILITY

"Use your brain, adapt". War and battle are complex, varying, and uncertain environments. That's why battles are so rarely fought as planned. That's why commanders of all ranks should constantly judge the situation and be flexible enough to find the best way to achieve the objective in the changing circumstances. Rigidly following orders, plans, or a doctrine in battle is often fatal. The fact that until the end of the war the Japanese Navy refused to adopt the convoy tactic to adapt to the threat of American submarines cost them their entire merchant fleet, a loss which resulted in severe shortage in most war materials. The British Navy and Air Force adapted to the German submarine threat with increasing efficiency, survived and even defeated it.

INITIATIVE

"Be active, always". In battle, sitting still, or even just being predictable, often leaves control of events to the enemy, which simply means that your side is much more likely to lose the battle.

This is true not just for the attacking side. In the battle of Kursk, the defending Russian side was almost hyperactive in constantly intensifying and enhancing their defensive fortifications and readiness for the expected German attack. That's why they won the battle as the German side crashed when it finally attacked.

ATTACK

You simply can't win a war without eventually attacking. That's why armies mark it as a principle. It's simply a derivative of the initiative principle. The German army which attacked Stalingrad was weakened by the horrible bloodshed in Stalingrad, but a large scale flanking attack was required to exploit that. The Russian attack completely encircled the Germans and their allies, resulted in the greatest single defeat in the history of the German military.

MANEUVER

Since wisely moving your forces before and during battle is the most common way to take the initiative, it's also marked as a principle. Maneuver is usually the way to produce local superiority which is often a key for victory.

The British victory in the Battle of Britain owes a lot to the Royal Air Force's ability to outmaneuver the Luftwaffe (in operational terms, not in dogfight terms) thanks to its effective use of the new RADAR technology.

The British use of RADAR gave them the ability to engage the German formations almost every time they came, and in much greater numbers (concentration of effort) than was possible without RADAR. This technological force multiplier greatly improved their success rate in each engagement, as if they had a much larger Air Force.

ECONOMY

"Don't be wasteful, use your forces efficiently" Make the best effort, not the maximum effort. There's a big difference. In the Russian front, the Russians, and later the Germans, suffered huge unnecessary losses simply by throwing every available unit directly at the enemy or by not allowing it to retreat, with total disregard to whether this is the right way to use these forces. The lack of economy of force is almost a trademark of totalitarian regimes.

SURPRISE AND DECEPTION

The idea is to use secrecy, speed, and deception, to achieve the objective in a way that the enemy will be unable to efficiently resist. A dramatic example is the allied invasion of France in 1944. It was obvious to allied commanders that despite all their efforts and air power, a swift and massive German armored counter attack could smash their beachhead and throw them back to the sea.

To prevent that, a tremendous dual effort of secrecy on one hand and active deception on the other hand, succeeded in misleading the Germans about where and when they where going to attack.

The deception effort was so convincing that even after the invasion began, when the Germans obviously knew both the Where and When, they kept their main armor reserves away from the beachhead because they were still convinced that the invasion in Normandy is just a diversion attack to the main invasion which they expected in Calais. When they realized they were wrong it was much too late.

SECURITY AND RESERVE

A complementary principle to the concentration of effort principle. Don't leave unprotected sectors, and also keep a reserve force to block a breach by the enemy, or to add it to the main attack at the right time and place to achieve a breakthrough. Don't really concentrate everything in one point, because if the enemy will act elsewhere, you're in trouble.

In the battle of Kursk, although the Russians built several lines of defense, one behind the other, the spearhead of the German Panzer attack was still able to break through all of them, but then, after they passed all those lines, the remaining German tanks were engaged by the Russian reserve, a large force of T34 tanks which engaged them near the small village Prokhorovka and broke the German attack before it could do further damage behind the Russian lines.

In 1944, the Germans had a powerful armored strategic reserve in France. It was obvious that its job is to engage The Allies wherever they will invade and that it was capable of crushing the invasion force before it could be reinforced. A huge allied campaign of deception was performed mainly in order to mislead the Germans about where the invasion will take place. It's main purpose was to ensure that this strategic reserve will not be in Normandy and will not be sent to Normandy to stop the invasion. The deception succeeded, and so was the invasion of Normandy.

The French military in 1940 totally neglected to secure the West flank of France's northern border. In contradiction to their border with Germany which was very heavily fortified, the West flank, in the Ardennes, was very poorly defended by light infantry forces. It was so because the French Generals believed it was impassable (they also believed war was not likely..).

They never tested that belief, but others did, including the famous military author B.H LiddellHart, who personally tested the Ardennes with his bicycles years before the war. The inevitable result was that in May 1940 the German armor force rushed deep into France through this unsecured section of the border and nothing was there to stop it. German victory in France was very quick and very decisive.

COOPERATION

Different forces, especially from the different military branches, should cooperate and coordinate their efforts.

Other examples of good cooperation are when the artillery and air support attack where the ground forces need them to attack, the tanks and infantry protect each other, different ground forces coordinate their attacks, the intelligence provides the needed information when it's needed, fighter escorts and Navy warships are there where and when they're needed, and all forces are properly supplied.

Examples of bad cooperation are when forces are hit by their own air support, artillery fires at empty fields, the infantry is overrun by tanks, the tanks are ambushed by infantry in the woods or in urban areas, encirclement attempts fail, there's plenty of intelligence that doesn't help at all, fighter escorts and warship escorts are so far away when they're urgently needed, the tanks run out of fuel, and supplies are airdropped right to the hands of the enemy.

The German Blitzkrieg tactic was so successful because it for the first time closely coordinated the efforts of the advancing tanks with the crushing potential of close support aircraft which were assigned to help them.

The tactic was simple. The tanks should continue to advance rapidly, in order to keep their momentum and strength in the enemy territory in order to inflict maximum damage.. To achieve that they bypassed strong enemy positions where ever they could. Where they could not bypass the enemy, instead of stopping their advance to engage the enemy, they called for massive air support which rapidly removed the obstacle from the tanks' way. This allowed the Panzers to use their own firepower mainly for destroying light enemy units and Inflict maximum damage, instead of engaging strong enemy points. The result of this cooperation was shocking to the enemy.

UNITY OF COMMAND

A modern version of the cooperation principle. The idea is that to ensure optimal cooperation between the many commanders of all the various units and branches, which naturally have different views of the situation, different tactics and doctrines, and sometimes unrelated or even contradicting orders, is to bring all the units in the area of operations into one chain of command, so that all commanders receive their orders from one source, a supreme commander. This obviously results in better cooperation between the units under his command.

A negative example of the lack of unity of command can be found in the Japanese High Command, where the Japanese army and Navy almost fought two different wars. The army remained focused in its war in China while the Navy was focused in Pacific operations.

The result was of course damaging, and so when US Marines occupied islands closer and closer to Japan, millions of Japanese army soldiers were practically stuck in China, unable to save their own country from invasion.

A positive example of unity of command is when Admiral Max Horton, a former submarine captain and commander of the British submarine force, took command of the battle against the German submarines in the North atlantic. Horton demanded and received command authority over all the naval and air units which were involved in antisubmarine warfare, and this allowed him to significantly improve their combined effort, achieve much better results than before, and defeat the Uboats.

CHASE

"Don't stop, exploit success"a victory in one battle can sometimes save other battles or even win the war if right after the battle is won, your forces continue to push forward, chase and decimate the retreating enemy forces, instead of giving them time to recover and build a second line of defence.

Dunkirk is perhaps the best example of the result of failing to exploit success by chase. At the peak of their successful Blitzkrieg advance into northern France in mid 1940, the

German tanks were stopped, because General von Rundstedt still doubted their potential and tactics and insisted that they should wait for the infantry to catch up with them. The British army in France, as well as French forces, had no chance of survival against the German forces there at that time.

To save them, an immediate naval operation was made to rapidly evacuate them across the British Channel. 338,226 British and French soldiers were successfully evacuated. If the Germans continued their assault without stopping, those 338,226 men, the majority of the British army and a large French force, would have been destroyed or forced to surrender, and the war would have developed very differently.

SIMPLICITY

"Keep it simple". Since battle is so complex and unpredictable, complex plans almost always fail. To succeed, a battle plan must be simple. Simple to understand, simple to execute, and simple to adapt to changes.

The most famous example of a battle plan which failed to achieve its objective because it required too much in order to succeed, even became a language term. "A bridge too far" is now a common language term for "too much", named after the movie about British operation "Market Garden" in September 1944. Operation Market Garden was a daring attempt to advance a long way, across several successive guarded river bridges in one strike, right into Germany. One bridge was not captured and so the heroic attempt failed to achieve its objective.

The principle of simplicity is also true for the design of weapon systems. While German tanks were sensitive to technical failures, needed a lot of maintenance, and were complex to produce, Russian and American tanks were massproduced and were able to fight a long time with minimal field maintenance.

LOGISTICS

During all of history, it was too common that proud and aggressive military leaders were too focused with their grand battle plans and with the mission and fighting, that they neglected the plain basic needs of their combat forces, and their unheroic but essential auxiliary units.

Typical results were that brave soldiers could not fight effectively because their military failed to properly provide them with (pick your favorite) water, food, fuel, ammunition, medical supplies, proper clothing, proper transportation, technical maintenance, spare parts, communication, proper intelligence gathering, proper intelligence distribution, digging equipment, worthy weapons that kill the target when aimed and fired properly, and the list goes on and on...

Neglecting to provide those brave soldiers with those essential needs is mostly stupid, sometimes even criminal, and many times it meant that the proud leader lost the war and his brave soldiers died, many of them not even by enemy fire, and it could all be prevented if they just did not so stupidly neglect a few basic needs.

The fact that the German army that invaded Russia in the summer of 1941 was so unequipped for the Russian winter, eight full years after Hitler became the dictator of Germany (with a firm intention to invade Russia), and over a century after Napoleon's grand army was decimated by the same Russian winter, was a criminal neglect. It cost the lives of so many thousands of dedicated German soldiers who died because they lacked all types of winterready equipment.

They lacked not just winter clothing, but a large variety of types of equipment that they needed in order for them and their weapons and vehicles to continue to function in winter as they did in the summer. The only reason they lacked that was the neglect and overconfidence of Adolf Hitler and his top military planners. It cost them the entire war.

MORALE

The psychological factor. The largest army, the best weapons, and the brightest Generals, are not enough if the soldiers don't believe in what they do, or in their ability to achieve the objective, so much that instead of fighting bravely and decisively they just want to get back to safety as soon as possible anyway possible. Low morale doesn't always means losing the war, but it's a major factor. To ensure high morale, the war objective, or even battle objective, should be perceived a reasonable, achievable, one that the soldiers will identify with, or at least accept.

The series of great successes of Japan's assault in South East Asia between December 1941 and February 1942 eroded the morale of British defenders in the strategically important Singapore to such a level that when they were eventually attacked, they quickly surrendered. General Yamashita who captured Singapore said after the war that his attack was a bluff, a bluff which succeeded. His force was very low on water, ammunition, and fuel, and the Japanese estimated that if the defenders held for one more week, and they could, the Japanese attack would have failed.

A lack of morale in a larger scale was seen in the French military and political leadership in 1940. The German attack was a great victory not just because of the Blitzkrieg tactic and the quality of the German military which was then at its best, but also because of the paralysis and inactivity of the French Generals.

They thought there will be no war in their time, they didn't think that kind of modern war was possible, they were not prepared for any scenario other than the one they expected, and therefore they were totally shocked when it came to them at such force. A classic example of being mentally unprepared for war.

SUMMARY

Some of the principles of war overlap. Some of them seem to contradict each other. That's because in different situations some principles are more suitable than others. As Sun Tzu said, the wise commander will adapt the principles to the specific situation. If we try to group those principles into a shorter generic list, this is what we get :

- Concentration concentrate your effort, decisively and efficiently.
- Activity prepare well, take the initiative, surprise and deceive the enemy, secure your positions, move, attack.

- Simplicity clear and simple objective, battle plan, and commands. One good commander in chief.

Sea and Air warfare

While in land warfare occupation of land, or specific places, is often more important than the killing of enemy forces, the unique nature of the mediums of sea and air makes killing targets the essence of fighting in those mediums. There are other missions, but essentially, war at sea is mainly sinking enemy ships while protecting yours. And air war is mainly destroying enemy planes and attacking specific ground and sea targets. Advanced technology and professionalism were also always much more crucial in sea and air warfare than in land warfare. Here are some subprinciples for air war, which are an adaptation of the general principles of war to the specific features of air war:

Air Superiority

"Air superiority is the ultimate expression of military power." Winston Churchill.

"Air superiority is a condition for all operations, at sea, in land, and in the air."

—Air Marshal Arthur Tedder.

In order to fully use its war potential, and to deny it from the enemy Air Force, the Air Force should first focus on winning its own war against the enemy Air Force, so that it would then be able to fly quite freely over the theater of operations, and massively attack the targets below.

Killing Targets

"Anyone who fights, even with the most modern weapons, against an enemy who dominates the air, is like a primitive warrior who stands against modern forces, with the same limitations and the same chance of success." —Field Marshal Erwin Rommel

The Air Force should focus on its ability to rapidly destroy many targets of various types. That's what gives it its decisive strength.

Prioritization, Operational Strategic Warfare

For optimal results, the Air Force should prioritize its target list. More decisive results are usually achieved by attacking strategic and operational targets, rather than tactical targets.

Example: to support the ground forces in stopping an enemy armor attack, attacking the enemy ammunition and fuel convoys that supply the tanks is better than attacking the tanks themselves in the battlefield.

Destroying bridges to slow down their advancement to the battlefield is even better, and destroying the enemy's national fuel sources or depots, or the tank industry (in case of a long war), is even better.

2

AMERICAN MILITARY HISTORY

The history of the United States Army lies firmly in the mainstream of modern Western military development. Heir to European traditions, the American Army has both borrowed from and contributed to that main current. Molded by the New World environment, a product of democratic and industrial revolutions, it has at the same time evolved, along with the nation it serves, uniquely. To the present generation of Americans faced by continuing challenges to their national security, the role that force and military institutions have played in American history becomes of increasing interest and importance. This volume is an introduction to the story of the U.S. Army and the American military history of which the Army's story is an integral part.

MILITARY HISTORY

Military history today has a much wider scope than previous generations of scholars granted it. More than simply the story of armed conflict, of campaigns and battles, it is the story of how societies form their institutions for their collective security and how those institutions operate in peace and war. It is the story of soldiers and the subculture of which they are a part. It includes the entire range of economic, social, legal, political, technological, and cultural issues that arise from the state's need to organize violence to preserve its existence and accomplish its national goals. Military history cannot be viewed as a separate, quaint, subset of the wider history of a society. It is an integral part of a society; and the essence of a military, the armed citizen, is a reflection of that society.

War is only one aspect of military history, though it remains the critical test for any military establishment and thus an essential aspect. The changes in warfare over time are thus a legitimate focus for the student of military history. The American Army has been both a recipient of and a contributor to the fruits of the changes in warfare pioneered by the Western world. The United States was born in the eighteenth century, during the great age of European dynastic wars involving, generally, armies of professional, uniformed soldiers whose maneuvers and battles left the civilian masses of a nationstate largely unaffected. Until the latter part of that century, wars were relatively simple and restricted in area, forces, and objectives. This changed with the advent of the "nation in arms" during the French Revolution and Napoleonic Wars. Warfare became conflicts of mass armies of conscripts, motivated by revolutionary ideology.

With the spread of the industrial revolution in the following century, warfare grew even more complex and exerted an everincreasing influence on more elements of society. This new era in warfare coincided with the evolution of the United States as an independent nation. In the first half of the twentieth century the effects of largescale wars became so pervasive that they were felt not only by the combatant nations but throughout the entire world, now seemingly grown more compact due to the advent of faster transportation and communications means. The outcome in those wars was no longer measured in terms of the preservation of national honor or the conquest of territory, familiar in eighteenth century warfare, but in terms of national survival. Thus, as warfare in the past two centuries broadened to involve more and more people and more and more of the energies and resources of society to fight itor during the Cold War, to deter itthe definition was extended to encompass more activities.

Broadly defined, military history lies on the frontier between general history and military art and science. It deals with the confluence and interaction of military affairs with diplomatic, political, social, economic, and intellectual trends in society. To understand it therefore requires some knowledge of both general history and military art. In its American context it represents many interrelated facets. Certainly it involves warsall kinds of wars. It may surprise Americans, who traditionally have regarded themselves as a peaceable and unmilitary people, to learn that the range of warfare in their national experience has been quite wide, and the incidence quite frequent.

Born in a revolution, a violent struggle often considered a prelude to modern ideological struggles, the United States has since endured a bitter Civil War, participated in numerous international wars, and has recently been thrust into a global war on terrorism. In American national experience, war itself has undergone considerable change and oscillation from one mode to another. The American Revolution was a limited war of the eighteenth century variety, although one fought on the backdrop of a "people's war" between Tories and Patriots over the loyalty of each small village and town.

The War of 1812, the Korean conflict of 19501953, and the Gulf War in 1991 were later models of limited conflict fought for specific, limited objectives short of the total destruction and occupation of the foes' homelands. The American Civil War introduced the age of total war to which World Wars I and II added their bloody chapters. The Cold War involved mobilizing and militarizing huge segments of society never before affected by warfare.

The current war on terrorism, with its potential for direct attacks on the American homeland and the pervasive (and invasive) security requirements for defending against such attacks, affects all aspects of American society. Over the centuries, war has cut deeper and deeper into the life of the nation.

Broadly defined, military history lies on the frontier between general history and military art and science.

After World War II, under the shadow of nuclear weapons that threaten all civilization with annihilation, warfare returned to earlier forms. Guerrilla wars, foreshadowed in American experience by the longcontinuing Indian Wars and the Philippine Insurrection of 18991902, returned as American forces became engaged in counterinsurgency warfare during the Vietnam War (19641973) and in support to various Central American nations, notably El Salvador, in the 1980s.

Today, modern conflicts include operations that could be classified as "small wars" such as Operation JUST CAUSE in Panama in 1989 and humanitarian and peacekeeping operations in Haiti, Somalia, and the former Yugoslavia. The line between war and peace, already blurred by nationbuilding operations and "police actions," grew even more difficult to discern as the twentieth century drew to a close with the U.S. Army involved in dozens of smallscale operations around the world. The direct attack on America on September 11, 2001, featuring the use of terrorism to kill over 3,000 Americans at the World Trade Center towers and the Pentagon, further changed the equation in ways still not fully known.

Wars used to be regarded as clearly definable exercises in violence when diplomacy failed and statesmen handed over to soldiers the burden of achieving victory. They were usually marked by formal ceremonies: a declaration at the beginning and a surrender and peace treaty at the end. Since World War II these formalities are no longer the fashion. War and peace have become blurred. Neither in Korea nor in Vietnam was war officially declared. The debate in Congress before the initiation of hostilities in the Gulf War led only to a congressional resolution of support, not a declaration of war.

Endings of military operations also are not clearly marked. No peace treaty followed the surrender of Germany in World War II or the truce in Korea in 1953. The Vietnam War ended with a treaty, but one the North Vietnamese promptly violated. Despite a decisive tactical victory for the United States, the confused political and diplomatic situation after the Gulf War continued to simmer, with United Nations resolutions and arms inspection programs in shambles and economic embargoes rapidly disappearing. The renewal of the war with Iraq in March 2003 resolved many of the problems of a stilldangerous regime at the cost of creating a host of others. While changes in the nature of warfare have affected the conduct of war and the role of the military and society in it, participation in organized violence in all its forms is still a vital component of military history that must be studied. Not only must the causes, conduct, and consequences of a war be analyzed, but as the line between war and peace becomes more indistinct, the periods between the wars require renewed interest from students of military history.

Besides war in the broad sense, there is another major facet that military history must address and that military historians of this generation have found more and more integral to their subject. That is the study of the military as an institution and a manifestation of state power. The way in which a state organizes for violence and the multifaceted effects of that effort are critical to understanding war and its impact on the society of which the military is often but a reflection. To apply force, societies organize armies. Reflecting the national culture and varying in their impact on it, armies are institutions, social entities in themselves. Some armies have close relations with the societies from which they are drawn; others are a class apart. For example, during much of U.S. history the Army was scattered in frontier posts and physically isolated from the rest of society. But in the period since World War II, civilmilitary relations have been close.

As institutions, armies take form and character. Their institutional outlines are manifested in a number of ways, some overt, some subtle: organization and administration, system of training, mode of supply, planning for mobilization and the conduct of war, methods of fighting on the battlefield, weaponry and utilization of technology, system of command and control, selection of manpower and leaders, and relations with the civilian population and authorities. The whole host of policies, doctrines, customs, traditions, values, and practices that have grown up about armies is an important part of the institutional story. The impact of the selective service system (the draft) on many aspects of American life in this century is in itself a significant story. Its ending, for all intents and purposes, in 1973 and the creation of the all volunteer Army has equal and farreaching significance. Many elements of that significance are still not yet fully revealed.

> *Wars used to be regarded as clearly definable exercises in violence when diplomacy failed and statesmen handed over to soldiers the burden of achieving victory.*

All the facets of change in the military as an institution thus represent histories in themselves and reflect other changes in the nature of warfare, technology, and a country's internal development and external responsibilities. A shift in one component will inevitably have an impact on the institutional structure. For example, a fundamental change in weaponry, equipment, or technology, be it the adoption of gunpowder, the rifled musket, the airplane, the tank, the atomic bomb, nightvision devices, or precisionguided munitions, will inevitably affect the traditional modes of fighting and reverberate throughout the institutional framework. The phenomenon of cultural lag evident in other human institutions also applies to military organizations, and some armies have been slower to adopt changes than others, often with fatal results in the test of battle.

While the U.S. Army as a social entity has evolved to meet its primary mission to fightin its American institutional context military history must also treat the Army as a social force in peace. From the beginning the Army has played a role in developing the country: in exploring, guarding the frontier, and constructing roads; in engineering, transportation, communication, sanitation, and medicine; and in flood control. At the same time the Army has served as a vehicle for social mobility of certain disadvantaged groups, for example, European immigrants in the nineteenth century, African Americans in the 1950s and 1960s, and Hispanic Americans today.

The mixture of the European legacy, native environment, democratic ideals and values, and national experience in war and peace have combined to mold the Army into a distinct institution in American life, a unique blend of professional and civilian elements. Indeed, as Russell F. Weigley, a student of the Army's institutional history, has well expressed it, the story of the American Army is really a history of "two armies": "a Regular Army of professional soldiers and a citizen army of various components variously known as militia, National Guards, Organized Reserves, selectees."

THE ARMY SEAL

The Army Seal was used originally during the American Revolution to authenticate documents. It displayed the designation "War Office," which was synonymous with Headquarters of the Army, and the Roman date MDCCLXXVIII (1778) the first time it was used. It remained unchanged until 1974, when the War Office banner was replaced with "Department of the Army" and the date was changed to 1775, the year in which the Army was established. The seal embodies the Army's ideals of loyalty, vigilance, perseverance, truth, courage, zeal, fortitude, remembrance, determination, constancy, achievement, dignity, and honor.

It has been said that every generation rewrites its history. Its own needs and problems inevitably make it take fresh looks at its own past for light, understanding, guidance, and alternative courses of action. Nowhere is this necessity more evident than in the field of American military history todaybroadly conceived. During most of the national existence of the United States the liberal democratic tradition and geographic isolation combined to subordinate in the public mind the role of force and military institutions in its history. Blessed by relatively weak neighbors on the north and south and safe behind its ocean barriers, the United States could define its security in terms of its own boundaries and frontiers. The military factor in its heritage, birth, and development tended to be discounted. But when scientists began to conquer space and time in the twentieth century and the European system that had maintained order in the nineteenth century began to crumble under the impact of two world wars, Americans began to find their security bound up with the fates of other countries.

The nation that began the twentieth century with a strong sense of security by midcentury began to feel insecure. George F. Kennan, former director of the Policy Planning Staff of the Department of State, elaborates, "A country which in 1900 had no thought that its prosperity and way of life could in any way be threatened by the outside world had arrived by 1950 at a point where it seemed to be able to think of little else but this danger." The Cold War and then our involvement in the Global War on Terrorism put an end to America's lingering beliefs in isolation and safety. Not since the era of the founding fathers has survival in a dangerous world become such an urgent issue and the foundations of national security of such concern. An essential element of maintaining that national security must be the study of war in theory and practice. Both the theory and the practice of war must be analyzed together to gain the fullest perspective.

THEORY AND PRACTICE OF WAR

One question that has long interested students of the theory and practice of military affairs is whether war is an art or a science. This is no small question in an age when the lure of technology seeks to reduce so much of human behavior to scientific principles or mechanistic templates. In the eighteenth century, the age of enlightenment, when the systematic study of war began, military theory regarded warfare as mathematical and scientific. A general who knew mathematics and topography, the theorists optimistically maintained, could conduct campaigns with geometrical precision and win wars without bloody battles.

Not since the era of the founding fathers has survival in a dangerous world become such an urgent issue.

In Europe, the violent shock of Napoleonic warfare brought a rude end to the notion of war as a purely scientific or mathematical game. But insofar as the application of physical pressure upon the enemy involves the use of mechanical tools under certain predictable or calculable conditions, it is possible to speak in terms of military science. The systematic application of science to the development of weapons and to technology in general is a comparatively recent development. Since World War II, techniques of research and analysis have been enlisted from scientific fields to make calculations and choices among complex weapon systems and in the management of huge defense programs more exact. Over and above the techniques, the successful conduct of war at all levels of command requires assessing unpredictable variables and taking calculated risks under circumstances for which no precise precedent exists. Since the "fog of war" still holds and wars involve men as well as machines, warfare remains in many ways what it has always been essentiallyan art.

Military theorists have long searched for the principles underlying the art of war. They have sought to distill from the great mass of military experience over the centuries simple but fundamental truths to guide commanders through the fog of war. They have evolved lists of principles from an analysis of the campaigns and the writings of the great captains of war, such as Julius Caesar, Frederick the Great, Napoleon Bonaparte, and Helmuth von Moltke. Occasionally the masters have provided their own set of precepts. Foremost among the analysts have been Henri de Jomini, Carl von Clausewitz, Ardant du Picq, Alfred Thayer Mahan, Ferdinand Foch, Giulio Douhet, Basil H. Liddell Hart, J. F. C. Fuller, and Sun Tzu. The axioms range from the Confederate Lt. Gen. Nathan B. Forrest's oftmisquoted advice, "Git thar fustest with the mostest men," to Napoleon's 115 maxims. The lists differ in emphasis as well as in number. Some theorists have stressed that the battle is all and the defeat of the enemy's armed forces the correct objective, others that the best path to victory is by indirect methods and approaches that avoid confrontations and rely upon maneuver and psychological pressure.

Today, all great nations recognize principles of war and incorporate them in one manner or another into military doctrine. The lists vary from nation to nation. In the modern dress of the Western world, the accepted principles are essentially a postNapoleonic conception, advanced by Clausewitz, the great Prussian philosopher of war of the early nineteenth century, and his contemporary, Jomini, the wellknown French general and theorist. Since the United States shares a common military heritage and a common body of military thought with Europe, American students of war have also sought to reduce the conduct of war to certain essential premises. The U.S. Army recognizes nine such principles:

objective, offensive, maneuver, mass, economy of force, unity of command, security, surprise, and simplicity. The proper application of these principles is still essential to the exercise of effective military operations. First, let us define them.

American students of war have also sought to reduce the conduct of war to certain essential premises.

Objective: Direct every military operation toward a clearly defined, decisive, and attainable objective. The ultimate military objective may be the complete destruction of an enemy's armed forces and his will to fight. The wider political objective may be the complete defeat and reconstruction of an enemy nation that will involve regime change and political, economic, and social reshaping. Each intermediate objective must have the precise mix of force applied to it to attain decisive results. Every commander must understand the overall military and political objectives of the application of force and how his element will contribute to attain those goals. The principle of objective, with a series of intermediate objectives, helps all elements of an operation focus on what must be done and by whom.

Offensive: Seize, retain, and exploit the initiative. In order to achieve victory, a commander must undertake offensive operations. Offensive operations make the enemy react to your moves and keep him on the defensive and off balance. Offensive permits the commander to retain the initiative. This does not mean that defensive operations have no place on the battlefield. Going onto the defensive can conserve forces, allow for a logistical pause, or force an enemy to attack to his distinct disadvantage. However, a defensive mindset ultimately surrenders the initiative to the enemy. Only offensive operations can, in the end, force your will on the enemy.

Maneuver: Place the enemy in a disadvantageous position through the flexible application of combat power. Maneuver is an essential ingredient of combat power. It contributes materially to exploiting successes and in preserving freedom of action and reducing vulnerability. The object of maneuver is to dispose a force in such a manner as to place the enemy at a relative disadvantage and thus achieve results that would otherwise be more costly in men and materiel. Successful maneuver requires flexibility in organization, administrative support, and especially command and control. It is the antithesis of permanence of location and implies avoidance of stereotyped patterns of operation.

Mass: Concentrate the effects of combat power at the decisive place and time. Mass is much more than mere numbers. Many armies through the years have had a greater number of soldiers on any given battlefield but still have failed to win. Mass is thus the concentration of military assets against a specific target. Mass focuses the right mix of combined arms (infantry, armor, artillery) and airpower to overcome even an otherwise superior enemy force.

Proper application of mass can permit numerically inferior forces to achieve decisive combat results. Economy of Force. Allocate minimum essential combat power to secondary efforts. Skillful and prudent use of combat power will enable the commander to accomplish the mission with minimum expenditure of resources. Combat power on the battlefield is a limited resource. If you use it in one place, it is not available in another. Commanders must choose carefully how to use the exact amount of necessary force in the primary and secondary attacks to ensure sufficient combat power at the right place and time. This will allow other assets to focus on other targets. At times, a commander may use his forces in one area to defend, deceive, or delay the enemy or even to conduct retrograde operations to free up the necessary forces for decisive operations in another area.

Unity of Command: For every objective, ensure unity of effort under one responsible commander. The decisive application of full combat power requires unity of command, which obtains unity of effort by the coordinated action of all forces toward a common goal. While coordination may be attained by cooperation, it is best achieved by vesting a single commander with the requisite authority to get the job done. Security. Never permit the enemy to acquire an unexpected advantage. Security is essential to the preservation of combat power and is achieved by measures taken to prevent surprise, preserve freedom of action, and deny the enemy information of friendly forces. Since risk is inherent in war, application of the principle of security does not imply undue caution and the avoidance of all risk. Security frequently is enhanced by bold seizure and retention of the initiative, which denies the enemy the opportunity to interfere. The principle of security does require, however, that risks be calculated carefully and that no unnecessary chances are taken.

THE ARMY FLAG AND CAMPAIGN STREAMERS

Prior to 1956 the Army was the only armed service without a flag to represent the entire service. Prompted by the need for a flag to represent the Army in joint service ceremonies, in 1955 Secretary of the Army Wilber M. Brucker requested the creation of the Army Flag. The design was a simplified version of the Army Seal placed on a white background that included a scroll designation United States Army with the numerals 1775 displayed below and the Army's campaign streamers attached to the spearhead of the flagstaff.

The Army has defined an official campaign as a particular combat action or series of actions that has historical significance or military importance to the Army and the nation. The concept of campaign streamers began during the Civil War, when the War Department instructed regiments to inscribe the names of their meritorious battles on their national colors. In 1890 the War Department directed that regimental honors be engraved on silver rings placed on the staffs of regimental flags. In 1920 the War Department ordered that each regimental color would bear streamers, in the colors of the campaign medal ribbon, for each campaign in which the regiment had fought. The creation of the Army Flag provided a means to display all the Army's campaigns (175 in 2003).

Battle Streamers

Richard Hasenauer, 1976

Surprise: Strike the enemy at a time or place or in a manner for which he is unprepared. Surprise can decisively shift the balance of combat power. Surprise may allow for success out of proportion to the effort expended. It is not essential that the enemy be taken completely unaware, but only that he becomes aware too late to react effectively. Factors contributing to surprise include speed, deception, application of unexpected combat power, effective intelligence and counterintelligence (including communications and electronic intelligence and security), and variations in tactics and methods of operation.

Simplicity: Prepare clear, uncomplicated plans and clear, concise orders to ensure thorough understanding and minimize confusion. Simplicity contributes to successful operations. If other factors are equal, the simplest plan is preferred. In multinational operations, differences in language, culture, and doctrine complicate the situation; simple plans and orders can help minimize the confusion inherent in such environments.

Many examples of the successful employment or violation of these principles can be cited in American military history, and illustrations will be given in appropriate places in subsequent chapters. Each case requires careful study in its own context. For example, we may note briefly that the proper objective has often eluded commanders in war. The British in the American Revolution, for example, were never clear as to their prime objective: whether to capture strategic positions, to destroy the Continental Army, or simply to try by an appropriate show of force to woo the Americans back to their allegiance to the Crown. As a result, their victories over Washington's army in the field seldom had much meaning. In another case, not until after many years of fighting the elusive Seminoles in the Florida swamps did Col. William J. Worth realize that the destruction of their villages and sources of supply would end the conflict.

In the limited wars and expeditions since 1945, however, the United States has sought to achieve objectives short of the total destruction of the enemy or of his productive capacity. What was the objective in Vietnam? It was not the conquest of the North, but the establishment of a viable political entity in South Vietnam. That did not require so much military force as political. The objective is often even more elusive, and can change over time, in peacekeeping or humanitarian relief operations. In Somalia, the original mission in 1992 of providing food to a starving people changed over time into the objective of remaking a country and achieving political stability. A violent reaction by a number of factions resulted in an American retreat from that country. The traditional concept of "victory" and "winning" has taken on a different meaning in the new political context of warfare in the postCold War age. Overwhelming force has often been replaced with the necessity for restraint and only carefully applied military force. Fresh support has been given to Clausewitz's reminder that a successful war is one in which the political objectives for which it is waged are achieved by suitable means and at appropriate cost. Wars are fought to achieve political aims.

No principle has been more ingrained in American military thinking than the belief that only offensive action can achieve decisive results. Offensive action seizes and retains the initiative. One of many examples is Washington's brilliant attack at Trenton in 1776, when his small, tattered, and nearly starving force turned on their pursuers with a lightning attack against a Hessian outpost to revitalize the Revolution. There are some instances, however, when the defense has in certain cases more advantages than the offensive. Some of the most notable actions in American military history, such as Maj. Gen. Andrew Jackson's stand at New Orleans at the end of the War of 1812, have involved the defense. Yet it is offensive action that achieves the most decisive results and wins wars. No one would deny the necessity of maneuver to success in military operations. Brilliant examples have occurred throughout American military history.

During Operation DESERT STORM in 1991, the forces of General H. Norman Schwarzkopf's army moved hundreds of miles through the Saudi Arabian desert in a "great wheel" to attack the Iraqi flank. Attempts at direct assault, rather than maneuver, have often led to bloody and indecisive actions. In the Civil War, Maj. Gen. Ambrose E. Burnside of the Army of the Potomac conducted one of the bloodiest and most useless attacks of the war when he launched his army in a massive frontal assault against Confederate positions on Marye's Heights at Fredericksburg in 1862. Even a successful maneuver can be subject to criticismwitness the controversy over General of the Army Dwight D. Eisenhower's decision to advance across Europe along a continuous broad front rather than permit one of his major forces to thrust deep into Germany during World War II. Nevertheless, a wellorganized and controlled force can often maneuver successfully to achieve victory over a larger, but more ponderous, enemy force.

Many examples of the successful employment or violation of these principles can be cited in American military history.

The principle of mass, often called concentration, probably offers more examples of successful and unsuccessful application than any other. Eisenhower's invasion of the Normandy beaches in 1944 is a brilliant example of the massing of all elements of combat power at the decisive time and place. Conversely, those commanders who fail to mass enough forces or combat power often suffer defeat. On the second day at Gettysburg in 1863, General Robert E. Lee attacked the supposedly "undefended" high ground on the Union left at Little Round Top, but late in the day and with insufficient strength. However, earlier in 1863, Lee's division of his army at Chancellorsville into three separate elements is a classic success. He left one portion to engage the enemy in a holding battle at Fredericksburg while striking with the rest against the advancing Union Maj. Gen. Joseph Hooker. After halting Hooker in his tracks, Lee divided his army again and sent Lt. Gen. Thomas J. "Stonewall" Jackson around the Union right to launch a surprise attack on the enemy flank. The risk involved in this violation of the principle of mass was carefully calculated and brilliantly executed.

The successful application of economy of force has usually resulted in brilliant gains. MacArthur's "island hopping" strategy in World War II is an excellent example of economizing force by bypassing Japanese island strongholds and isolating them with air and naval power, while using the freedup forces to strike elsewhere and keep the enemy off balance. No principle of war is probably more important today, in this era of limited war, than restraint in the use of force and the precise calculation of only the exact amount of force needed.

Unity of command was successfully achieved for the Union under Lt. Gen. Ulysses S. Grant, but only in 1864 after three years of confused leadership and divided objectives. In World War II, the interservice conflicts between General Douglas S. MacArthur and Admiral Chester W. Nimitz, each engaged in major offensive operations against Japan along two disparate axes of advance, indicate that this principle can in some respects be violated and military victory gained. But often lack of unity of command leads to misunderstandings, wasted resources, and confused objectives.

A commander has to do all he can to make elements of the overall plan clear, concise, and direct.

Security and surprise are obvious necessities and closely related. In the Civil War at Antietam, there were security violations on both sides. General Lee's orders for the concentrations of his forces were wrapped in some cigars and found by a Union soldier. Maj. Gen. George B. McClellan, the Union commander, failed to reconnoiter the approaches to the battlefield before the action took place. The success of the Chinese Communist intervention in Korea in November 1950 resulted both from a United Nations security failure and from a carefully planned surprise movement into Korea by massive Communist forces. Surprise can achieve startling results; security lapses can also achieve startling resultsfor the other side.

Of all the principles of war, none is now probably harder to follow above the battalion level than the principle of simplicity. Modern warfare, involving mechanization, electronic equipment, airborne and amphibious operations, joint or even combined operations with foreign forces, is inherently not simple. Even the ostensibly easy movement of a small tankinfantryartillery team cannot be termed simple. In counterinsurgency operations or nationbuilding missions the integration of military with political, economic, sociological, and psychological factors often leads to an even higher degree of complexity. But a commander has to do all he can to make elements of the overall plan clear, concise, and direct. Even tactical operations can sometimes become too complex for the commanders to execute. Washington, fresh from a series of brilliant maneuvers at Trenton and Princeton, planned to use a complex attack against a British outpost at Germantown in 1777. His plan involved coordinating the movement and convergence of four columns of inexperienced troops moving over different roads at night. Columns got lost, delayed, and confused. Washington thus lost the advantage of surprise and failed to mass his forces; he was forced to retreat in defeat. The plan proved too complicated for successful execution.

The growing complexity and variety of modern warfare has led students of military affairs to take a fresh look at these principles. Since World War II a debate has been raging in military literature over the precise meaning and application of the principles, a debate fed by the new circumstances of nuclear and counterinsurgency warfare. The discussion revolves around four major questions: Are the present principles too exclusive? Are they too inclusive? Does modern insurgent and nuclear warfare make them obsolete? To what degree does technology change any of the principles? To some extent this is a debate over semantics.

The defenders point out that the principles are as valid in modern as in ancient warfare; that each age must make its own applications of the "fundamental truths." Critics argue that they are not immutable scientific laws of universal applicability; that they require constant reexamination; that no two military situations are ever completely alike; that the principles are merely methods and commonsense procedures adopted by great captains in the past; and that changes in the conditions of war alter their relative importance. Moreover, some claim that new technology, computers and weapon systems, have destroyed whatever validity remained in the principles. The principles, these critics conclude, are no substitute for imaginative thinking, logical analysis, broad professional knowledge, and highly developed qualities of leadership. Perhaps the key point to remember, whatever the outcome of the ongoing debate among the theorists, is that war remains fundamentally an art. Dennis Hart Mahan, famed West Point professor and teacher of the Civil War generals, put it well: "In war as in every other art based upon settled principles there are exceptions to all general rules. It is in discovering these cases that the talent of the general is shown." Even the defenders of the principles stress that the art of war lies in their interpretation and application. Within limits, the principles of war nevertheless remain a useful tool for analysis, a general frame of reference, and a checklist for examining past campaigns. Themselves an inheritance from the past, these adages offer no substitute for real historical inquiry or for thinking and action on the part of the officer. They represent generalizations and premises rather than fixed immutable rules. They provide general guides that on the whole have in the past led to military success. As in the past, the victorious captain will have to adapt concepts or improvise others most suitable to the particular circumstances facing him.

All theorists agree that in the final analysis the art of war is what men make it. To quote Mahan again, "No soldier who has made himself conversant with the resources of his art, will allow himself to be trammeled by an exclusive system." He must be flexible. He must learn to deal with men. Moreover, Napoleon stated that in war, "The moral is to the physical as three to one." The ability to penetrate the fog of war and make the correct decision is the heart of leadership, and leadership is at the heart of war. Indeed, flexibility and leadership might well be added as tenth and eleventh principles, basic concepts inherent to all the others. It is not surprising, therefore, that the qualities that make for good leadership have long interested the Army and that a whole body of literature has grown up about the theoretical and practical foundations of this phase of the military art.

The military like other professions has developed its own language to allow easy communication. Aside from the principles of war, it is useful for the student of military history to become familiar with other terms commonly encountered in the literature. In the theory of warfare, strategy and tactics have usually been put into separate categories. Strategy deals with both the preparation for and the waging of war and has often been defined as the art of projecting and directing campaigns. To tactics, its close partner, military jargon has reserved the art of executing plans and handling troops in battle. Strategy is usually regarded as the prelude to the battlefield, tactics as the action on the battlefield. As society and warfare have grown more complex, the term strategy has been gradually broadened from its eighteenth century connotation as the "art of the general," far beyond its original, narrow military meaning. In the nineteenth century, and even more in the twentieth, distinctions began to be blurred between strategy as a purely military phenomenon and national strategy of a broader variety involving a combination of political, economic, technological, and psychological factors, along with the military elements, in the management of national policy.

As a result, the term grand strategy (or higher strategy) has come to connote the art of employing all the resources of a nation or coalition of nations to achieve the objects of war (and peace). The broad policy decisions governing the overall conduct of war or its deterrence are the prerogative of the chief of state and his principal advisers. The strategist, whether in the narrower or broader sense, deals in many uncertainties and his art is the calculated risk. At the opposite end of the scale are minor tactics, the term used to describe the maneuver of small units. Falling in between is the concept of operational art that involves the maneuver of large scale units (divisions and corps) to achieve victory that often has strategic results. Despite distinctions in theory, strategy, operational art, and tactics cannot always be easily separated in practice. The language of operational maneuverputting one's army into the most favorable position to engage the enemy and depriving the enemy of freedom of movementis also largely the language of tactics. Thus, envelopment is an attack on an enemy's flank and toward his rear, usually accompanied by an attack on his front. A turning movement is a wide enveloping maneuver, passing around the side of the enemy's main forces and attacking him from the rear. Double envelopment involves an attack on both flanks of the enemy while his center is held in check. A penetration is an attack on the enemy's front by driving a wedge into it or piercing it completely.

It may be followed by an enveloping attack on one or both flanks. In connection with these four basic forms of attack, two terms are often used: main effort, concentrating on the critical point in the enemy's position, and secondary effort, pinning down the remainder of the enemy or moving against a secondary objective to obtain an important but less critical result.

Linking strategy, operational art, and tactics and attracting more and more attention is logistics, defined simply as the art of planning and carrying out the movement and maintenance of forces. This field also has been greatly broadened as warfare has expanded and grown more technological and complex. Logistics deals with the deployment of military forces and their equipment to the theater of operations, along with innumerable services, to feed, clothe, supply, transport, and house the troops. The connecting linksthe network of railways, waterways, roads, and air routes by which an armed force in the field is reinforced and supplied from its base of operations in the home or friendly areaare the lines of communications. The theater of operations comprises the combat zone as well as the supply and administration area directly connected with military operations.

In modern warfare the major divisions of the military art (strategy, logistics, operational art, and tactics) are closely interdependent. One field merges into the others, and changes in one inevitably lead to changes in the others. Sometimes weapons have appeared on the battlefield before military theory and planning have fully absorbed them, and adjustments throughout the art have been slow to follow. In the Civil War, for example, the widespread use of the rifled musket upset the relation among the combat arms; the range and accuracy of these weapons in the hands of defending infantry shattered the effectiveness of the concentrated attack in which Napoleonic strategy culminated. But, as often has been observed in the history of warfare, armaments and weapons are more readily changed than ideas. Napoleon's principles continued to be upheld, sometimes with disastrous consequences on the battlefield. An oftcited case of the appalling repercussions of holding concepts too long or rigidly is the French offensive spirit in World War I that led to massed infantry attacks against entrenched German troops with machine guns.

> *The strategist, whether in the narrower or broader sense, deals in many uncertainties and his art is the calculated risk.*

It is clear that in modern warfare theory and practice have not always been the same. Wars, particularly in the great coalition conflicts of the twentieth century, are not run by rules or theories. Once joined, modern war has had a way of breeding its own strategy, tactics, and weapons. More than ever, for successful commanders, flexibility has become the only sure guide. World War I, beginning as a war of mass offensives, was a classic case of arrested strategy that required new tactics and weapons to dig the war out of the trenches. The AngloAmerican strategy against Germany in World War II proved a compromise of the theory of mass and concentration upheld by the U.S. Army and Prime Minister Winston Churchill's attack on the periphery. Despite attention to principles, Allied strategy in World War II was a hybrid product hammered out largely on the "anvil of necessity." In war, moreover, military strategy varies with political direction and goals. In this vein, Clausewitz had argued that military strategy must respond to national policy and political aims. Perhaps he best summed up the political context of modern war in his assertion, "War is not merely a political act, but also a real political instrument, a continuation of policy carried out by other means." "War," he concluded, "admittedly has its own grammar, but not its own logic."

AMERICAN MILITARY SYSTEM

To organize for national security, each nation adopts the military system most suited to its culture, needs, and policies. Some nations have traditionally tended to concentrate significant segments of their economy on the maintenance of huge military forces and to determine national policies largely in terms of their military implications. While the United States shares with Europe a legacy of military thought and practice whose roots lie deep in the past, its military system has grown out of its own national experience.

The form of government, the traditions of the people, the nature of the country, and its geographical position in relation to other powers have had a profound influence upon American military institutions. In turn, those institutions reflect the American culture and way of life. Indeed, the Army is essentially an institutional form adapted by American society to meet military requirements. The American military system has been developed to place a minimum burden on the people and give the nation a reasonable defense without sacrificing its fundamental values. From the beginning, the United States has sought to reconcile individual liberty with national security without becoming a nation in arms. The balance is often difficult to achieve.

Chief characteristics of American culture that have a bearing on its military system include the value placed upon human beings as individuals; life, liberty, and the pursuit of happiness and peace; the desire to achieve decisive results quickly; a talent for the design and use of machinery; highly developed productive capacity and managerial skills; and great material wealth.

These characteristics underline the American penchant for absolutes: the sharp distinction between war and peace; the insistence on complete victory; an abhorrence of casualties; and the desire for short, decisive, offensive action in warfare. They help account for the traditional American attitude toward war as an aberration in which the bully who disturbed the peace must be soundly and quickly thrashed so American society can return to normalcy. They also point to the importance of public opinion in a democracy in raising and supporting armed forces and to the reason why wars against disturbers of the peace are apt to take on the character of moral crusades. They help explain the traditional rhythm of sharp expansion of the armed forces in wartime and precipitate contraction after the end of hostilities.

While the United States shares with Europe a legacy of military thought and practice whose roots lie deep in the past, its military system has grown out of its own national experience.

In turn, these characteristics and attitudes have shaped the Army in its organizational relationships and in its philosophy of operations. They account also for such distinctive Army features as the development of great mechanical power, the stress on firepower rather than sheer manpower, and the concentration on quick victory by offensive operations.

Throughout its existence the United States has been compelled to provide for military security. The degree to which the provisions were made has varied with the nature and magnitude of the particular threat. Until technology reduced the distance separating the United States from the Old World, the forces in being could be, and were, small.

At the same time the deepseated American reluctance to devote a large proportion of the national wealth to the support of a standing military force played an important part in the development of a system based upon a small professional nucleus that could be expanded in time of need by the induction of citizensoldiers.

This initial system took advantage of the ocean barriers favoring the United States and the balance of power existing in Europe. In accord with Washington's injunction, it held forth the possibility of acquiring greater strength by temporary alliances during extraordinary emergencies but the avoidance of permanent, "entangling" alliances.

Since World War II the rise of new foes and the destruction of the balance of power in Europe and the Far East caused a drastic change in the American military system. During the Cold War, the United States maintained relatively large standing air, land, and sea forces around the world, ready for immediate action and for cooperation with the forces of its many allies. Even with the collapse of the Soviet Union in 1991 and the end of the Cold War, American standing forces remained comparatively larger and more powerful than at any other time in our history. The challenge of worldwide terrorism will doubtless see new changes in our military system.

The American Army as it exists today has evolved through a historical process that parallels the social, economic, and political development of the United States. Its evolution may in general be divided into three periods: colonial, continental expansion, and global operations. During the colonial period (16071775), the militia of the various colonies defended the settlers while they were establishing themselves in America and helped England eliminate the French from North America.

This was the period of roots and origins, of the transplanting of military institutions from abroad, particularly from England, and of their modification in the New World. During the era of continental expansion (17751898), the militia and volunteers and the Continental Army and its successor, the Regular Army, played a significant role in bringing the United States into being, in winning important extensions of national territory, in saving the nation from internal destruction, and in exploring, policing, and governing the vast regions of the West.

This was the period of national independence and consolidation. In the wars of this era, the Army's activities were concentrated on problems vital to the establishment, maintenance, and expansion of a nation based on new concepts of individual freedom and representative government. Only once in this period, during the Revolutionary War, did the Army fight with the help of allies and then only on a temporary basis.

The year 1898, which saw the outbreak of the SpanishAmerican War, the symbol of "looking outward," was an important turning point. It marked the emergence of the United States as a world power.

In the third period (1898 to the present), the Army has carried the flag to the four corners of the earth. Its assigned role has been to serve as a principal instrument for promoting American policies and American interests overseas and protecting the nation against the menace of tyrannical power. In the two great world wars of the twentieth century, as well as in Korea and Vietnam, the United States fought alongside associated or allied nations. In the increasing complexity of modern war, its operations have become inseparably intertwined with those of the Navy and the Air Force. In the history of the nation and the Army of the twentieth century, World War II became an important dividing line whose full implications are still not entirely clear.

Since World War II the revolution in the strategic position of the United States, its emergence as leader of the free world and of allies in military combination, the Cold War, the nuclear age, and the Global War on Terrorism have presented unprecedented challenges to traditional American concepts and institutions in national security.

Whatever the U.S. Army's future contribution, it is as an instrument of force, the primary mission of an army, that it has played its major role in American history. From desperate handtohand engagements with the American Indian to vast battles with motorized and armored forces, from revolutionary war to world war, civil to foreign war, guerrilla to counterguerrilla war, from hot to cold war, and to the war on terrorism, the Army has figured prominently in the nation's conflicts while continuing to make important contributions to the general welfare and to the preservation of domestic order in peacetime.

One final point must be made about the essence of the American Army. We should always remember that it is the Army of the nation and as such responds to the nation's elected leaders. The leaders of the U.S. Army have consistently adhered to a principle basic to the American military system, that the Army is an instrument of civilian authority.

This principle, which General Washington firmly established in practice during the Revolutionary War, was embodied in the Constitution of the United States as a fundamental safeguard of republican institutions. The supremacy of civilian authority is the American solution to the problem of forestalling any possible danger from a standing army. Until World War II, American military policy was centered on the maintenance of very small regular forces and reliance on citizensoldiers in cases of national emergency.

In the colonial period almost every ablebodied man was a member of the militia and could be called out in case of need; and this system continued in force at least theoretically during the first two centuries of national existence. It was usually, nonetheless, the citizenvolunteer who swelled the Army's ranks in earlier wars.

This changed during the Cold War with the continuation of the idea of universal obligation for military duty under selective service in time of national emergency. The return to the earlier idea of a small professional regular army, backed up by an organized militia, the National Guard and Army Reserves, has changed the equation again. Yet this relatively small professional force undergoes other risks such as being separated physically, socially, and even culturally from society as a whole with all that entails for a nation that values civilian control of the military.

It remains to be seen to what degree this return to a regular volunteer force, this time under the pressure of a worldwide struggle against terror, creates tensions between the military and society at large.

In an age when forces in being may determine the outcome of a war or an emergency action in peacetime, the principle of reliance on masses of citizensoldiers has given way to the concept of small, efficient professional forces supported by a select body of trained reserves.

The increasing complications of modern warfare, the great rapidity with which attacks can be launched with modern weapons, and the extensive overseas commitments of the United States have negated the traditional American habit of preparing for wars after they have begun. But whatever the future composition of the Army, it will still have to incorporate the historic principle, ingrained in the nation's military system, of being representative of the people and subject to civilian control.

To be truly progressive, a military system, like most evolving human institutions, must operate in two planes of time: the present and the future. In the field of national security, the choices in the twentieth century were never easy; those for the twentyfirst promise to be even more challenging. The citizen and the soldier cannot know what path to follow unless they are aware of the breadth of alternatives that have been accepted or rejected in the past. Philosopher George Santayana's dictum that those who ignore the past are condemned to repeat its mistakes is nowhere more apt than in military history.

At the same time the blend of the historical with the military art reinforces the caution that no two periods or operations are precisely alike, that the easy analogy and the false comparison must be avoided, and that the past must be interpreted in proper context and depth. For the fledgling officer, as well as for the citizen, American military history provides a laboratory of experience; an accumulation of continuities and disparities; a rich storehouse of courage, sacrifice, and knowledge; and a source of inspiration and wisdom. It is to the multifaceted story of the American Army, how it originated and developed and what it contributed to the nation in war and peace, that we now turn.

3

PRINCIPLES FOR WAR IN GENERAL

The theory of warfare tries to discover how we may gain a preponderance of physical forces and material advantages at the decisive point. As this is not always possible, theory also teaches us to calculate moral factors: the likely mistakes of the enemy, the impression created by a daring action,... yes, even our own desperation. None of these things lie outside the realm of the theory and art of war, which is nothing but the result of reasonable reflection on all the possible situations encountered during a war. We should think very frequently of the most dangerous of these situations and familiarize ourselves with it. Only thus shall we reach heroic decisions based on reason, which no critic can ever shake.

Any person who may present this matter differently to Your Royal Highness is a pedant, whose views will only be harmful to you. In the decisive moments of your life, in the turmoil of battle, you will some day feel that this view alone can help where help is needed most, and where a dry pedantry of figures will forsake you.

Whether counting on physical or moral advantages, we should always try, in time of war, to have the probability of victory on our side. But this is not always possible. Often we must act AGAINST this probability, SHOULD THERE BE NOTHING BETTER TO DO. Were we to despair here, we would abandon the use of reason just when it becomes most necessary, when everything seems to be conspiring against us. Therefore, even when the likelihood of success is against us, we must not think of our undertaking as unreasonable or impossible; for it is always reasonable, if we do not know of anything better to do, and if we make the best use of the few means at our disposal.

We must never lack calmness and firmness, which are so hard to preserve in time of war. Without them the most brilliant qualities of mind are wasted. We must therefore familiarize ourselves with the thought of an honorable defeat. We must always nourish this thought within ourselves, and we must get completely used to it. Be convinced, Most Gracious Master, that without this firm resolution no great results can be achieved in the most successful war, let alone in the most unsuccessful.

Certainly this thought frequently occupied the mind of Frederick II during his first Silesian wars. Because he was familiar with it he undertook his attack near Leuthen, on that memorable fifth of December, and not because he believed that his oblique formation would very likely beat the Austrians.

In any specific action, in any measure we may undertake, we always have the choice between the most audacious and the most careful solution. Some people think that the theory of war always advises the latter. That assumption is false. If the theory does advise anything, it is the nature of war to advise the most decisive, that is, the most audacious. Theory leaves it to the military leader, however, to act according to his own courage, according to his spirit of enterprise, and his selfconfidence. Make your choice, therefore, according to this inner force; but never forget that no military leader has ever become great without audacity.

TACTICS OR THE THEORY OF COMBAT

War is a combination of many distinct engagements. Such a combination may or may not be reasonable, and success depends very much on this. Yet the engagement itself is for the moment more important. For only a combination of successful engagements can lead to good results. The most important thing in war will always be the art of defeating our opponent in combat. To this matter Your Royal Highness can never turn enough attention and thought. I think the following principles the most important:

General Principles For Defense

1. To keep our troops covered as long as possible. Since we are always open to attack, except when we ourselves are attacking, we must at every instant be on the defensive and thus should place our forces as much under cover as possible.
2. Not to bring all our troops into combat immediately. With such action all wisdom in conducting a battle disappears. It is only with troops left at our disposal that we can turn the tide of battle.
3. To be little or not at all concerned about the extent of our front. This in itself is unimportant, and an extension of the front limits the depth of our formation (that is, the number of units which are lined up one behind the other). Troops which are kept in the rear are always available. We can use them either to renew combat at the same point, or to carry the fight to other neighboring points. This principle is a corollary of the previous one.
4. The enemy, while attacking one section of the front, often seeks to outflank and envelop us at the same time. The units which are kept in the background can meet this attempt and thus make up for the support usually derived from obstacles in the terrain. They are better suited for this than if they were standing in line and extending the front. For in this case the enemy could easily outflank them. This principle again is a closer definition of the second.
5. If we have many troops to hold in reserve, only part of them should stand directly behind the front. The rest we should put obliquely behind.

   From this position they in turn can attack the flank of the enemy columns which are seeking to envelop us.
6. A fundamental principle is never to remain completely passive, but to attack the enemy frontally and from the flanks, even while he is attacking us. We should, therefore, defend ourselves on a given front merely to

induce the enemy to deploy his forces in an attack on this front. Then we in turn attack with those of our troops which we have kept back. The art of entrenchment, as Your Royal Highness expressed so excellently at one time, shall serve the defender not to defend himself more securely behind a rampart, but to attack the enemy more successfully. This idea should be applied to any passive defense. Such defense is nothing more than a means by which to attack the enemy most advantageously, in a terrain chosen in advance, where we have drawn up our troops and have arranged things to our advantage.

7. This attack from a defensive position can take place the moment the enemy actually attacks, or while he is still on the march. I can also, at the moment the attack is about to be delivered, withdraw my troops, luring the enemy into unknown territory and attacking him from all sides. The formation in depth i.e., the formation in which only twothirds or half or still less of the army is drawnup in front and the rest directly or obliquely behind and hidden, if possibleis very suitable for all these moves. This type of formation is, therefore, of immense importance.

8. If, for example, I had two divisions, I would prefer to keep one in the rear. If I had three, I would keep at least one in the rear, and if four probably two. If I had five, I should hold at least two in reserve and in many cases even three, etc.

9. At those points where we remain passive we must make use of the art of fortification. This should be done with many independent works, completely closed and with very strong profiles.

10. In our plan of battle we must set this great aim: the attack on a large enemy column and its complete destruction. If our aim is low, while that of the enemy is high, we will naturally get the worst of it. We are pennywise and poundfoolish.

11. Having set a high goal in our plan of defense (the annihilation of an enemy column, etc.), we must pursue this goal with the greatest energy and with the last ounce of our strength. In most cases the aggressor will pursue his own aim at some other point. While we fall upon his right wing, for example, he will try to win decisive advantages with his left. Consequently, if we should slacken before the enemy does, if we should pursue our aim with less energy than he does, he will gain his advantage completely, while we shall only half gain ours. He will thus achieve preponderance of power; the victory will be his, and we shall have to give up even our partly gained advantages. If Your Royal Highness will read with attention the history of the battles of Ratisbon and Wagram, all this will seem true and important.

    In both these battles the Emperor Napoleon attacked with his right wing and tried to hold out with his left. The Archduke Charles did exactly the same. But, while the former acted with great determination and energy, the latter was wavering and always stopped halfway. That is why the advantages which Charles gained with the victorious part of his army were without consequence, while those which Napoleon gained at the opposite end were decisive.

12. Let me sum up once more the last two principles. Their combination gives us a maxim which should take first place among all causes of victory in the modern art of war: "Pursue one great decisive aim with force and determination."

13. If we follow this and fail, the danger will be even greater, it is true. But to increase caution at the expense of the final goal is no military art. It is the wrong kind of caution, which, as I have said already in my "General Principles," is contrary to the nature of war. For great aims we must dare great things. When we are engaged in a daring enterprise, the right caution consists in not neglecting out of laziness, indolence, or carelessness

those measures which help us to gain our aim. Such was the case of Napoleon, who never pursued great aims in a timid or halfhearted way out of caution.

If you remember, Most Gracious Master, the few defensive battles that have ever been won, you will find that the best of them have been conducted in the spirit of the principles voiced here. For it is the study of the history of war which has given us these principles.

At Minden, Duke Ferdinand suddenly appeared where the enemy did not expect him and took the offensive, while at Tannhausen he defended himself passively behind earthworks. At Rossbach, Frederick II threw himself against the enemy at an unexpected point and an unexpected moment.

At Liegnitz, the Austrians found the King at night in a position very different from that in which they had seen him the previous day. He fell with his whole army upon one enemy column and defeated it before the others could start fighting.

At Hohenlinden, Moreau had five divisions in his front line and four directly behind and on his flanks. He outflanked the enemy and fell upon his right wing before it could attack.

At Ratisbon, Marshal Davout defended himself passively, while Napoleon attacked the fifth and sixth armycorps with his right wing and beat them completely.

Though the Austrians were the real defenders at Wagram, they did attack the emperor on the second day with the greater part of their forces. Therefore Napoleon can also be considered a defender. With his right wing he attacked, outflanked and defeated the Austrian left wing. At the same time he paid little attention to his weak left wing (consisting of a single division), which was resting on the Danube. Yet through strong reserves (i.e., formation in depth), he prevented the victory of the Austrian right wing from having any influence on his own victory gained on the Rossbach. He used these reserves to retake Aderklaa.

Not all the principles mentioned earlier are clearly contained in each of these battles, but all are examples of active defense.

The mobility of the Prussian army under Frederick II was a means towards victory on which we can no longer count, since the other armies are at least as mobile as we are. On the other hand, outflanking was less common at that time and formation in depth, therefore, less imperative.

General Principles For Offense

1. We must select for our attack one point of the enemy's position (i.e., one section of his troopsa division, a corps) and attack it with great superiority, leaving the rest of his army in uncertainty but keeping it occupied. This is the only way that we can use an equal or smaller force to fight with advantage and thus with a chance of success. The weaker we are, the fewer troops we should use to keep the enemy occupied at unimportant points, in order to be as strong as possible at the decisive point. Frederick II doubtlessly won the battle of Leuthen only because he massed his small army together in one place and thus was very concentrated, as compared to the enemy.
2. We should direct our main thrust against an enemy wing by attacking it from the front and from the flank, or by turning it completely and attacking it from the rear. Only when we cut off the enemy's line of retreat are we assured of great success in victory.
3. Even though we are strong, we should still direct our main attack against one point only. In that way we shall gain more strength at this point. For to surround an army completely is possible only in rare cases and requires tremendous physical or moral superiority. It is possible, however, to cut off the enemy's line of retreat at one point of his flank and thereby already gain great success.
4. Generally speaking, the chief aim is the certainty (high probability) of victory, that is, the certainty of driving the enemy from the field of battle. The plan of battle must be directed towards this end. For it is easy to change an indecisive victory into a decisive one through energetic pursuit of the enemy.
5. Let us assume that the enemy has troops enough on one wing to make a front in all directions. Our main force

should try to attack the wing concentrically, so his troops find themselves assailed from all sides. Under these circumstances his troops will get discouraged much more quickly; they suffer more, get disorderedin short, we can hope to turn them to flight much more easily.

6. This encirclement of the enemy necessitates a greater deployment of forces in the front line for the aggressor than for the defender.

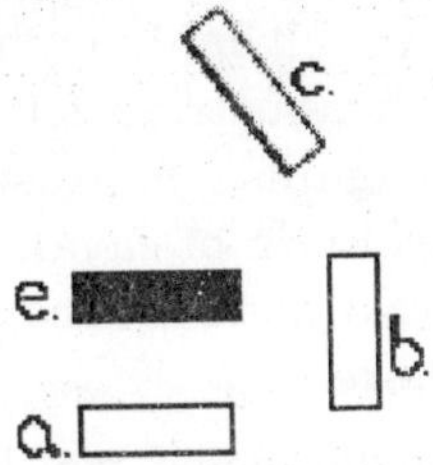

If the corps a b c should make a concentric attack on the section e of the enemy army, they should, of course, be next to each other. But we should never have so many forces in the front line that we have none in reserve. That would be a very great error which would lead to defeat, should the enemy be in the least prepared for an encirclement.

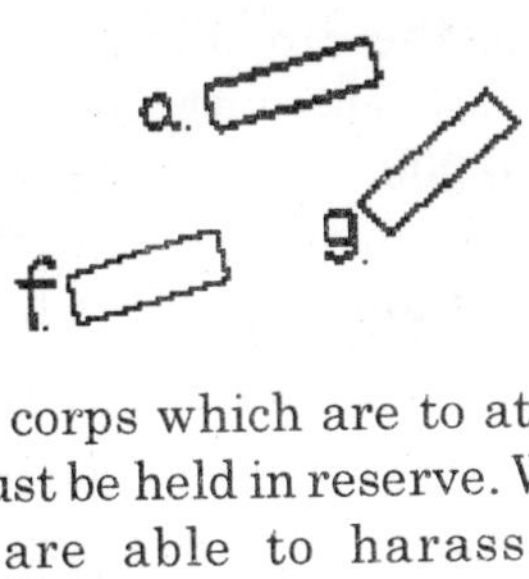

If a b c are the corps which are to attack section e, the corps f and g must be held in reserve. With this formation in depth we are able to harass the same point continuously. And in case our troops should be beaten at the opposite end of the line, we do not need to give up immediately our attack at this end, since we still have reserves with which to oppose the enemy. The French did this in the battle of Wagram. Their left wing, which opposed the Austrian right wing resting on the Danube, was extremely weak and was completely defeated. Even their center at Aderklaa was not very strong and was forced by the Austrians to retreat on the first day of battle. But all this did not matter because Napoleon had such depth on his right wing, with which he attacked the Austrian left from the front and side. He advanced against the Austrians at Aderklaa with a tremendous column of cavalry and horseartillery and, though he could not beat them, he at least was able to hold them there.

7. Just as on the defensive, we should choose as the object of our offensive that section of the enemy's army whose defeat will give us decisive advantages.

8. As in defense, as long as any resources are left, we must not give up until our purpose has been reached. Should the defender likewise be active, should he attack us at other points, we shall be able to gain victory only if we surpass him in energy and boldness. On the other hand, should he be passive, we really run no great danger.

9. Long and unbroken lines of troops should be avoided completely. They would lead only to parallel attacks, which today are no longer feasible.

   Each division makes its attack separately, though according to the directions of a higher command and thus in agreement with each other. Yet one division (8,000 to 10,000 men) is never formed into one single line, but into two, three, or even four. From this it follows that a long unbroken line is no longer possible.

10. The concerted attacks of the divisions and army corps should not be obtained by trying to direct them from a central point, so that they maintain contact and even align themselves on each other, though they may be far

apart or even separated by the enemy. This is a faulty method of bringing about cooperation, open to a thousand mischances. Nothing great can be achieved with it and we are certain to be thoroughly beaten by a strong opponent.

The true method consists in giving each commander of an army corps or a division the main direction of his march, and in pointing out the enemy as the objective and victory as the goal.

Each commander of a column, therefore, has the order to attack the enemy wherever he may find him and to do so with all his strength. He must not be made responsible for the success of his attack, for that would lead to indecision. But he is responsible for seeing that his corps will take part in battle with all its energy and with a spirit of selfsacrifice.

11. A wellorganized, independent corps can withstand the best attack for some time (several hours) and thus can not be annihilated in a moment. Thus, even if it engaged the enemy prematurely and was defeated, its fight will not have been in vain. The enemy will unfold and expend his strength against this one corps, offering the rest a good chance for an attack.

The way in which a corps should be organized for this purpose will be treated later.

We therefore assure the cooperation of all forces by giving each corps a certain amount of independence, but seeing to it that each seeks out the enemy and attacks him with all possible selfsacrifice.

12. One of the strongest weapons of offensive warfare is the surprise attack. The closer we come to it, the more fortunate we shall be. The unexpected element which the defender creates through secret preparations and through the concealed disposition of his troops, can be counterbalanced on the part of the aggressor only by a surprise attack.

Such action, however, has been very rare in recent wars, partly because of the more advanced precautionary measures, partly because of the rapid conduct of campaigns. There seldom arises a long suspension of activities, which lulls one side into security and thus gives the other an opportunity to attack unexpectedly.

Under these circumstancesexcept for nightly assaults which are always possible (as at Hochkirch) we can surprise our opponent only by marching to the side or to the rear and then suddenly advancing again. Or, should we be far from the enemy, we can through unusual energy and activity arrive faster than he expects us.

13. The regular surprise attack (by night as at Hochkirch) is the best way to get the most out of a very small army. But the aggressor, who is not as well acquainted with the terrain as the defender, is open to many risks. The less well one knows the terrain and the preparations of the enemy, the greater these risks become. In many instances, therefore, these attacks must be considered only as desperate means.

14. This kind of attack demands simpler preparations and a greater concentration of our troops than in the daytime.

Principles Governing the Use of Troops

If we cannot dispense with firearms (and if we could, why should we bring them along?), we must use them to open combat. Cavalry must not be used before the enemy has suffered considerably from our infantry and artillery. From this it follows:

That we must place the cavalry behind the infantry. That we must not be easily led to use it in opening combat. Only when the enemy's disorder or his rapid retreat offer the hope of success, should we use our cavalry for an audacious attack.

Artillery fire is much more effective than that of infantry. A battery of eight sixpounders takes up less than onethird of the front taken up by an infantry battalion; it has less than oneeighth the men of a battalion, and yet its fire is two to three times as effective.

On the other hand, artillery has the disadvantage of being less mobile than infantry. This is true, on the whole, even of the lightest horseartillery, for it cannot, like infantry, be used in any kind of terrain.

It is necessary, therefore, to direct the artillery from the start against the most important points, since it cannot, like infantry, concentrate against these points as the battle progresses. A large battery of 20 to 30 pieces usually decides the battle for that section where it is placed.

From these and other apparent characteristics the following rules can be drawn for the use of the different arms:

(a) We should begin combat with the larger part of our artillery. Only when we have large masses of troops at our disposal should we keep horse and footartillery in reserve. We should use artillery in great batteries massed against one point. Twenty to thirty pieces combined into one battery defend the chief part of our line, or shell that part of the enemy position which we plan to attack.

(b) After this we use light infantry either marksmen, riflemen, or fusileers being careful not to put too many forces into play at the beginning. We try first to discover what lies ahead of us (for we can seldom see that clearly in advance), and which way the battle is turning, etc.

If this firing line is sufficient to counteract the enemy's troops, and if there is no need to hurry, we should do wrong to hasten the use of our remaining forces. We must try to exhaust the enemy as much as possible with this preliminary skirmish.

(c) If the enemy should lead so many troops into combat that our firing line is about to fall back, or if for some other reason we should no longer hesitate, we must draw up a full line of infantry. This will deploy between 100 and 200 paces from the enemy and will fire or charge, as matters may be.

(d) This is the main purpose of the infantry. If, at the same time, the battle array is deep enough, leaving us another line of infantry (arranged in columns) as reserve, we shall be sufficiently master of the situation at this sector. This second line of infantry should, if possible, be used only in columns to bring about a decision.

(e) The cavalry should be as close behind the fighting troops during battle as is possible without great loss; that is, it should be out of the enemy's grapeshot or musket fire. On the other hand, it should be close enough to take quick advantage of any favorable turn of battle.

In obeying these rules more or less closely, we should never lose sight of the following principle, which I cannot stress enough:

> *Never bring all our forces into play haphazardly and at one time, thereby losing all means of directing the battle; but fatigue the opponent, if possible, with few forces and conserve a decisive mass for the critical moment. Once this decisive mass has been thrown in, it must be used with the greatest audacity.*

We should establish one battleorder (the arrangement of troops before and during combat) for the whole campaign or the whole war. This order will serve in all cases when there is no time for a special disposition of troops. It should, therefore, be calculated primarily for the defensive.

This battle array will introduce a certain uniformity into the fightingmethod of the army, which will be useful and advantageous. For it is inevitable that a large part of the lower generals and other officers at the head of small contingents have no special knowledge of tactics and perhaps no outstanding aptitude for the conduct of war.

Thus there arises a certain methodism in warfare to take the place of art, wherever the latter is absent. In my opinion this is to the highest degree the case in the French armies.

After what we have discussed about the use of weapons, this battleorder, applied to a brigade, would be approximately as follows:

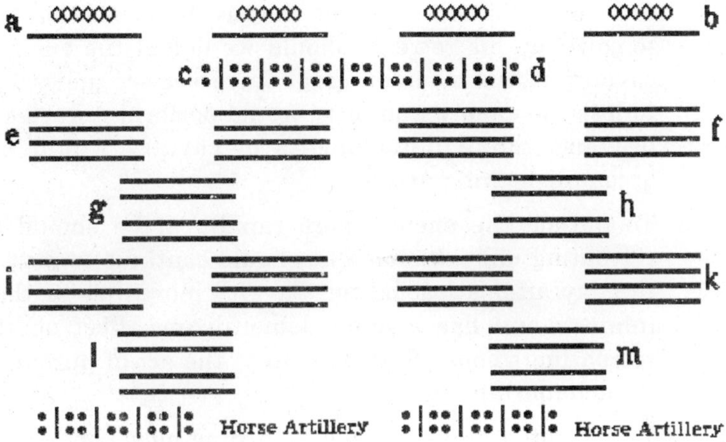

ab is the line of light infantry, which opens combat and which in rough terrain serves to some extent as an advanced guard. Then comes the artillery, cd, to be set up at advantageous points. As long as it is not set up, it remains behind the first line of infantry. ef is the first line of infantry (in this case four battalions) whose purpose is to form into line and to open fire, and gh are a few regiments of cavalry. ik is the second line of infantry, which is held in reserve for the decisive stage of the battle, and lm is its cavalry.

A strong corps would be drawn up according to the same principles and in a similar manner. At the same time, it is not essential that the battle array be exactly like this. It may differ slightly provided that the above principles are followed. So, for instance, in ordinary battleorder the first line of cavalry gh can remain with the second line of cavalry, lm. It is to be advanced only in particular cases, when this position should prove to be too far back.

The army consists of several such independent corps, which have their own general and staff. They are drawn up in line and behind each other, as described in the general rules for combat. It should be observed at this point that, unless we are very weak in cavalry, we should create a special cavalry reserve, which, of course, is kept in the rear. Its purpose is as follows:

(a) To fall upon the enemy when he is retreating from the field of battle and to attack the cavalry which he uses to cover up his retreat. Should we defeat the enemy's cavalry at this moment, great successes are inevitable, unless the enemy's infantry would perform miracles of bravery. Small detachments of cavalry would not accomplish this purpose.

(b) To pursue the enemy more rapidly, if he should be retreating unbeaten or if he should continue to retreat the day after a lost battle. Cavalry moves faster than infantry and has a more demoralizing effect on the retreating troops. Next to victory, the act of pursuit is most important in war.

(c) To execute a great (strategic) turning move, should we need, because of the detour, a branch of the army which moves more rapidly than the infantry.

In order to make this corps more independent, we should attach a considerable mass of horse artillery; for a combination of several types of arms can only give greater strength.

The battleorder of troops described thus far was intended for combat; it was the formation of troops for battle.

The order of march is essentially as follows:

Each independent corps (whether brigade or division) has its own advancedand rearguard and forms its own column. That, however, does not prevent several corps from marching one behind the other on the same road, and thus, as it were, forming a single column.

The corps march according to their position in the general formation of battle. They march beside or behind each other, just as they would stand on the battlefield. In the corps themselves the following order is invariably observed: the light infantry, with the addition of one regiment of cavalry, forming the advanced and rearguard, then the infantry, the artillery, and last the remaining cavalry.

This order stands, whether we are moving against the

enemyin which case it is the natural order or parallel with him. In the latter case we should assume that those troops which in the battle formation were behind each other should march side by side. But when we have to draw up the troops for battle, there will always be sufficient time to move the cavalry and the second line of infantry either to the right or left.

Principles for the Use of Terrain

The terrain (the ground or country) offers two advantages in warfare.

The first is that it presents obstacles to the enemy's approach. These either make his advance impossible at a given point, or force him to march more slowly and to maintain his formation in columns, etc.

The second advantage is that obstacles in the terrain enable us to place our troops under cover.

Although both advantages are very important, I think the second more important than the first. In any event, it is certain that we profit from it more frequently, since in most cases even the simplest terrain permits us to place ourselves more or less under cover. Formerly only the first of these advantages was known and the second was rarely used. But today the greater mobility of all armies has led us to use the former less frequently, and therefore the latter more frequently. The first of these two advantages is useful for defense alone, the second for both offense and defense. The terrain as an obstacle to approach serves chiefly to support our flank, and to strengthen our front.

To support our flank it must be absolutely impassable, such as a large river, a lake, an impenetrable morass. These obstacles, however, are very rare, and a complete protection of our flank is, therefore, hard to find. It is rarer today than ever before, since we do not stay in one position very long, but move about a great deal. Consequently we need more positions in the theater of war.

An obstacle to approach which is not wholly impassable is really no point d'appui for our flank, but only a reinforcement. In that case troops must be drawn up behind it, and for them in turn it becomes an obstacle to approach.

Yet it is always advantageous to secure our flank in this way, for then we shall need fewer troops at this point. But we must beware of two things: first, of relying so completely on this protection that we do not keep a strong reserve in the rear; second, of surrounding ourselves on both flanks with such obstacles, for, since they do not protect us completely, they do not always prevent fighting on our flanks. They are, therefore, highly detrimental to our defense, for they do not permit us to engage easily in active defense on either wing. We shall be reduced to defense under the most disadvantageous conditions, with both flanks, a d and c b, thrown back.

The observations just made furnish new arguments for the formation in depth. The less we can find secure support for our flanks, the more corps we must have in the rear to envelop those troops of the enemy which are surrounding us.

All kinds of terrain, which cannot be passed by troops marching in line, all villages, all enclosures surrounded by hedges or ditches, marshy meadows, finally all mountains which are crossed only with difficulty, constitute obstacles of this kind. We can pass them, but only slowly and with effort. They increase, therefore, the power of resistance of troops drawn up behind them. Forests are to be included only if they are thickly wooded and marshy. An ordinary timberforest can be passed as easily as a plain. But we must not overlook the fact that a forest may hide the enemy. If we conceal ourselves in it, this disadvantage affects both sides. But it is very dangerous, and thus a grave mistake, to leave forests on our front or flank unoccupied, unless the forest can be traversed only by a few paths. Barricades built as obstacles are of little help, since they can easily be removed.

From all this it follows that we should use such obstacles on one flank to put up a relatively strong resistance with few troops, while executing our planned offensive on the other flank. It is very advantageous to combine the use of entrenchments with such natural obstacles, because then, if the enemy should pass the obstacle, the fire from these entrenchments will protect our weak troops against too great superiority and sudden rout.

When we are defending ourselves, any obstacle on our front is of great value.

Mountains are occupied only for this reason. For an elevated position seldom has any important influence, often none at all, on the effectiveness of arms. But if we stand on a height, the enemy, in order to approach us, must climb laboriously. He will advance but slowly, become separated, and arrive with his forces exhausted. Given equal bravery and strength, these advantages may be decisive. On no account should we overlook the moral effect of a rapid, running assault. It hardens the advancing soldier against danger, while the stationary soldier loses his presence of mind. It is, therefore, always very advantageous to put our first line of infantry and artillery upon a mountain.

Often the grade of the mountain is so steep, or its slope so undulating and uneven, that it cannot be effectively swept by gunfire. In that case we should not place our first line, but at the most only our sharpshooters, at the edge of the mountain. Our full line we should place in such a way that the enemy is subject to its most effective fire the moment he reaches the top and reassembles his forces.

All other obstacles to approach, such as small rivers, brooks, ravines, etc., serve to break the enemy's front. He will have to reform his lines after passing them and thus will be delayed. These obstacles must, therefore, be placed under our most effective fire, which is grapeshot (400 to 600 paces), if we have a great deal of artillery or musketshot (150 to 200 paces), if we have little artillery at this point.

It is, therefore, a basic law to place all obstacles to approach, which are to strengthen our front, under our most effective fire.

But it is important to notice that we must never completely limit our resistance to this fire but must hold ready for a bayonetcharge an important part of our troops (1/3 to 1/2) organized into columns. Should we be very weak, therefore, we must place only our firingline, composed of riflemen and artillery, close enough to keep the obstacle under fire. The rest of our troops, organized into columns, we should keep 600 to 800 paces back, if possible under cover.

Another method of using these obstacles to protect our front is to leave them a short distance ahead. They are thus within the effective range of our cannon (1000 to 2000 paces) and we can attack the enemy's columns from all sides, as they emerge. (Something like this was done by Duke Ferdinand at Minden. In this way the obstacle contributes to our plan of active defense, and this active defense, of which we spoke earlier, will be executed on our front.

Thus far we have considered the obstacles of the ground and country primarily as connected lines related to extended positions. It is still necessary to say something about isolated points.

On the whole we can defend single, isolated points only by entrenchments or strong obstacles of terrain. We shall not discuss the first here. The only obstacles of terrain which can be held by themselves are:

(a) *Isolated, steep heights:* Here entrenchments are likewise indispensable; for the enemy can always move against the defender with a more or less extended front. And the latter will always end up by being taken from the rear, since one is rarely strong enough to make front towards all sides.

(b) *Defiles:* By this term we mean any narrow path, through which the enemy can advance only against one point. Bridges, dams, and steep ravines belong here.

We should observe that these obstacles fall into two categories: either the aggressor can in no way avoid them, as for example bridges across large rivers, in which case the defender can boldly draw up his whole force so as to fire upon the point of crossing as effectively as possible. Or we are not absolutely sure that the enemy can not turn the obstacle, as with bridges across small streams and most mountain defiles. In that case it is necessary to reserve a considerable part of our troops 1/3 to 1/2 for an attack in close order.

(c) *Localities, villages, small towns, etc.* : With very brave troops, who fight enthusiastically, houses offer a unique defense for few against many. But, if we are not sure of the individual soldier, it is preferable to occupy the houses, gardens, etc., only with sharpshooters and the entrances to the village with cannons. The greater part of our troops (1/2 to 3/4) we should keep in close columns and hidden in the locality or behind it, so as to fall upon the enemy while he is invading.

These isolated posts serve in large operations partly as outposts, in which case they serve not as absolute defense but only as a delay to the enemy, and partly to hold points which are important for the combinations we have planned for our army. Also it is often necessary to hold on to a remote point in order to gain time for the development of active measures of defense which we may have planned. But, if a point is remote, it is ipso facto isolated.

Two more observations about isolated obstacles are necessary. The first is that we must keep troops ready behind them to receive detachments that have been thrown back. The second is that whoever includes such isolated obstacles in his defensive combinations should never count on them too much, no matter how strong the obstacle may be. On the other hand, the military leader to whom the defense of the obstacle has been entrusted must always try to hold out, even under the most adverse circumstances. For this there is needed a spirit of determination and selfsacrifice, which finds its source only in ambition and enthusiasm. We must, therefore, choose men for this mission who are not lacking in these noble qualities.

Using terrain to cover the disposition and advance of troops needs no detailed exposition. We should not occupy the crest of the mountain which we intend to defend (as has been done so frequently in the past) but draw up behind it. We should not take our position in front of a forest, but inside or behind it; the latter only if we are able to survey the forest or thicket. We should keep our troops in columns, so as to find cover more easily. We must make use of villages, small thickets, and rolling terrain to hide our troops. For our advance we should choose the most intersected country, etc.

In cultivated country, which can be reconnoitered so easily, there is almost no region that can not hide a large part of the defender's troops if they have made clever use of obstacles. To cover the aggressor's advance is more difficult, since he must follow the roads.

It goes without saying that in using the terrain to hide our troops, we must never lose sight of the goal and combinations we have set for ourselves. Above all things we should not break up our battleorder completely, even though we may deviate slightly from it.

If we recapitulate what has been said about terrain, the following appears most important for the defender, i.e., for the choice of positions:

(a) Support of one or both flanks.

(b) Open view on front and flanks.

(c) Obstacles to approach on the front.

(d) Masked disposition of troops. And finally

(e) Intersected country in the rear, to render pursuit more difficult in case of defeat. But no defiles too near (as at Friedland), since they cause delay and confusion.

It would be pedantic to believe that all these advantages could be found in any position we may take up during a war. Not all positions are of equal importance: the most important are those in which we most likely may be attacked. It is here that we should try to have all these advantages, while in others we only need part.

The two main points which the aggressor should consider in regard to the choice of terrain are not to select too difficult a terrain for the attack, but on the other hand to advance, if possible, through a terrain in which the enemy can least survey our force. I close these observations with a principle which is of highest significance, and which must be considered the keystone of the whole defensive theory:

Never to depend completely on the strength of the terrain and consequently never to be enticed into passive defense by a strong terrain.

For if the terrain is really so strong that the aggressor cannot possibly expel us, he will turn it, which is always possible, and thus render the strongest terrain useless. We shall be forced into battle under very different circumstances, and in a completely different terrain, and we might as well not have included the first terrain in our plans. But if the terrain is not so strong, and if an attack within its confines is still possible, its advantages can never make up for the disadvantages of passive defense. All obstacles are useful, therefore, only for partial defense, in order that we may put up a relatively strong resistance with few troops and gain time for the offensive, through which we try to win a real victory elsewhere.

STRATEGY

This term means the combination of individual engagements to attain the goal of the campaign or war. If we know how to fight and how to win, little more knowledge is needed. For it is easy to combine fortunate results. It is merely a matter of experienced judgment and does not depend on special knowledge, as does the direction of battle.

The few principles, therefore, which come up in this connection, and which depend primarily on the condition of the respective states and armies, can in their essential parts be very briefly summarized:

General Principles

Warfare has three main objects:

(a) To conquer and destroy the armed power of the enemy;

(b) To take possession of his material and other sources of strength, and

(c) To gain public opinion.

To accomplish the first purpose, we should always direct our principal operation against the main body of the enemy army or at least against an important portion of his forces. For only after defeating these can we pursue the other two objects successfully.

In order to seize the enemy's material forces we should direct our operations against the places where most of these resources are concentrated: principal cities, storehouses, and large fortresses. On the way to these objectives we shall encounter the enemy's main force or at least a considerable part of it.

Public opinion is won through great victories and the occupation of the enemy's capital.

The first and most important rule to observe in order to accomplish these purposes, is to use our entire forces with the utmost energy. Any moderation shown would leave us short of our aim. Even with everything in our favor, we should be unwise not to make the greatest effort in order to make the result perfectly certain. For such effort can never produce negative results. Suppose the country suffers greatly from this, no lasting disadvantage will arise; for the greater the effort, the sooner the suffering will cease.

The moral impression created by these actions is of infinite importance. They make everyone confident of success, which is the best means for suddenly raising the nation's morale.

The second rule is to concentrate our power as much as possible against that section where the chief blows are to be delivered and to incur disadvantages elsewhere, so that our chances of success may increase at the decisive point. This will compensate for all other disadvantages.

The third rule is never to waste time. Unless important advantages are to be gained from hesitation, it is necessary to set to work at once. By this speed a hundred enemy measures are nipped in the bud, and public opinion is won most rapidly.

Surprise plays a much greater role in strategy than in tactics. It is the most important element of victory. Napoleon, Frederick II, Gustavus Adolphus, Caesar, Hannibal, and

Alexander owe the brightest rays of their fame to their swiftness. Finally, the fourth rule is to follow up our successes with the utmost energy. Only pursuit of the beaten enemy gives the fruits of victory.

The first of these rules serves as a basis for the other three. If we have observed it, we can be as daring as possible with the last three, and yet not risk our all. For it provides us with the means of constantly creating new forces in our rear, and with fresh forces any misfortune can be remedied.

Therein lies the caution which deserves to be called wise, and not in taking each step forward with timidity.

Small states cannot wage wars of conquest in our times. But in defensive warfare even the means of small states are infinitely great. I am, therefore, firmly convinced that if we spare no effort to reappear again and again with new masses of troops, if we use all possible means of preparation and keep our forces concentrated at the main point, and if we, thus prepared, pursue a great aim with determination and energy, we have done all that can be done on a large scale for the strategic direction of the war. And unless we are very unfortunate in battle we are bound to be victorious to the same extent that our opponent lags behind in effort and energy.

In observing these principles little depends on the form in which the operations are carried out. I shall try, nevertheless, to make clear in a few words the most important aspects of this question.

In tactics we always seek to envelop that part of the enemy against which we direct our main attack. We do this partly because our forces are more effective in a concentric than in a parallel attack, and further because we can only thus cut off the enemy from his line of retreat.

But if we apply this to the whole theater of war (and consequently to the enemy's lines of communication), the individual columns and armies, which are to envelop the enemy, are in most cases too far away from each other to participate in one and the same engagement. The opponent will find himself in the middle and will be able to turn against the corps one by one and defeat them all with a single army. Frederick II's campaigns may serve as examples, especially those of 1757 and 1758.

The individual engagement, therefore, remains the principal decisive event. Consequently, if we attack concentrically without having decisive superiority, we shall lose in battle all the advantages, which we expected from our enveloping attack on the enemy. For an attack on the lines of communication takes effect only very slowly, while victory on the field of battle bears fruit immediately.

In strategy, therefore, the side that is surrounded by the enemy is better off than the side which surrounds its opponent, especially with equal or even weaker forces.

Colonel Jomini was right in this, and if Mr. von Bülow has demonstrated the opposite with so much semblance of truth, it is only because he attributed too great an importance to the interruption of provisions and carelessly and completely denied the inevitable success of battle.

To cut the enemy's line of retreat, however, strategic envelopment or a turning movement is very effective. But we can achieve this, if necessary, through tactical envelopment. A strategic move is, therefore, advisable only if we are so superior (physically and morally) that we shall be strong enough at the principal point to dispense with the detached corps.

The Emperor Napoleon never engaged in strategic envelopment, although he was often, indeed almost always, both physically and morally superior.

Frederick II used it only once, in 1757, in his invasion of Bohemia. To be sure, the result was that the Austrians could not give battle until Prague, and what good was the conquest of Bohemia as far as Prague without a decisive victory? The battle of Kolin forced him to give up all this territory again, which proves that battles decide everything. At the same time he was obviously in danger at Prague of being attacked by the whole Austrian force, before Schwerin arrived. He would not have run this risk had he passed through Saxony with all his forces. In that case the first battle would have been fought perhaps near Budin, on the Eger, and it would have been as decisive as that of Prague. The dislocation of the Prussian army during the winter in Silesia and Saxony undoubtedly caused this concentric maneuver. It is important to notice that circumstances of this kind are generally more influential than the advantages to be gained by the form of attack. For facility of operations increases their speed, and the friction inherent in the tremendous warmachine of an armed power is so great in itself that it should not be increased unnecessarily.

Moreover, the principle of concentrating our forces as much as possible on the main point diverts us from the idea of strategic envelopment and the deployment of our forces follows automatically. I was right, therefore, in saying that the form of this deployment is of little consequence. There is, however, one case in which a strategic move against the enemy's flank will lead to great successes similar to those of a battle: if in a poor country the enemy has accumulated with great effort stores of supplies, on whose preservation his operations absolutely depend. In this case it may be advisable not to march our main forces against those of the enemy, but to attack his base of supply. For this, however, two conditions are essential:

(a) The enemy must be so far from his base that our threat will force him into a considerable retreat, and

(b) We must be able to obstruct his advance in the direction followed by his principal force with only a few troops (thanks to natural and artificial obstacles), so that he cannot make conquests somewhere else which will compensate for the loss of his base.

The provisioning of troops is a necessary condition of warfare and thus has great influence on the operations, especially since it permits only a limited concentration of troops and since it helps to determine the theater of war through the choice of a line of operations.

The provisioning of troops is carried on, if a region possibly permits it, through requisitions at the expense of the region.

In the modern method of war armies take up considerably more territory than before. The creation of distinct, independent corps has made this possible, without putting ourselves at a disadvantage before an adversary who follows the old method of concentration at a single point (with from 70,000 to 100,000 men). For an independent corps, organized as they now are, can withstand for some time an enemy two or three times its superior. Then the others will arrive and, even if the first corps has already been beaten, it has not fought in vain, as we have had occasion to remark.

Today, therefore, the divisions and corps move into battle independently, marching side by side or behind each other and only close enough to take part in the same battle, if they belong to the same army.

This makes possible immediate provisioning without storehouses. The very organization of the corps with their General Staff and their Commissariat facilitates this.

If there are no MORE decisive motives (as for example the location of the enemy's main army), we choose the most fertile provinces for our operations; for facility of provisioning increases the speed of our actions. Only the situation of the enemy's main force which we are seeking out, only the location of his capital and the place of arms which we wish to conquer are more important than provisioning. All other considerations, such as the advantageous disposition of our forces, of which we have already spoken, are as a rule much less important.

In spite of these new methods of provisioning, it is quite impossible to do without any depots whatever. Therefore, even when the resources of the region are quite sufficient, a wise military leader does not fail to establish depots in his rear for unexpected emergencies and in order to be able to concentrate his forces at certain points. This precaution is of the sort which are not taken at the expense of the final goal.

Defensive

Politically speaking defensive war is a war which we wage for our independence. Strategically it is the kind of campaign in which we limit ourselves to fighting the enemy in a theater of war which we have prepared for this purpose. Whether the battles which we wage in this theater of war are offensive or defensive, makes no difference. We adopt a strategic defensive mainly when the enemy is superior. Fortresses and entrenched camps, which constitute the chief preparations for a theater of war, afford, of course, great advantages, to which may be added the knowledge of the terrain and the possession of good maps. A smaller army, or an army which is based on a smaller state and more limited resources, will be better able to withstand the enemy WITH these advantages than without them.

In addition there are the following two reasons which can lead us to choose a defensive war.

First, when the regions surrounding the theater of war render operations extremely difficult because of lack of provisions. In this case we avoid a disadvantage which the enemy is forced to undergo. This is the case now (1812) with the Russian army.

Second, when the enemy is superior in warfare. In a theater of war which we have prepared, which we know, and in which all minor conditions are in our favor, war is easier to conduct, and we commit fewer mistakes. When lack of trust in our troops and generals forces us to wage defensive war, we often like to combine tactical with strategic defensive. In that case we fight battles in prepared positions because we are thus again exposed to fewer mistakes.

In defensive just as in offensive warfare, it is necessary to pursue a great aim: the destruction of the enemy army, either by battle or by rendering its subsistence extremely difficult. Thus we shall disorganize it and force it into a retreat, during which it will necessarily suffer great losses. Wellington's campaign in 1810 and 1811 is a good example.

Defensive warfare, therefore, does not consist of waiting idly for things to happen. We must wait only if it brings us visible and decisive advantages. That calm before the storm, when the aggressor is gathering new forces for a great blow, is most dangerous for the defender.

If the Austrians after the battle of Aspern had increased their forces threefold, as they might have and as the Emperor Napoleon did, then and only then would they have made good use of the lull which lasted until the battle of Wagram. This they did not do, and consequently the time was lost. It would have been wiser to profit from Napoleon's disadvantageous position, and to gather the fruits of the battle of Aspern.

The purpose of fortifications is to keep a considerable part of the enemy's army occupied as siege troops, to give us an opportunity to defeat the rest of his army. Consequently, it is best to fight our battles behind our fortifications and not in front of them. But we must not stand by idly, while they are being conquered, as Bennigsen did during the siege of Danzig.

Large rivers, across which it is difficult to throw a bridge (such as the Danube below Vienna and the Lower Rhine), offer a natural line of defense. But we should not distribute our forces evenly along the river bank in order to prevent any crossing whatsoever. That would be most dangerous. On the contrary, we should watch the river and fall upon the enemy from all sides the minute he crosses, while he has not yet reassembled his forces and is still restricted to a narrow space on the river bank. The battle of Aspern offers a good illustration. At Wagram the Austrians had yielded to the French too much territory without the slightest necessity, so that the disadvantages inherent in a river crossing had disappeared.

Mountains are the second obstacle which offers a good line of defense. There are two ways of using them. The first is to leave them in front of us, occupying them only with light troops and considering them, so to speak, a river which the enemy will have to cross. As soon as his separated columns emerge from the passes, we fall upon one of them with all our force. The second is to occupy the mountains ourselves. In that case we must defend each pass with just a small corps and keep an important part of the army (1/31/2) in reserve, in order to attack with superior forces one of the enemy columns that succeed in breaking through. We must not divide up this large reserve to prevent completely the penetration of any enemy columns, but must plan from the outset to fall only upon those columns which we suppose to be the strongest. If we thus defeat an important part of the attacking army, any other columns which have succeeded in breaking through will withdraw of their own accord.

In the midst of most mountain formations we find more or less elevated plains (plateaus) whose slopes are cut by ravines serving as means of access. Mountains, therefore, offer the defender a region in which he can move rapidly to the right or left, while the columns of the aggressor remain separated by steep, inaccessible ridges. Only mountains of this kind are well adapted for defensive warfare. If, on the other hand, their whole interior is rough and inaccessible, leaving the defender dispersed and divided, their defense by the bulk of the army is a dangerous undertaking. For under these circumstances all advantages are on the side of the aggressor, who can attack certain points with great superiority, and no pass, no isolated point is so strong that it cannot be taken within a day by superior forces.

In regard to mountain warfare in general, we should observe that everything depends on the skill of our subordinate officers and still more on the morale of our soldiers. Here it is not a question of skillful maneuvering, but of warlike spirit and wholehearted devotion to the cause; for each man is left more or less to act independently. That is why national militias are especially suited for mountain warfare. While they lack the ability to maneuver, they possess the other qualities to the highest degree.

Finally, it should be observed that the strategic defensive, though it is stronger than the offensive, should serve only to win the first important successes. If these are won and peace does not follow immediately, we can gain further successes only through the offensive. For if we remain continually on the defensive, we run the great risk of always waging war at our own expense. This no state can endure indefinitely. If it submits to the blows of its adversary without ever striking back, it will very likely become exhausted and succumb. We must begin, therefore, using the defensive, so as to end more successfully by the offensive.

Offensive

The strategic offensive pursues the aim of the war directly, aiming straight at the destruction of the enemy's forces, while the strategic defensive seeks to reach this purpose indirectly.

The principles of the offensive are therefore already contained in the "General Principles" of strategy. Only two points need be mentioned more fully.

The first is constant replacement of troops and arms. This is easier for the defender, because of the proximity of his sources of supply. The aggressor, although he controls in most cases a larger state, must usually gather his forces from a distance and therefore with great difficulty. Lest he find himself short of effectives, he must organize the recruiting of troops and the transport of arms a long time before they are needed. The roads of our lines of operation must be covered constantly with transports of soldiers and supplies. We must establish military stations along these roads to hasten this rapid transport.

Even under the most favorable circumstances and with greatest moral and physical superiority, the aggressor should foresee a possibility of great disaster. He therefore must organize on his lines of operation strong points to which he can retreat with a defeated army. Such are fortresses with fortified camps or simply fortified camps. Large rivers offer the best means of halting the pursuing enemy for a while. We must therefore secure our crossing by means of bridgeheads, surrounded by a number of strong redoubts.

We must leave behind us a number of troops for the occupation of these strong points as well as the occupation of the most important cities and fortresses. Their number depends on how much we have to be afraid of invasions or of the attitude of the inhabitants. These troops, together with reinforcements, form new corps, which, in case of success, follow the advancing army, but in case of misfortune, occupy the fortified points in order to secure our retreat.

Napoleon always took great care with these measures for the protection of the rear of his army, and therefore, in his most audacious operations, risked less than was usually apparent.

APPLICATION OF THESE PRINCIPLES IN TIME OF WAR

The principles of the art of war are in themselves extremely simple and quite within the reach of sound common sense.

Even though they require more special knowledge in tactics than in strategy, this knowledge is of such small scope, that it does not compare with any other subject in extent and variety. Extensive knowledge and deep learning are by no means necessary, nor are extraordinary intellectual faculties. If, in addition to experienced judgment, a special mental quality IS required, it would be, after all that has been said cunning or shrewdness. For a long time the contrary has been maintained, either because of false veneration for the subject or because of the vanity of the authors who have written about it. Unprejudiced reflection should convince us of this, and experience only makes this conviction stronger. As recently as the Revolutionary War we find many men who proved themselves able military leaders, yes, even military leaders of the first order, without having had any military education. In the case of Condé, Wallenstein, Suvorov, and a multitude of others it is very doubtful whether or not they had the advantage of such education.

The conduct of war itself is without doubt very difficult. But the difficulty is not that erudition and great genius are necessary to understand the basic principles of warfare. These principles are within the reach of any wellorganized mind, which is unprejudiced and not entirely unfamiliar with the subject. Even the application of these principles on maps or on paper presents no difficulty, and to have devised a good plan of operations is no great masterpiece. The great difficulty is this:

To Remain Faithful Throughout To The Principles We Have Laid Down For Ourselves.

To call attention to this difficulty is the purpose of these closing remarks, and to give Your Royal Highness a clear idea of it I consider the most important object of this essay.

The conduct of war resembles the workings of an intricate machine with tremendous friction, so that combinations which are easily planned on paper can be executed only with great effort.

The free will and the mind of the military commander, therefore, find themselves constantly hampered, and one needs a remarkable strength of mind and soul to overcome this resistance. Many good ideas have perished because of this friction, and we must carry out more simply and moderately what under a more complicated form would have given greater results.

It may be impossible to enumerate exhaustively the causes of this friction; but the main ones are as follows:

1. Generally we are not nearly as well acquainted with the position and measures of the enemy as we assume in our plan of operations. The minute we begin carrying out our decision, a thousand doubts arise about the dangers which might develop if we have been seriously mistaken in our plan. A feeling of uneasiness, which often takes hold of a person about to perform something great, will take possession of us, and from this uneasiness to indecision, and from there to half measures are small, scarcely discernible steps.

2. Not only are we uncertain about the strength of the enemy, but in addition rumor (i.e., all the news which we obtain from outposts, through spies, or by accident) exaggerates his size. The majority of people are timid by nature, and that is why they constantly exaggerate danger. All influences on the military leader, therefore, combine to give him a false impression of his opponent's strength, and from this arises a new source of indecision.

   We cannot take this uncertainty too seriously, and it is important to be prepared for it from the beginning.

   After we have thought out everything carefully in advance and have sought and found without prejudice the most plausible plan, we must not be ready to abandon it at the slightest provocation. On the contrary, we must be prepared to submit the reports which reach us to careful criticism, we must compare them with each other, and send out for more. In this way false reports are very often disproved immediately, and the first reports confirmed. In both cases we gain certainty and can make our decision accordingly. Should this certainty be lacking, we must tell ourselves that nothing is accomplished in warfare without daring; that the nature of war certainly does not let us see at all times where we are going; that what is probable will always be probable though at the moment it may not seem so; and finally, that we cannot be readily ruined by a single error, if we have made reasonable preparations.

3. Our uncertainty about the situation at a given moment is not limited to the conditions of the enemy only but of our own army as well. The latter can rarely be kept together to the extent that we are able to survey all its parts at any moment, and if we are inclined to uneasiness, new doubts will arise. We shall want to wait, and a delay of our whole plan will be the inevitable resu't.

   We must, therefore, be confident that the general measures we have adopted will produce the results we expect. Most important in this connection is the trust which we must have in our lieutenants. Consequently, it is important to choose men on whom we can rely and to put aside all other considerations. If we have made appropriate preparations, taking into account all possible misfortunes, so that we shall not be lost immediately if they occur, we must boldly advance into the shadows of uncertainty.

4. If we wage war with all our strength, our subordinate commanders and even our troops (especially if they are not used to warfare) will frequently encounter difficulties which they declare insurmountable. They find the march too long, the fatigue too great, the provisions impossible. If we lend our ear to all these DIFFICULTIES, as Frederick II called them, we shall soon succumb completely, and instead of acting with force and determination, we shall be reduced to weakness and inactivity.

   To resist all this we must have faith in our own insight and convictions. At the time this often has the appearance of stubbornness. but in reality it is that strength of mind and character which is called firmness.

5. The results on which we count in warfare are never as precise as is imagined by someone who has not carefully observed a war and become used to it.

   Very often we miscalculate the march of a column by several hours, without being able to tell the cause of the delay. Often we encounter obstacles which were impossible to foresee. Often we intend to reach a certain place with our army and fall short of it by several hours. Often a small outpost which we have set up achieves much less than we expected, while an enemy outpost achieves much more. Often the resources of a region do not amount to as much as we expected, etc.

   We can triumph over such obstacles only with very great exertion, and to accomplish this the leader must show a severity bordering on cruelty. Only when he knows that everything possible is always being done, can he be sure that these small difficulties will not have a great influence on his operations. Only then can he be sure that he will not fall too far short of the aim which he could have reached.

6. We may be sure that an army will never be in the condition supposed by someone following its operations from an armchair. If he is sympathetic to the army he will imagine it from a third to a half stronger and better than it really is. It is quite natural that the military commander will make the same mistake in planning his first operations. Consequently, he will see his army melt away as he never thought it would, and his cavalry and artillery become useless. What appeared possible and easy to the observer and to the commander at the opening of a campaign is often difficult and even impossible to carry out. If the military leader is filled with high ambition and if he pursues his aims with audacity and strength of will, he will reach them in spite of all obstacles; while an ordinary person would have found in the condition of his army a sufficient excuse for giving in.

Masséna proved at Genoa and in Portugal the influence of a strongwilled leader over his troops. At Genoa, the limitless exertion to which his strength of will, not to say his harshness, forced people, was crowned with success. In Portugal he at least retreated later than anyone else would have.

Most of the time the enemy army is in the same position. For example, Wallenstein and Gustavus Adolphus at Nuremberg, and Napoleon and Bennigsen after the battle of Eylau. But while we do not see the condition of the enemy, our own is right before our eyes. The latter, therefore, makes a greater impression on ordinary people than the first, since sensuous impressions are stronger for such people than the language of reason.

7. The provisioning of troops, no matter how it is done, whether through storehouses or requisitions, always presents such difficulty that it must have a decisive influence on the choice of operations. It is often contrary to the most effective combination, and forces us to search for provisions when we would like to pursue victory and brilliant success. This is the main cause for the unwieldiness of the whole war machine which keeps the results so far beneath the flight of our great plans.

   A general, who with tyrannical authority demands of his troops the most extreme exertions and the greatest privations, and an army which in the course of long wars has become hardened to such sacrifices will have a tremendous advantage over their adversaries and will reach their aim much faster in spite of all obstacles. With equally good plans, what a difference of result!

8. We cannot stress the following too much: Visual impressions gained during actual combat are more vivid than those gained beforehand by mature reflection. But they give us only the outward appearance of things, which, as we know, rarely corresponds to their essence. We therefore run the risk of sacrificing mature reflection for first impression.

The natural timidity of humans, which sees only one side to everything, makes this first impression incline toward fear and exaggerated caution.

Therefore we must fortify ourselves against this impression and have blind faith in the results of our own earlier reflections, in order to strengthen ourselves against the weakening impressions of the moment.

These difficulties, therefore, demand confidence and firmness of conviction. That is why the study of military history is so important; for it makes us see things as they are and as they function. The principles which we can learn from theoretical instruction are only suited to facilitate this study and to call our attention to the most important elements in the history of war.

Your Royal Highness, therefore, must become acquainted with these principles in order to check them against the history of war, to see whether they are in agreement with it and to discover where they are corrected or even contradicted by the course of events.

In addition, only the study of military history is capable of giving those who have no experience of their own a clear impression of what I have just called the friction of the whole machine.

Of course, we must not be satisfied with its main conclusions, and still less with the reasoning of historians, but we must penetrate as deeply as possible into the details. For the aim of historians rarely is to present the absolute truth. Usually they wish to embellish the deeds of their army or to demonstrate the concordance of events with their imaginary rules. They invent history instead of writing it. We need not study much history for the purpose we propose. The detailed knowledge of a few individual engagements is more useful than the general knowledge of a great many campaigns. It is therefore more useful to read detailed accounts and diaries than regular works of history. An example of such an account, which cannot be surpassed, is the description of the defense of Menin in 1794, in the memoirs of General von Scharnhorst. This narrative, especially the part which tells of the sortie and break through the enemy lines, gives Your Royal Highness an example of how to write military history.

No battle in history has convinced me as much as this one that we must not despair of success in war until the last moment. It proves that the influence of good principles, which never manifests itself as often as we expect, can suddenly reappear, even under the most unfortunate circumstances, and when we have already given up hope of their influence.

A powerful emotion must stimulate the great ability of a military leader, whether it be ambition as in Caesar, hatred of the enemy as in Hannibal, or the pride in a glorious defeat, as in Frederick the Great.

Open your heart to such emotion. Be audacious and cunning in your plans, firm and persevering in their execution, determined to find a glorious end, and fate will crown your youthful brow with a shining glory, which is the ornament of princes, and engrave your image in the hearts of your last descendants.

4

STATIC PRINCIPLES OF WAR IN A CHANGING WORLD

The 20th century has seen veritable successive 'revolutions' in warfare, starting with the advent of air power in World War I, and cemented by aircraft carriers further extending this reach across the oceans by World War II. This was followed by the introduction of nuclear weapons, development of nuclear warfighting doctrines, growth of missile and electronic warfare, and a move towards increasing coordination and jointness between the single Services. In the last two decades, technological advances have provided near realtime situational awareness and minimal sensorshooter cycle, even as the reach, accuracy and lethality of modern weapons have attained unprecedented levels. Over this period, the 'ways and means' of war have undergone constant transformation. The ends for which war was waged have also expanded, from territorial ambitions to increasing geostrategic spheres of influence, to pursuit of religiousideological conflicts, and again a reversion towards safeguarding of territorial and socioeconomic interests. The nature of war, as seen through its ways, means and ends, has probably traversed its largest arc of change in the last 100 years.

The evolutionary trends of war led to several assessments, even before 9/11, of the emerging nature of 21st century warfare.

This was appreciated as being more diverse and divisive, with the ways, means and ends of war continuing to change, along with traditional rationale and actors, and expectations of a transmutation of conflict, from total to limited war, from interstate to intrastate war, and from regular, structured warfare to irregular warfare.

Wars of choice were assessed to more likely dominate the 21st century, with significant effort required to keep them limited amidst a danger of cascading effect upon wider areas in the world.

The tragic events of 9/11 and the ensuing wars against (and by) terrorism have exemplified these earlier estimates and the wider spectrum of modern war.

In the constant evolution of the nature of war, it is reasonable to expect that changes would be reflected in revision of not only the doctrines of warfighting, but also the underlying Principles of War (PoW). However, whilst warfighting doctrines have undergone significant changes in the last two decades, there has been little debate on the corresponding evolution of the PoW, which provide the (conceptual) foundation for building these warfighting doctrines. A review of the prevailing PoW, in the light of the current nature and spectrum of war, would reveal significant deficiencies and point out the revisions necessary for the principles to have continued relevance in the 21st century.

The PoW have been codified from the time of Sun Tzu, and evolved/refined by Napoleon, Clausewitz, J.F.C. Fuller, and thence given institutionalised definition and interpretation by various nations and militaries. The fact that there is still no consensus on a single list of PoW underscores the complexities in addressing war across time and space.

A glance at the table shows there is a fair degree of commonality in the list and understanding of the PoW amongst the various nations, though some emphases and nuances would naturally vary. In the modern spectrum of war, however, some of these principles appear excessively focussed on conventional, unlimited, war, and do not adequately cover the imperatives of other forms of war, such as limited conventional war and subconventional war, which are both more widespread and more likely in the postCold War geostrategic environment. Conventional limited wars are restricted in aim, scope and methods, and may require a broader canvas and interpretation of the PoW to meet their specific requirements. Subconventional war, where at least one actor is a nonstate and the war is characterised by an irregular and covert fabric such as for terrorism, militancy, insurgency, proxy war and civil war, may also need a more flexible interpretation of the PoW, especially since such warfare may take place in own territory and impose limitations on the applicability of the PoW.

However, even this would be more relevant for fighting against subconventional forces, rather than in the waging of such form of warfare, since the latter is the domain of mostly nonstate actors who do not follow established norms and laws of war. Hence, full application of the PoW to them would remain tenous. Some of the existing PoW, with slight amendments, would retain their validity in this context, even whilst others may be seen to suffer from limitations in addressing the wider spectrum of modern war.

The principle of Selection and Maintenance of Aim is the primary PoW, which entails that the desired 'endstate' must be clearly defined and selection of the attainable aim done after careful costbenefit analysis, keeping in mind the resources available. More often than not, this principle has been interpreted in purely military terms (since it is, after all, a principle of 'war'). But, accepting the Clausewitzian precept that war is an extension of politics by other means, the issue of politics can never be separated from the military objective. Military aims would have to be situated in the political purpose for the use of force. In the era of 'total wars,' the selection and maintenance of aim/objective was relatively simpler, with full national resources being devoted to the war and all costs deemed acceptable, since the purpose was survival on one side and 'unconditional surrender' or annihilation on the other. But the nature of war itself has been changing, with total, unlimited war becoming a considerably lesser viable option.

In an increasingly globalised and interdependent world, political restraints (including those of domestic pressures) would have a major influence in the way war can be waged, and what sort of endstate can be achieved. This is even more critical for countries that possess nuclear weapons. It can be argued that 'asymmetric warfare' has emerged primarily because of the politicomilitary restraints in an information age. The problem is that the 'endstate' is becoming less easy to define. For example, the war against global terrorism might seek to rid the world of the scourge of terrorism. But it obviously remains unachievable without a major politicalideological campaign of ideas.

Nuclear weapon states, in particular, have to seriously rethink the issue of military objectives and aims. Warfighting with nuclear weapons would defeat the very logic of war as a rational instrument of policy since it would destroy the very object it seeks to gain. Similarly, even a conventional war between nuclear weapon states would require redefinition of the traditional concepts of victory and defeat. Risk of escalation to nuclear weapons use can nullify what might have been seen as a 'decisive' military victory in a nonnuclear weapon environment.

This has wideranging implications for the way wars can be fought. But, from the point of view of this examination, the critical point is that the very concept of 'victory' would need to be redefined in a war using conventional weapons and forces under a nuclear overhang. Countries placed in such situations would either have to avoid a direct war (as indeed the two superpowers did during the Cold War), or plan and fight a limited war (e.g. SinoRussian border war 1969, and IndoPak Kargil War 1999). The former, avoidance of direct war, had led to the use of proxy wars; while the latter permits only a war with limited objectives. It is not surprising, therefore, that China has adopted a military doctrine of "local, border war under hightech conditions." This, in turn, would require far greater synergy between political aims and military goals.

The military aim of modern war may accordingly require refinement, with consequent shift in focus onto attaining key objective areas that signify political victory or provide the postwar political leverage for conflict resolution, rather than seeking 'decisive' military victory as defined in the past. In the case of fighting insurgency/militancy/terrorism, the military objective may need to be similarly attuned to the political purpose, and limited to providing the modicum of security necessary for generating movement towards a politicoeconomic solution.

An excessively ambitious aim, such as "stamping out all violent opposition" or "overthrow of the state" through the use of military force is more likely to fuel that very violence, and also provide nonstate actors with an image of victory even if they merely survive or avoid total military defeat. This has been evinced in the ongoing Iraq War, where the desire to crush militant opposition has been faulted as an inappropriate and inapplicable politicomilitary aim and military strategy, and has probably instead contributed to deterioration of the security environment, rather than provide stability for attaining the political objectives.

The nature of modern warfare emphasises the need to synergise military objectives with political goals, with an inherent recognition of the fact that the latter could change frequently and demand similar readjustment of military objectives and strategy. Such continued synergy was demonstrated in the IndoPak Kargil War 1999, where Indian political desire to limit the war to the Indian side of the Line of Control (LoC) was supported by a military strategy to "containevictdeny," and included political clearance for use of air power in India's own territory.

Inversely, political goals may also be affected by the military situation, and require reorientation according to the military gains or losses in order to derive the best 'endstate' possible, as seen in the IndiaPakistan War 1971, where the capture of Dhaka was reportedly not part of the original aim.

Hence, while "Selection and Maintenance of Aim" as a PoW remains at the core of modern warfare, its application has undergone significant change with the need for maintaining greater and constant synergy with the political purpose of the war, particularly in the case of limited and subconventional wars. Accordingly, the "aim" in the earlier Principle of War needs a more comprehensive and representative interpretation to encompass both political and military aims and, most importantly, the maintenance of synergy between them. The revisions in interpretation warrant a more appropriate term, such as Maintenance of Synergy in PoliticoMilitary Aims.

The principle of Offensive Action, which is often held as the chief means of achieving victory, entails control over the purpose, scope, intensity and pace of operations, and retention of initiative at all times. This places a premium on early action, even preemption. But the nature of subconventional warfare, especially terrorism, inherently provides early initiative to the nonstate actor. Preemptive action here is difficult, and may well prove counterproductive, such as in the case of faulty intelligence, or due to collateral damage in the apparent absence of adequate justification. This would push the civil populace to favour the nonstate actors, as partly experienced in the current Iraq War, and provide strategiclevel backlash for tactical actions. In such cases, a higher level of own security and rapid response capability would serve the war aims better than focus on offensive action per se. In the case of conventional limited war, with an inherently higher premium on preemption, there may be less scope for regaining the offensive or dictating fresh parameters against preemptive strike, within the limitations of time, area, scale and methods available.

This was seen in the IndoPak War in Kargil, 1999, wherein any Indian attempt to develop military offensive action beyond the tactical level purely on military logic could have escalated the war to the detriment of the war's politicostrategic objective. Hence, the view that offensive action per se is the means to attaining the initiative and freedom of action, and positive results thereby, needs adjustment. In the available technological environment, and ongoing technodoctrinal focus on rapid response capability, the requirement is not so much on maintaining offensive action, but rather on the maintenance and exploitation of Freedom of Action (FoA) by a variety of measures, since the latter would provide broader options and initiative for decisive, including offensive, action.

Freedom of Action has, accordingly, become a core principle across the spectrum of modern warfare, with the requirements extending from its attainment and maintenance for own forces, across all levels and dimensions of war, to the disruption and denial of similar freedom to the opponent. Freedom of Action would need to cover the various dimensions of war, viz. land, sea, air and information. This would also entail the exploitation of own Freedom of Action by the employment of offensive doctrines, such as attainment and utilisation of favourable situation or air superiority, sea control, command of the air/sea, information superiority, escalation control/dominance, etc. The development and exploitation of Freedom of Action in all dimensions and theatres/battlefields would require the support of robust physical and information security, sound logistics and administration, exercise of mobility, maintenance of initiative, suitable deployment of offensive forces, etc. Each of these aspects would need to be addressed in the military doctrines flowing from the overarching PoW, of maintenance and exploitation of Freedom of Action. It stands to reason that the side losing freedom of action would thereby lose its ability to influence the conduct of the war, and be forced to constantly react to the exercise of corresponding freedom by the opponent.

The principle of Mass/Concentration of Force is viewed as the concentration of combat power at the decisive time and place, to achieve decisive results. This principle has been highly valued, from SunTzu through Napoleon to World War II, wherein it denoted the destructive power of a force. The principle of mass providing a distinct advantage is perhaps embedded in Napoleon's supposed remarks that even God is on the side of the bigger battalions! Mass, no doubt, denoted the killing power of a force, seen essentially in terms of quantity. This was the logic that gave the Roman Phalanx its distinct advantage in battle, and why modern militaries still look at a 3:1 favourable ratio of forces as a doctrinal parameter for successful offensive action. But, if viewed more closely, what we can observe is that killing power as a function of mass was true when the quantum of killing power in a unit element of force was limited. Hence, to maximise the overall impact of killing power, mass and concentration of force became a necessary principle. In substance, since the accuracy, rate of fire, and range of the manmachine combination that produced the weapon system was limited, this was sought to be compensated by concentrating combat power, so that the friendly force could kill the maximum number of enemy forces/weapon systems. In battlefields that were concentrated in space, mass also provided enhanced moral power because of the emotional psychological support derived from a greater number of friendly forces.

Generation of mass, whether by massing more soldiers or by dispensing more projectiles onto the target, remained intrinsically important because of the limitations of range, target location and acquisition, accuracy and lethality of weapons, and the friction in war (that Clausewitz talked of). This also placed limits on the quantum of combat power that could be concentrated in time and space. In reality, however, the foundations of this principle started getting eroded with the advancement of technology. For example, the carnage at Verdun in World War I demonstrated how even a single machine gun could concentrate more firepower in the hands of a single soldier than what was possible earlier. Advances in military technology have been rapidly altering the traditional aggregative relation between quantum of forces and their combat power. Nowhere has this been more obvious than in the advent of air power, which provided the means to outflank the enemy from the third dimension. This changed the battlefield completely, and rendered the surface forces vulnerable except through acquiring a counter outflanking capability with their own air power.

Even here, technological changes have determined a continuous expansion of the 'engagement zone', which itself challenges the traditional concept of concentration of force, as brought about by advances in air power. One element of this was airtoair warfare becoming allweather with beyond visual range (BVR) capability soon after the end of World War II. However, employment of air power against surface targets remained limited to what was essentially 'lineofsight' targeting till recently, when improvements in targeting technology have enabled the application of combat power by diverse and geographically separated force elements. Space capabilities are expected to further expand this envelope, and in fact have already done so in the form of surveillance and information warfare, e.g. target spotting by an unmanned aerial vehicle

(UAV), its classification and targeting by a centre possibly in another continent, and prosecution by a cruise missile launched from a submarine in another theatre, more than 1,000 km away. Expansion of the battlefield along with compression of time has provided a totally different dimension to concentration of combat power in time and space compared to what the principle of mass/concentration of force conveys. In determining the nature of change in this principle, we need to revisit the purpose of concentration of force and augmentation of combat power. Simply, this was to attain a certain destructive effect, wherein the massing of force appeared to provide the best means for attaining this end.

Consequently, this assumed the status of a PoW. The impact of advanced weapon technologies in terms of range, accuracy and lethality, synergised with parallel advancements in sensor and command and control (C_2) technologies, has led to a situation wherein firepowereffect, as a derivative of cosmbat power, is no longer a summation of the mass of forces. All other things being equal, and leaving the intangibles like morale, etc. out of consideration for the time being, effective combat power could be denoted normatively by the equation:

Combat Power CP = Q x D x M

where Q is Quantity,

D is Destructive Power (a combination of range, accuracy and lethality) per unit weapon, and

M is Mobility (or manoeuvre to enable concentration in time and space)

It is obvious that if D, the destructive power of the force (weapon/soldier) is low, then Q, the quantity of force needed, would have to be high. In other words, a greater mass would be necessary to maintain the requisite combat power as constant. But, where D is higher, and M is developed, the Q quotient could be much lower, i.e. concentration of force would not be required, as the requisite combat power was being applied by the other components. The applicability of the above can be seen even in World War II, wherein the combination of German Panzer Divisions and aerial dive bombers in the Blitzkrieg in

France, and Allied "thousand bomber raids" over Germany, were examples of augmenting combat power through enhancing Mobility, Destructive Power and Quantity, respectively.

The recent wars in Iraq and Afghanistan have further demonstrated the applicability of the above, wherein requisite combat power was attained with a lesser concentration of forces than would have been the case earlier, by a corresponding increase in precision strike, destructive power and mobility of the forces used. This fact has also been evident throughout military history, where lesser numbers of higher range and accuracy weapons, with higher rates of fire and speed of delivery, have habitually prevailed against larger concentration of opposing forces, due to their relatively higher concentration of firepower.

But, since the weapons and systems in most wars, including the Napoleonic and two World Wars, tended to be comparable for the opposing sides, concentration of forces was perceived as providing the decisive edge, whereas it was actually the concentration of firepower enabled by the massing of forces that was responsible for this effect. In other words, it was the Q+Q, that is (Quality +Quantity) paradigm (both of firepower and manpower) that held the key.

The distinction is important today, when advanced military technologies have led to provision of unprecedented levels of discriminate destructive power in small elements of force, which can be delivered more accurately, at longer ranges, and in smaller timeframes, upon the desired target. The source of that firepower could be naval, air or land power, which is also the central logic for joint operations. The most recent and dramatic example in support of the need to replace the existing principle of mass/concentration of force to one of concentration of firepower is to be found in the Iraq War where the United States reversed the traditionally accepted force ratios necessary for offensive action completely on their head.

Similarly, the United States employed forces widely dispersed across the globe, ranging from home bases to warships and aircraft carriers, and special forces operating with missiles, UAVs, space assets, etc. in the 200102 War in Afghanistan, so as to bring firepower concentrated on specific tactical targetseven employing B52 strategic bombers for close air support missions with the barest minimum military force deployed on land. This did not mean that the principle of concentration of force per se was ignored, but that its effect was attained through concentration of effective firepower, independent of the position and number of weapon firing platforms rather than from the aggregation of combat power platforms in time and space. Today, two B2s can provide the same effect, through accurate delivery of firepower, which required 50 B52s a decade ago, and 1,000 bombers in World War II.

Modern battlefields are expanding in space, even as they are contracting in time, due to the speed and reach of modern firepower. Hence, there will continue to be greater dispersion of forces, especially amongst naval and air platforms. This would seem to violate the principle of concentration of force, as understood hitherto. However, there is no contradiction if the principle is viewed instead as Concentration of Firepower, with its components being the emulative effect of the Quantity, Destructive Power and Mobility paradigm.

Economy of Effort is the principle requiring forces to be judiciously employed so as to maximise the effect of available resources, including through apportionment of resources between the main and secondary efforts. This has been seen as an adjunct to the principle of Concentration of Force (or firepower, as suggested above), and the focus is on the availability of forces. The core, however, relies on attaining the maximum effect for available resources, which also provides the conceptual foundation for the modern doctrine of "EffectsBased Operations." Hence, it may be more appropriate to view this principle instead as the Attainment of Effect, i.e. expand the current understanding from merely fullest use of available forces, to production of the desired effect through best employment of these resources, including by development of different strategies/tactics. For example, guerrilla warfare was developed in response to the adversary's superior force and firepower, wherein it neutralised own inferiority by exploiting potential strengths in relation to the prevailing environment (jungles, mountains, and now also urban areas). This, and also terrorist methods of waging war, such as 9/11 or the Madrid bombings, are not adequately covered under the principle of Economy of Force/Effort, but would be well supported by a shift in focus on production of effect using available resources. The relation between "Effect" and 'Force" may be considered as an equation:

E = F x S

Where E is Effect,

F is Force/Firepower, and

S is Strategy

Thus, while the old principle of Economy of Effort sought to maximise the effect for a given force, it inherently accepted that this maximum effect need not correspond to what was required. This was in consonance with wars being 'total' or unlimited, where the emphasis was on maximum effective utilisation, rather than on utilisation for maximum (desired) effect. However, by shifting focus on attaining the desired effect, rather than on economising the effort, we emphasise the goal more than the means.

Thus, the earlier 'economy' of effort would correspond to the component of strategy in the above equation, as a means to attaining the goal. However, strategy would also have other components, and not just judicious employment of forces. Effect could also be achieved by enhancing the firepower and other strategy quotients. Hence, attainment of effect would provide a more useful principle. The principle of Flexibility has been replaced by Manoeuvre, Initiative and/or Mobility by some countries (Table 1). The principle is looked at in both active and reactive manner, leading to different interpretations and terms used by various nations. For example the US definition of manoeuvre is more active, in that it entails placing the enemy at disadvantage through the flexible application of own combat power at the strategic, operational and tactical levels of war. The Indian Army Doctrine is, however, somewhat reactive, in that it deems flexibility as the capability to react appropriately to changing situations.

The Indian Maritime Doctrine is a mix of both, and views flexibility as the capacity to cope with a rapidly changing situation and seize fleeting opportunities, wherein it entails both physical mobility and reaction capability, with the latter accruing from planning, staffwork and the commander's mental outlook.

In the various definitions/interpretations, we can see two themes: first, the ability to respond to change and, second, the ability to impose change. In essence, the principle of Flexibility/Manoeuvre/Initiative/Mobility all look at the Management of Change, both in imposition upon the enemy, by the use of manoeuvre and 'flexible' application of combat power, and in reacting to change that is imposed by the enemy or that occurs otherwise.

The purpose, in both cases, is to derive advantage from a change in situation that could occur or be created by either side. The change may occur in the various dimensions of war, i.e. through forces arrayed on land, sea or air, and also at the various levels of warfare, viz. tactical, operational or strategic.

Thus, change may be introduced by the application or redeployment of physical forces in the three dimensions, by the timing of executing change, and also by the very rate of change. In fact, the rate of change or pace/tempo of battle is increasingly being recognised as a key factor in introducing and exploiting vulnerabilities in the enemy's Information Decision Action (IDA) Cycle, also leading to suggestions of time becoming an independent dimension of war.

The 'manoeuvrist' concept of warfare, espoused in the UK Joint Warfare Doctrine, also envisages application of multiple lines of operation, in physical dimensions, at a higher speed and tempo, so as to overwhelm the enemy's mental and moral capability to cope/respond.

It may be seen, therefore, that the current principle of flexibility, whilst constituting a valid concept, is inadequate as it does not address the advantages provided in imposing change on the enemy, which are inherent in the corresponding principles of initiative, manoeuvre, and mobility. However, these latter principles on their part do not address the value of flexibility in enabling rapid and appropriate response to changes in situations that occur or are imposed by the enemy, or the developments in using time/tempo in unsettling the enemy's management of change. Hence, this principle needs to be expanded in scope, and the concepts of Flexibility, Initiative, Manoeuvre, and Mobility all subsumed into a more inclusive term, such as the

MANAGEMENT OF CHANGE

Cooperation/Unity of Command has been viewed as the coordination of efforts to attain a common goal. In India and UK, this is seen as emanating from 'jointness', wherein cooperation is the vehicle by which the necessary coordination is sought to be delivered.

In the US interpretation of this PoW, coordination is sought to be attained by vesting a single commander with the requisite authority, viz. unity of command, which would allow him to direct all forces in coordinated action. The moot and common point here is in the need for coordination of effort and actions by multiple forces, of the same and also allied nations, so as to avoid mutual interference and synergise their effect upon the opponent.

This clearly brings out that the principle is simply Coordination, as already adapted by Russia and China. The concepts of unity of command or cooperation are, thus, not principles in themselves, but merely the tools used to comply with the core, common principle and organisational method of attaining coordination. In an era of growing joint and combined complex and specialised operations, there is increasing focus on effective coordination, through a variety of means.

This becomes even more valid in the case of limited conventional wars, where limitations in time, space or methods employable necessitate synchronisation of efforts, as also in subconventional wars, where there is likely to be a larger number of actors and resources involved, including nonmilitary resources. In these cases, unity of command per se may not be feasible and is less likely to provide the result by itself. Additional tools to strengthen coordination, through joint planning training, perspective and organisations, and experience of combined, multinational operations have accordingly become increasingly important.

The principle of Security refers to protection of own forces from enemy action. In essence this points to the factor of vulnerability, in turn, therefore, this is aimed at enhancing own freedom of action. The utility of this concept is certainly evident, but not as an independent principle in the light of the arguments made earlier for replacing the principle of offensive action by Freedom of Action (FoA).

It follows that this latter new principle of FoAwould subsume the principle of security as well, wherein the concept of maintaining security is inherent in the maintenance of own FoA. The converse of the principle of security is also covered in FoA, viz. attacking the enemy's security through denying him FoA through manoeuvre and offensive counter FoA operations.

The principle of security is, thus, deemed limited in scope, and not worthy of categorisation as an independent principle. Its replacement and absorption by FoA would provide a more robust and inclusive principle. The principle of Surprise has long been seen as a necessary force multiplier, to provide the decisive edge at strategic, operational and tactical levels of warfare. It entails catching the enemy offbalance and thereby forcing him to give battle in circumstances unfavourable to him.

There is a growing realisation, however, that surprise is increasingly difficult to attain at the strategic and operational levels, as a result of the increasing transparency of the battlespace and effect of the Information Age.

The reduced attainability of this condition in modern warfare would lead to its reduced applicability as a principle, which gravitates against its viability and status as an independent Principle of War. It is important to examine the purpose and limitations of surprise, in relation to modern warfare, to identify and rectify the flaw.

The purpose of surprise is, very evidently, to provide an advantage, by pushing the enemy 'offbalance'. The purpose itself indicates that surprise is only 'a', and not necessarily 'the', means to an end, let alone being considered as an end/goal in itself, even though it has been hitherto a primary means in attaining the above purpose.

But, in the modern technotactical environment, the attainability and sustainability of surprise is coming increasingly under question, whereby combat power would still need to be applied in significant measure to achieve dominance and victory. A great deal would also depend upon a common but frequently ignored aspect of warfare, i.e. the enemy and his ability to cope with surprise.

After all, once the initial surprise and possible dislocation due to it is over, the enemy could well convert the disadvantage of being tactically surprised into an advantage of his own, through a technological surprise or a countertactical surprise move. Hence, surprise also has to be converted into continuing operational/tactical advantage, rather than be limited to an initial action or early advantage, which has sometimes been deemed adequate.

The foregoing does not lend support to the qualification of surprise per se as an independent principle. On the other hand, credible nuclear deterrence relies on reducing surprise and ensuring transparency to allow for successful deterrence.

The excessive focus on surprise as a PoW, and its centrality in avoiding casualties or attrition warfare, appears to have masked the fact that it is merely a tool and not the main principle, as borne out by its stated purpose of "catching the enemy offbalance."

The principle, in fact, lies in pushing and then keeping the enemy 'offbalance', rather than in attaining surprise per se. This would require the generation of an asymmetry, which would allow application of combat power in own favour, and then sustaining the same so as to develop a favourable momentum (in other words, a continuing competitive advantage) in the war/battle and thereby attain the overall aims.

Hence, it could also be expressed in terms of a 'competitive advantage' in strategic, operational, tactical and also technological terms. Technological asymmetry and surprise is perhaps even more important, but would provide its best value where the doctrine has been developed to support and exploit its potential, so that it can be used in ways superior to that of the enemy, even where the technological level of the opposing forces may be similar.

Hence, the key point is the need for a more comprehensive concept, such as Generation and Sustenance of Favourable Asymmetry, to provide the guidelines in waging of warfare in modern conditions. Surprise, as such, would be one facet of establishing continuing favourable asymmetry in the application of combat power, even while generation and sustenance of favourable asymmetry as a principle would employ a broader range of technical and tactical tools.

The attainment of favourable asymmetry has been the basic theme in warfare through history. The methods used have included use of surprise in terms of time and space, advantages of new technology, exploitation of operational art and environment, use of stratagem, information superiority, etc.

Technological tools have arguably been as, if not more, effective than surprise in time and space, for generating favourable asymmetry.

The Israeli actions at Beka'a Valley in June 1982 relied on integration of technology with doctrine, leading to spectacular results, and became the forerunner of modern joint operations and the "Revolution in Military Affairs."

In World War II, Rommel marshalled his forces and used them in superior tactical manner to generate local favourable asymmetry against superior forces, mostly by sheer speed of advance. However, he did not possess the means to sustain that advantage due to poor logistics backup and inferior air power. The Allied forces, on the other hand, were able to generate sustained favourable asymmetry with airland cohesion and better logistics, and were thereby able to push Rommel back.

This revised approach to the PoW would also recognise logistics as an important ingredient in generating and sustaining favourable asymmetry. The use of pace and tempo of operations, discussed above in the context of flexibility/manoeuvre and the manoeuvrist approach to warfare, also provides another tool for generation of asymmetry, even in the absence of strategic or operational surprise.

For example Op Cactus Lily, the Indian military strike through East Pakistan in 1971 in 12 days, led to the collapse of Pakistani defences and capture of 90,000 Pakistani military prisoners of war.

It follows, therefore, that the attainment of favourable asymmetry sets the conditions for military victory and is its prerequisite at some stage of the operation. Further, its maintenance enables the avoidance of defeat by denying the enemy the conditions for victory. Asymmetry is not generated automatically through its potential or possession, but by the specific interaction in time and space against the opponent, employing various tools, such as the above. Hence, generation and sustenance of favourable asymmetry deserves to be viewed as an independent PoW, with surprise as its subset.

The principle of Administration primarily covers logistics, and also welfare and discipline. The use and value of Logistics in winning wars has been amply demonstrated throughout history, such as its effect on Rommel's operations in North Africa despite tactical superiority, and bears no further reiteration. Based on its timetested central role in the history of warfare, and its continued relevance today, such as in expanding the reach and reducing the time for response of a force, logistics merits recognition as an independent principle of war.

Its inclusion within the principle of administration, as presently done, tends to dilute the value of this concept and limit the scope as long as it is yoked to administration. The aspects of welfare and discipline, which have been dovetailed with logistics in the principle of administration, are certainly important, but need mix up with logistics, which stands on its own merit. In fact, welfare and discipline are more relevant to, and better covered under, the existing, separate principle of Maintenance of Morale, as they are contributory factors to the same.

In the practice of maintenance of morale, another aspect that bears recognition is the new challenges thrown against it by the modern technotactical environment, where morale has to be maintained for forces spread across different dimensions and separated theatres, amidst higher intensity and increasing opaqueness of operations, and an increasingly deleterious and visible effect of war and its human cost. This is more so in the case of prolonged counterinsurgency and antiterrorist warfare, in own and foreign lands.

There are a couple of principles that have been enunciated by some countries, but which do not have a parallel amongst other nations. These include "simplicity" in the USA, and "political mobilisation" in China. A closer look at these 'principles' reveals that they do not really merit independent status. Simplicity simply entails avoiding 'complexity' in military operations. In essence, it addresses the need to maintain clarity and cohesion at all levels, and avoidance of unnecessary complications.

However, this principle is inherent in the application of the first PoW of aim/objective, and flows from the same, whilst also forming part of the execution of some others, such as "coordination" and "logistics." Hence, its value as an independent PoW is questionable, and it belongs more at the doctrinal level than amongst the higher PoW. Similarly, "political mobilisation" is inherent in the "maintenance of synergy" in politicomilitary aims.

In conclusion, it may be seen that the present definitions of the PoW have been tailored to the wars of the 19th and early 20th centuries. The nature and spectrum of war have been changing over the last halfcentury, and particularly in the postCold War era. Doctrinal changes have been introduced by many countries to address the modern requirements and threats, but these have been mostly done without formal review of the PoW upon which the original doctrines were based. The PoW as a concept and as underlying guidelines remain valid, but the specific understanding and scope of PoW as hitherto defined and interpreted bear revision, in keeping with the imperatives of changes in warfare. This is necessary to avoid the principles becoming static in a changing world, including in geopolitical, technological, and doctrinal terms. There is a need, therefore, to evolve our definitions and interpretations of the principles of modern war.

JOMINIAN PRINCIPLES OF WAR

The following are three perspectives relating to the study of Jominian principles of strategy as they were applied during the Civil War. John Shy speaks to each of Jomini's defined principles, calling them timeless in their application, while Archer Jones relates strategy to specific battles.

T. Harry Williams asserts that Jominian principles didn't work during the Civil War because the Civil War was the first "modern war" which called for strategies beyond Jominian concepts, labeling Union command failures during the first two years of the war as failed attempts by commanders to fight a modern war with outdated Jominian techniques. This situation changed only when Grant came East in 1864 and modified the techniques.

John Shy meticulously traces the development of Jominian principles on warfare from origin during the years of the French Revolution through the RussoTurkish War of 182829 and the Crimean War 185456.

Jomini's key principles centered upon the fundamental premise that an effective strategy was the very key to warfare controlled by certain invariable principles, which focused on the offensive, the massing of forces, and the striking of a weaker enemy force at some decisive point.

Shy points to the influence of German Karl von Clausewitz on Jomini's writings, but also points to an important distinction in the way both men looked at warfare. Clausewitz saw war as a tragic, complex enterprise, always threatening to escape human control, while Jomini saw war in terms of simplicity and clarity, viewing it in personal or heroic terms, but always under the control of a masterful commander.

In addition, Jomini emphasized "lines of operation" as an essential principle of warfare which he categorized as natural lines of operation, i.e., topographical barriers (including manmade fortifications, etc.) which he called "territorial lines" and the strategic choices, i.e., where to fight, how to fight, etc. which he called "maneuver lines."

Shy believes that although Jomini purported to follow simplicity and clarity, his works often become ambiguous. On one occasion victory would seem to depend upon strict adherence to principles of strategy, while on another, victory seems to depend upon the genius of the commander.

Another important principle to Jomini is that of the pursuit of a beaten foe. This point is driven home by T. Harry Williams who points to Lincoln's frustration with his commanders in the East who constantly sought to capture Richmond, rather than placing their focus upon destroying Lee's army. If the Army of Northern Virginia could be destroyed, Richmond would soon fall.

Archer Jones looks at Jominian principles articulated by Shy in a more practical straight forward application of their use in specific engagements. This works well In the case of the East where there were abundant examples of textbook Jominiantype battles.

However, the West was a totally different story due to the vastness of the territory and the openness of the terrain.

IN THESE AREAS WEST OF THE APPALACHIANS

Jomini found less application to his principles. Good examples of this were Sidney Albert Johnston, upon being given a unified command, formed a cordon defense and tried to protect every foot of Confederate territory possible. Likewise, Henry Halleck's slow and methodical advance on a defeated Confederate Army at Corinth ran counter to Jominian principles.

On the other hand there were some resounding Jominiantype successes in the East. Jackson's Valley Campaign during the spring and Lee's maneuvers during the summer of 1862 were textbook Jominian, where interior lines were employed, bringing Jackson from the Valley to reinforce Lee during Seven Days, and later to concentrate Confederate forces against Pope at Second Manassas.

Jones identifies the railroad and the telegraph as the major innovations of the Civil War, both being successfully employed to implement interior lines on several occasions, i.e., Johnston to reinforce Beauregard at First Manassas, and Bragg's 1862 Kentucky Campaign.

Jones point out that although Sherman's raids into Georgia and the Carolinas were actually contrary to Jominian principles for dealing with conquered populations, both had a dramatic impact politically as well as and psychologically, contributing significantly to killing the rebel spirit in the South.

Jones concludes that in reality, the continual use of interior lines by the Confederates, while effective in the short term, only served to prolong the war, and contribute to the indecisiveness of battles which contributed heavily to the human cost of the war.

Actually, the most effective principal strategic innovation employed during the war was the strategy of exhaustion used to ultimately strangle the Confederacy. T. Harry Williams seems to agree with historian David Donald who makes the point that Jominian principles didn't work in the Civil War because the Civil War was a modern war, while Jominian principles had been designed for earlier wars fought under different circumstances and views about warfare. To Williams as well as Donald the Civil War being a war of ideas which contained no limitations upon its objectives. In other words, war had become a zero sum game. The South fought for its independence and the North fought to preserve the Union. There could be no in between. One side had to win and one side had to lose.

Williams continues his argument for the modern war theory by pointing to the fact that this was the first time that largescale weapons, techniques, and technologies were being employed; many of the same techniques and equipment that would become common in the wars of the twentieth century.

Williams calls the American Civil War as a kind of a laboratory where the weapons of modern warfare were tested for their use in future battles. Williams concludes that by 1862 the war had become a no holds barred struggle which demanded a different kind of strategy than could be gleaned from Jomini.

For the first time massive armies were raised and arms and supplies massproduced resulting in a profound experience in warfare and serving as a catalyst for many changes that would come about in military thinking.

Williams views Jones as contradicting himself in his adherence to Jominian principles when advocated two conflicting strategies. In the case of Frederick the Great (18th Century) he recommended the destruction of the enemy's army, and in the case of Napoleon (early 19th century) he recommended a strategy of exhaustion. Jones resolves this apparent contradiction by stating although he favored Napoleonic strategy of battle and annihilation, he believed that the destruction of an enemy army was hard to achieve and that a strategy of exhaustion was usually more practical. Thus, Williams concludes that Jones looked at the nonJominian strategy of exhaustion as not only more practical but also a more humane way of waging war.

The primary argument made by Williams in his book Lincoln and His Generals is that the Civil War was the first modern war, and therefore, a new kind of strategy was necessary incorporating a much wider view than Jomini would ever have envisioned. Within in this context, Williams makes some very key points, the most salient of which was that because of its nature as the first modern war, Jominian principles just didn't apply.

In fact, Williams would likely view the successful employment of Jominian principles during the early years of the war as suggested by Jones, as isolated and misleading, and in fact, most often resulting in high casualties, indecisive battles, and a war that drug on for four years.

A second important point made by Williams is that although Abraham Lincoln was a man of humble origins, he possessed great talent and vision, and found himself totally out of sync, both politically, and in terms of military strategy with his early commanders. Not only did he find himself struggling and out of sync with his commanders, he would continue to be so until he brought Grant east in 1864.

It was not until this time that he finally had the general who would implement his ideas of strategic warfare and bring the war to a conclusion.

For the first two years of the war, Lincoln had been frustrated with the likes of McClellan, Burnside, Hooker, Pope, Buell and Rosecrans; field commanders who just didn't get when it came to grasping the concept of total war. They failed to grasp the concept of what constituted "Union Territory," and most either failed or refused to adhere to the importance of the strategic value in destroying the Confederate Armies as their objective, instead of focusing on capturing Richmond.

And most certainly he had been frustrated by McClellan who consistently misjudged his abilities and underestimated his character.

Had McClellan been willing to communicate with Lincoln and incorporate the president's thought into his own, and by doing so forge a strategic partnership, his command might have had a chance for success.

Upon bringing Grant east in the spring of 1864, Lincoln realigned the Union Armies under commanders who saw the war in the same manner as did he, and as a result, unleashed coordinated attacks in Virginia and northern Georgia, which ultimately crushed the Confederacy.

The Civil War was a war which had to happen in order to bring about the development of our federalist system we enjoy today. Consequently, it can be equally said that the war was as significant to the evolution of the modern American military and strategy as the Industrial Revolution was to the development of the American economy.

SIMPLICITY

For anyone who has studied them closely, the principles of war sometimes seem as if they are deliberately contradictory: they tell you to sit down while standing and face left while facing right. The principle of security, for example, clashes with both maneuver and offensive, because in order to accomplish either, an army must compromise its security, at least to a degree.

The same is true for the principle of simplicity. The principle advises modern commanders to "prepare clear, uncomplicated plans and concise orders to ensure thorough understanding." Yet the very nature of operations today mandate detailed coordination on land, sea, air, and space. Modern plans and orders are anything but uncomplicated and concise. A typical divisionlevel order today is several inches thick and replete with cryptic annexes, matrices, and templates.

Commanders and their planners acknowledge that modern warfare is inherently complex and requires detailed coordination. So what of simplicity?

Simplicity, while it has some points in its favor, should not be a principle of war. At best, it represents good advice, but advice that is often laid aside.

The principle of simplicity derives from an age when Newtonian science and drunken grenadiers vied for control of the battlefield. As the science of war developed from the time of Frederick the Great to the eve of the Great War, plans for mobilization, force development, weapons technology, and tactical maneuver became ever more complex. At the same time, European armies were populated by the scum of the earthoften illiterate soldiers shanghaied from public houses, where they drank themselves into unconsciousness only to wake up the next morning in uniform.

These reluctant grenadiers became the stuff of legends spun by Kipling as they marched, conquered, and secured the Empire. They were brave and capable in battle, honed by harsh discipline, paid next to nothing, and proud of their regiments. But they were not mental giants. To employ the infantry soldiers of the British army or its European counterparts, commanders had to keep things simple. As pundits and historians took note of battles lost through confusion, counterorders, and chaos, they hit upon some wise counsel:

keep it simple, stupid!

America's military today is a vastly different enterprise. Soldiers, sailors, airmen, and Marines are almost invariably high school graduates, and not a few of them have college degrees. The officers are all college graduates, and many (if not most) go on to earn advanced degrees. In short, modern armies are smarter and better equipped to deal with complexity.

The proliferation of computers has also impacted the anachronistic principle of simplicity. The essential problem that underlies the principle is that human cognition is greater than human memory.

That isI can concoct a more complicated plan than I can remember in battle. This memory shortfall mandates that armies of the past compensated with simple plans. But with the arrival of the computer, the modern warrior now has a memory aid that helps him to get his arms around complex maneuvers. (One could argue persuasively that computers also add their own level of complexity, but the latest generation of Americans grew up with them and can assimilate that complexity with relative ease.)

The casual observer who wanders into a modern tactical operations center (or air operations center, or combat direction center on an aircraft carrier) will be challenged to find evidence of simplicity. In its place are highly educated, thoroughly trained warriortechnicians who thrive in complexity. Does this mean that we should throw out the whole notion of simplicity altogether? Not at all.

The issue in modern war is not simplicity, which doesn't exist, but rather simplification. A good commander and his staff constantly strive to elicit and understand the details of the battlespace, but they simultaneously try to simplify their plans and orders as best they can. The science and art of command thus looks like a constant sine wave, oscillating back and forth between complexity and simplification.

The science of war (the word 'science' has the same etymology as 'scissors' and 'scythe') is all about cutting things into their component partsanalyzing and ferreting out critical facts. As staffs perform mission analysis or course of action analysis, they delve deep into the complexities of modern combat in order to understand the situation better than the enemy does.

In short, the scientific part of command searches for truth. In theory, this quest is endless, but in practice there are limits to how much the commander can analyze. There is never enough time to analyze thoroughly, because to prevail in battle, the army must act. Time is of the essence.

The art of war ('art' has the same root as 'artificial' or 'artisan') is all about bringing things together into an integrated whole. It is the opposite of science, in that it creates and simplifies, rather than breaking things down for analysis. In war, a commander must simplify in order to act. He evaluates the analyzed facts and makes a decision. He then communicates that decision as rapidly and clearly as he can. The art of war, then, focuses on action.

The principle of simplicity ignored this crucial balance between the science of war and the art of war. The reality of modern war depends to a large degree on concepts, technologies, and systems that are inherently complex.

To embrace a principle that eschews complexity is unrealistic and inapplicable to experience. At the same time, the science of war must be balanced with the art of war through the process of simplification. The result is a commander who can effectively balance the neverending quest for truth with the need for prompt action.

SCIENCE ART

** Conversely, there is the danger of overanalyzing and thus failing to act in time.*

** There is a danger of acting too rashly, ignoring the science of war.*

There is another aspect to the requirement for simplification: the ubiquitous, global media that accompanies military operations. One of the salient characteristics of modern war is the sensitivity and immediacy of public opinion.

This trend has been growing ever since an ambitious photographer snapped pictures of the piles of corpses on the

Antietam battlefield in 1862. Public reaction was immediate and dramatic. Vietnam illustrated how public opinion is both central to success in war and at the same time easily manipulated by the press. In our latest conflicts, each skirmish, each minor incident is instantly broadcast to the world and evaluated in excruciating detail.

In order to gain or retain public approval, governments and military authorities must simplify the situation. Modern mediatelevision in particulardoes not excel at dealing with details and complexity. Even weighty decisions concerning major national policies must confront fidgety anchorpersons anxious to cut to commercial. An official trying to explain a complicated plan will come across as incompetent, unsure, and untrustworthy. Media managers within military organizations have become experts at presenting the bottom line in a simplified manner in order to retain public confidence.

There remains, then, some good horse sense to the old principle of simplicity, even if the principle itself does not measure up. By appreciating the inherent complexity of modern military operations, commanders and their staffs can nonetheless strive to simplify, so that our armies, navies, and air forces can act swiftly and operate in the context of a population that understands our efforts. By balancing the science of war with the art of war through simplification of detail, today's commander can dominate the cognitive domain of modern war...

5

PRINCIPLES OF WAR FOR THE NEW AGE

PRINCIPLES OF A PAST AGE

For most of recorded history, principles of war were also principles of life, applied to both peace and war.

Sun Tzu's Bing Fa laid out 36 principles to guide dealings with friend and foe, in business and in conflict, and they applied to both competitive and consensual relationships.

Only recently did this changein 1648 with the Treaty of Westphalia. It ushered in the era of the nationstate as the focal point of international relations. The sovereignty of territory and the authority exercised therein became the symbols of statehood. Interstate wars became the preeminent form of conflict for governments.

Amaturing industrial revolution, spurred on by advances in technology, provided the weapons, the mobility, and the communications demanded by larger wars fought over more territory by more states.

Principles of Waror, more accurately, principles of warfightingbecame the warriors' 'bible,' in every sense of that term. They provided direction, doctrine, ideology, and a basis for hope and salvationhope for victory, and salvation from defeat.

The Principles codified in the 17 th Century have proven to be remarkably resilient. The 10 in vogue today 2 are little changed from then, even though war and its sustainment have undergone a number of major transformations.

PRESSURES PLACED UPON PRINCIPLES

Set piece, shortduration, close quarter, rulesbased, politely managed, if nonetheless gory 'settos' eventually morphed into the lengthy, massive, but generally continentallycontained carnage of the Great War.

That saga and its aftermath led to the even longer Second World War, unique for both its truly global participation and its atomic finale. Its outcome, and the concomitant management of the 'victory,' heralded in the halfcentury long Cold War; a geopolitical oxymoron during which the main obstacle to global apocalypse eventually became the concept of Mutually Assured Destruction (MAD). Now, the predominant scenario has become a contest of wills affecting everyone on the globe. The new War on Terrorism is unique, as is every war, with respect to the unpredictability of its outcomes, but also because it resembles so much more closely the War on Drugs than, for example, combat waged during the Second World War. When discussing principles of war generally, this is one characteristic that must not be ignored.

The business of arming forces military industrial complexes has provided ever more goods and services for warfighting, relentlessly exploiting a combination of technological progress and near universal obsession with sovereignty, once being claimed by a mere handful of states and now by 200plus national entities or claimants. But, throughout more than three centuries, dozens of different wars, hundreds of defeats and victories large and small, millions of dead, wounded, and dispossessed, and trillions of dollars in cost, the Principles of War have remained generally the same.

Indeed, in this fifth year of the War on Terrorisma global conflict unlike either of the previous world wars the Principles dating from the 17 th Century continue to command compliance, even though armed forces doctrines are changing apace. This trend should constitute yet another reason to reexamine the Principles of War.

That the same Principles were respected and universally followed for centuries, until the Soviet Union imploded at the end of the 1980s, should not be surprising. Security throughout that period was framed by and handled as an exclusively state centred concern. But that is no longer the case, and this constitutes perhaps the strongest reason for considering new Principles of War.

In just 15 years, the causes and effects of globalization have spawned a broad new paradigm of security. Although awareness of an expanded and more inclusive security environment is growing everywhere, it is a sad testimonial to politicians, civil societies, and soldiers alike, just how many are unprepared, or unwilling, or unableindividually or collectively to adapt to, and to adopt processes for, the new and powerful security realities.

The realities of the 21 st Century are new. They reflect the increasing spread and pervasiveness of a contemporary security paradigm, one that is both multidimensional and not constrainable. Two of the main reasons for this state of affairs involve trade and human security.

Much of international relations is now designed and carried out more by 'marketstates' than by 'nationstates,' so powerful are the needs of, desires for, and efforts to trade anywhere there exists a market. The exploding demand for human securitythe security of the individual at the individual level, and legitimized by ever more declarations, treaties and courtshas become pervading. So much so that very few people will either ignore or dispute that security, now and for the foreseeable future, and this is an issue concerning far more than the sovereignty of state territory.

Clearly, 17th Century grounded Principles of War now constitute less than what is either required or even appropriate to engage in the likes of today's Trade Wars and Human Security Wars, many of which exist. They are even less appropriate for dealing with the consequences of those wars.

Indeed, the needs and demands of security from global to individual concerns have become so extensive, visible and convincing, it can be further argued that state sovereignty no longer deserves the status of 'the foundation security issue,' and it should be relegated in terms of time, effort and resources to a middle position on the list of components of contemporary security. The implication of such an action would be, at the least, a requirement for very different principles for warwar being taken in its broadest context.

PRINCIPLES AND WARS

Supporting this claim is experience garnered since the Second World War, including the Vietnam War. During this time frame, some of the traditional Principles of War have not been applied at all, and some that were used proved inappropriate at best and disastrous at worst under certain circumstances. Further, since the end of the Cold War, in conflicts such as those waged in Somalia during the early 1990s, more recently in the Balkans, and in Iraq today, either actual or attempted application of several of the old, 'tried and true' Principles of War has produced results that were at best unsuccessful, and, at worst, constituted military or political blunders. War in modern times, especially the War on Terrorism, is not waged in the traditional way.

The expanded security paradigm has become both cause and effect. War is now fought almost continuously on several very different fronts. The front one most commonly associates with war that is, actual combat 'in the field'is intermittent. But on such fronts as politics, economics, energy, health and mobility, engagement is necessarily virtually fulltime, especially for state governments.

Also, war in its new and fullest sense is more complex and unpredictable than before, because security within a context of globalization and instant communications is always, on all fronts, about both military and civilian concerns. In addition, actions and reactions on all fronts are interdependent, interrelated, or interconnected, meaning that a change in one, suddenly or over time, changes the other. This, of course, intensifies unpredictability.

ARMED FORCES: PRINCIPLES AND WARS

Armed forces know they need better Principles of War, even when they do not articulate that need. This is partially due to the following reasons:

- o Virtually all wars are now limited wars, most engaging both private and public armed organizations.

- o Contemporary conflict is rich in circumstances in which very junior soldiers and civilians from many sectors may, or are required to, take action that provokes strategic consequences.
- o Soldierwarriors are morphing, by design, from the soldier scholar, and, by default, the soldiersavior, into soldierdiplomats.
- o Technology no longer is an impartial, undiscriminating tool of the soldier. It has come so far and is moving forward so quickly that it is provoking increasing unevenness in military capabilities and security options. It has magnified the demands for, and on, interoperability in an era when interoperability is a key to success in any war. And, not incidentally, the technology explosion has all but destroyed any reason to hope for broad standardization.
- o War is both artin the minds and hearts and hopes of those warringand sciencein the weapons, goods, and services at their disposal. Superpower America has learned, again at huge and continuing cost in Iraq, that modern war constitutes much more than just combat, and that security needs encompass much, much more than just technology. New Principles of War have to recognize and embrace the 'art' of war.
- o There is now such a thing as an 'asymmetrical advantage.' A 'failure of imagination' by combatants can erase virtually every advantage provided by conventional power in a war against a committed, conscientious, clever adversary, on any security front.
- o Wars have no end. There is no longer permanent defeat or permanent victory. Life is becoming experiences of 'instances of war' in different places and in various forms, with diverse results and unpredictable, geographically unlimited consequences.
- o Conscript armies are on the way out. Recognizing that even national service armies, such as that of Singapore, need good fulltime professionals, volunteers are the

true foundation of service. Volunteers will expect the principles of their profession to be sensible in the sense that their 'unlimited liability' is at least hedged whenever possible.

- o Contracting for war services has been a longstanding military characteristic. Now renewed and already extensive, the practice may cause a knowledge shift not unlike business outsourcing, such that soldier knowhow, skills, and special capabilities may well weaken, and, in some cases, even vanish from the soldier's repertoire.

CIVILIANS

Civilians, if in different ways due to their nonmilitary cultures and ethos, are increasingly aware of the need for principles with respect to the wars that involve them. The 'homeland security' challenges imposed upon them may not all come as surprises, but they are extremely uncomfortable, since decisions and choices that have previously been made have become infinitely more difficult to do properly, especially in the almost total absence of relevant principles. Such decisions and choices include, but are not limited to:

- o Entry to war: When (time), for what (cause and values), against whom, with whom, and with what?
- o Exit from war: When (time), why (cause and values), how (means), and a notwithstanding consideration.
- o How much national human, monetary, and materiel treasure can be spent, and will be spent?

SOCIETY: PRINCIPLES AND WARS

Further complicating security is the fact that many modern issues engage both civilian and military camps seriously, if not always similarly. The recent emergence of human security expectations, norms, and standards is one such issue. At national and international levels there is now a need for principles to help:

- o Decide the degree of, and manage engagement with, the International Criminal Court (ICC), and

- o Manage compliance with the paradigm of The Responsibility to Protect, the Report of the International Commission on Intervention and State Sovereignty.

A second civilmilitary issue has already been referenced. Much of contemporary conflict is ethnic, religious, ideological, or intrastate, and it focuses intensely on mental and spiritual planes, as well as conventional materiel and technological planes. Consequences of such types of wars are more unpredictable than ever, and they are also more multidimensional than ever. They are also often global in reach. Therefore, military and civilian personnel have no choice but to be jointly aware of the urgent need for new ways of thinking, planning, operating, and sustaining security. Old, or 'stovepiped' methods are no longer sufficient.

Also, more servicepersons and civilians share an understanding that, whereas the fundamental characteristics of fighting a war of violencefire and manoeuvre, death and destructionremain, their features have been changed over time by the wars of the 20 th Century and by the contemporary global security paradigm. 'Fire' now often includes actions that create and maintain fear. 'Manoeuvre' now includes a global mobility offering unlimited choice of time, means, and location of target to an attacker. 'Death' no longer is the 'ultimate liability' of predominately soldiers in uniform, but increasingly, it has become the lot of modern mercenaries, and also the fate of even more civiliansinnocent and otherwisecaught up in war. 'Destruction' no longer rains down primarily on the people, goods, and services of the enemy's armed forces, but combinations of funds, technology, and commitment offer the power to threaten and to destroy the symbols, structures, and livelihoods of tens of thousands of military personnel and civilians in an instant.

Also, an adversary's success with any offensive form of fire, manoeuvre, death, or destruction reinforces its reputation and influence, and weakens the confidence of those on the defensive.

All the foregoing begs the question: Is it most appropriate to retain the old Principles of War, a set of principles assumed valid for fighting any war, and make changes to them only as and when necessary? Or, should there now be a determined effort to codify truly modern principles of war that begin with a consideration of the relevant subject, namely, modern war in its many forms and contexts?

If the former option holds sway, there is clearly an urgent need for changes to some of the old principles, and probably the addition of several new ones. Whatever a renewed list of principles would consider, it must address more thoroughly the new global security paradigm. Also, these principles, in today's context, could become realistically, and at best, only guides, and not rigid rules. And the same caveat would also apply to any other form of principles adopted. It is suggested that a far better choice would be to construct a set of Principles for War. These principles could be derived from a selection of war scenarios; scenarios that are plausible, that address context across the range of wars' military and civilian fronts, and that situatepossibly with a form of generative analysismajor consequences. With respect to such scenarios:

- o It should be easier and quicker to design and construct meaningful Principles for War that are not just about aspects of fighting wars.
- o Principles designed purely for warfighting could be based upon, and updated from, a broader foundation of realities and reasonable future conditions, and reflected in the Principles for War themselves.
- o Principles for War should be more broadly and more enthusiastically accepted, having been designed with consideration, not only of experience and of current knowledge and events, but also of what the future may entail. This latter point is extremely important, since it is obviously in the future when any existing principles would be put to the test.

THE PROTEUS FACTOR

How will these scenarios of wars be designed and constructed?

They have to be built in ways that recognize a key and fundamental need, namely, the requirement to prepare for and to navigate contexts occurring now and in the future. This concept involves 'getting one's temporal bearings' for peace and conflict (sometimes violent conflict) in the future. This formed the intellectual context for a study on strategic research, completed by the American National Reconnaissance Office (NRO) in 2001. The study was called Proteus, and it spawned a group in 2003 known as the Proteus Consortium. On 30 November 2005, a subset organization, Proteus Canada, was established.

The Proteus Consortium then constructed a dynamic strategic vision model. Initially called Protean Media, its first application was to experiment with a 'manytomany' interaction of eight factions actually existing in contemporary Iraq. The work was based partly upon the referenced study conducted at the NRO, as well as upon research into complex visualization systems at the US Naval Postgraduate School. The Proteus Consortium has also developed a novel business model that prototypes a technology designed to experience and to apply 'educated intuition' as knowledge 'sensors' and 'weapons' that can be used alongside classic force sensors and weapons, such as those used by the military for contemporary operations. While this technology is new, some results were surprisingly positive, and they portend a rigorous, realtime analytic capability for force application that could lead to a 'navigationofchange' tool for both nonmilitary and military purposes.

This business model is a networkcentric acquisition model. The technical construct is a game that applies a fourdimension knowledge query/acquisition function to a complex environment. The most novel feature of this game is its ability to adapt to the play and to the choices (actions) of the players. Thus, it does not follow or depend upon a prescribed and set scenario.

The temporal bearings construct mentioned earlier is based upon acquiring knowledge while operating with different time scales in an environment consisting of three operational zones for force projection. Those three zones, in which the complex environments carry on simultaneously, are:

- The source zone: analogous to an image, map, or chart, or a geographical context.

- o The local zone: analogous to the locale on the receiving end of a projected force.

"Old, or 'stovepiped' methods are no longer sufficient."

The internal zone: reflecting the human experience at the local zone involving perception, as well as psychological or emotional elements.

Projected force is characterized by the classical descriptions of hard, soft, coercive, and persuasive forces. Force modifiers take many forms, and they reflect key insights grounded in the Proteus Project's research. Game play reveals both effectsbased consequences, and the gaps in knowledge that need to be filled in order to navigate changing situations. Play has also highlighted the weaknesses and incompleteness of the traditional Westphalian Principles of War with respect to modern conflict and as criteria for strategy. This is not surprising, given that:

- o Every threat or target promoted or provoked by the hugely complicated and changing mix of human security, military security, global security, environmental security, state security, democratization security, social security, food security, water security, energy security, and culture security is a moving target.
- o It is either a military's established role, or its new responsibility, or its professional concern, or its fate, to have to be engaged, more or less, with all these security fronts.

New Principles of War must embrace changes in security contexts. Change demands better foresight, analysis of uncertainties, and consequence management. Needed are strategic charting, navigationofchange, and measurement and exploitation of relationships among temporal and positional bearings. Knowledge shifts associated with changing tasks, and even greater changes to traditional 'divisions of labour' have to be better appreciated, as does how and when to apply knowledge and experience to the internal zones, classical forces, and force modifiers within the scenarios we will use to prepare for the future.

PROPOSED PRINCIPLES FOR WAR

The collective experiences of the members of the Proteus Consortium, bolstered by the philosophy of principles expressed in earlier sections of this article, could become the basis for a first set of Principles for War. They flow from the Proteus insights and they reflect a belief that, for any scenario to be valid, intellectual space must be provided for all security fronts. In effect, the Principles for War that are itemized below are seen as dynamic boundary conditions for military and civilian actors to prepare for, and to make and to manage decisions for, future wars that will materialize, with or without warning. They are:

- o Intelligence in all directions, in time and space, using Proteus scenarios and responding to the capability gaps they expose.
- o Strategy criteria; ways and means, together with their metrics, to influence planning and decisionmaking for security futures.
- o Conciliation; active and patient tolerance for differences as a tool for preventing, when reasonable, or mitigating, when necessary, or bringing closure, when possible, to any form of conflict.
- o Cooperation; to foster interoperability. Cooperation includes 'neutral buyins,' or 'non buyins,' if there is no cost associated with the objective.
- o Arbitration; to recognize the potential for international treaties, laws, norms, and standards as a basis for conciliation. Particularly important issues are property rights and identity rights.
- o Readiness; to acknowledge the causes and effects of factors on all security fronts, as a means to ensure mental, materiel, and monetary readiness of processes and people to fight a necessary or discretionary war.
- o Objective; which is peace, not at any cost, but directed towards a state of affairs in the future more peaceful than that existing at present.

- o Economy; the design and maintenance of interactive overlapping business plans for the funds, manpower, power elements, and time required to stage a necessary or a chosen war.
- o Education; to equip every actor to be a better 'soldier statesman scholar saviour,' by promoting inter-disciplinary knowledge and skills, and by fostering an awareness of other players who possess what you do not.
- o Consequence criteria; to conduct impact measurement employing humanrun compatible process technologies.
- o Competence; including, among other components, 'farsight' (all foresight beyond the 'next' target of the Principles), willingness, ability, authority, means, legitimacy, and luck.

PRINCIPLES OF WARFIGHTING

The context for Principles of Warfighting is, not surprisingly, the Principles for War themselves.

Relative importance of the elements listed below will depend upon the war being fought. Also, varying customs and beliefs related to technology, the possession and use of weapons, fighting ethics, the perceived value of life, and 'Just War' considerations will promote different interpretations of the list's elements. The suggested Principles of Warfighting should look very familiar from a traditional vantage point. In no particular order of merit or importance, they are:

- o Security
- o Interoperability
- o Concentration
- o Objective
- o Mobility
- o Economy

CONCLUSIONS

The case for new Principles for War is based upon the fact that the security paradigm of the contemporary and foreseeable international system encompasses much more than the security of a sovereign state's territory. 'War' has many faces, all interconnected in ways of interest and concern to all human beings. Therefore, the need is for Principles for War, as well as for Principles of War.

The Principles for War recognize that wars often, but not always, include violent fighting. The Principles of Warfighting recognize that technological times are forever new, and they reflect that the traditional Principles of War are no longer suitable for today, or for the future.

The proposed Principles for War and Principles of Warfighting presented here are not 'cast in stone,' because that should never occur. The hopepersonal, professional, and protean, is that these proposals, and others, will promote an environment for peace, one of continuing review and renewal of all principles of all wars on all fronts. The goal, naturally, is fewer wars, and certainly no apocalypse.

As a postscript, it is hoped that somewhere, someone is working on a list of Principles of Peace. Surely, there should be codified principles for what rational man desires, not just for what he does not. Perhaps the answer lies in a 'return to the past,' to the Bing Fa and the Principles for Life.

6

SOCIALISM AND WAR

Socialists have always condemned war between nations as barbarous and brutal. But our attitude towards war is fundamentally different from that of the bourgeois pacifists (supporters and advocates of peace) and of the Anarchists. We differ froth the former in that we understand the inevitable connection between wars and the class struggle within the country; we understand that war cannot be abolished unless classes are abolished and Socialism is created; and we also differ in that we fully regard civil wars, i.e., wars waged by the oppressed class against the oppressing class, slaves against slaveowners, serfs against landowners, and wageworkers against the bourgeoisie, as legitimate, progressive and necessary. We Marxists differ from both the pacifists and the Anarchists in that we deem it necessary historically (from the standpoint of Marx's dialectical materialism) to study each war separately.

In history there have been numerous wars which, in spite of all the horrors, atrocities, distress and suffering that inevitably accompany alt wars, were progressive, i.e., benefited the development of mankind by helping to destroy the exceptionally harmful and reactionary institutions (for example, autocracy or serfdom), the most barbarous despotisms in Europe (Turkish and Russian). Therefore, it is necessary to examine the historically specific features of precisely the present war.

HISTORICAL TYPES OF WARS IN MODERN TIMES

The Great French Revolution ushered in a new epoch in the history of mankind. From that time to the Paris Commune, from 1789 to 1871, one of the types of wars were wars of a bourgeoisprogressive, nationalliberating character. In other words, the chief content and historical significance of these wars were the overthrow of absolutism and feudalism, the undermining of these institutions, the overthrow of alien oppression. Therefore, those were progressive wars, and during such wars, all honest, revolutionary democrats, and also all Socialists, always sympathised with the success of that country (i.e., with that bourgeoisie), which had helped to overthrow, or sap, the most dangerous foundation of feudalism, absolutism and the oppression of other nations. For example, the revolutionary wars waged by France contained an element of plunder and conquest of alien territory by the French, but this does not in the least alter the fundamental historical significance of these wars, which destroyed and shattered feudalism and absolutism in the whole of old, serfridden Europe. In the FrancoPrussian war, Germany plundered France, but this does not alter the fundamental historical significance of this war, which liberated tens of millions of German people from feudal disintegration and from the oppression of two despots, the Russian tsar and Napoleon III.

THE DIFFERENCE BETWEEN AGGRESSIVE AND DEFENSIVE WAR

The epoch of 17891871 left deep tracts and revolutionary memories. Before feudalism, absolutism and alien oppression were overthrown, the development of the proletarian struggle for Socialism was out of the question. When speaking of the legitimacy of "defensive" war in relation to the wars of such an epoch, Socialists always had in mind precisely these objects, which amounted to revolution against medievalism and serfdom. By "defensive" war Socialists always meant a "just" war in this sense (W. Liebknecht once expressed himself precisely in this way). Only in this sense have Socialists regarded, and now regard, wars "for the defence of the fatherland", or "defensive" wars, as legitimate, progressive and just. For example, if tomorrow, Morocco were to declare war on France, India on England, Persia or China on Russia, and so forth, those would be "just", "defensive" wars, irrespective of who attacked first; and every Socialist would sympathise with the victory of the oppressed, dependent, unequal states against the oppressing, slaveowning, predatory "great" powers.

But picture to yourselves a slaveowner who owned 100 slaves warring against a slaveowner who owned 200 slaves for a more "just" distribution of slaves. Clearly, the application of the term "defensive" war, or war "for the defence of the fatherland" in such a case would be historically false, and in practice would be sheer deception of the common people, of philistines, of ignorant people, by the astute slaveowners. Precisely in this way are the presentday imperialist bourgeoisie deceiving the peoples by means of "national ideology and the term "defence of the fatherland in the present war between slaveowners for fortifying and strengthening slavery.

THE PRESENT WAR IS AN IMPERIALIST WAR

Nearly everybody admits that the present war is an imperialist war, but in most cases this term is distorted or applied to one side, or a loophole is left for the assertion that this war may, after all, have a bourgeoisprogressive, nationalliberating significance. Imperialism is the highest stage in the development of capitalism, reached only in the twentieth century. Capitalism now finds the old national states, without the formation of which it could not have overthrown feudalism, too tight for it. Capitalism has developed concentration to such a degree that whole branches of industry have been seized by syndicates, trusts and associations of capitalist billionaires, and almost the entire globe has been divided up among the "lords of capital, either in the form of colonies, or by enmeshing other countries in thousands of threads of financial exploitation. Free trade and competition have been superseded by the striving for monopoly, for the seizure of territory for the investment of capital, for the export of raw materials from them, and so forth. From the liberator of nations that capitalism was in the struggle against feudalism, imperialist capitalism has become the greatest oppressor of nations. Formerly progressive, capitalism has become reactionary; it has developed the forces of production to such a degree that mankind is faced with the alternative of going over to Socialism or of suffering years and even decades of armed struggle between the "great powers for the artificial preservation of capitalism by means of colonies, monopolies, privileges and national oppression of every kind.

WAR BETWEEN THE BIGGEST SLAVEOWNERS FOR PRESERVING AND FORTIFYING SLAVERY

To explain the significance of imperialism, we will quote exact figures showing the division of the world among the socalled "great" (i.e., successful in great plunder) powers:

From this it is seen how most of the nations which fought at the head of others for freedom in 17981871, have now, after 1876. on the basis of highly developed and "overripe" capitalism, become the oppressors and enslavers of the majority of the populations and nations of the globe. From 1876 to 1914, six "great" powers grabbed 25 million sq. kilometres, i.e., an area two and a half times that of Europe! Six powers are enslaving over half a billion (521 million) inhabitants of colonies. For every four inhabitants of the "great" powers there are five inhabitants of "their" colonies. And everybody knows that colonies are conquered by fire and sword, that the populations of colonies are brutally treated, that they are exploited in a thousand ways (by exporting capital, concessions, etc., cheating when selling them goods, subordination to the authorities of the "ruling" nation, and so on and so forth). he AngloFrench bourgeoisie are deceiving the people when they say that they are waging war for the freedom of nations and for Belgium; actually they are waging war for the purpose of retaining the colonies they have inordinately grabbed. The German imperialists would free Belgium, etc., at once if the British and French would agree "fairly" to share their colonies with them.

The peculiarity of the situation lies in that in this war the fate of the colonies is being decided by war on the Continent. From the standpoint of bourgeois justice and national freedom (or the right of nations to existence), Germany would be absolutely right as against England and France, for she has been "done out" of colonies, her enemies are oppressing an immeasurably far larger number of nations than she is, and the Slays who are oppressed by her ally Austria undoubtedly enjoy far more freedom than those in tsarist Russia, that real "prison of nations".

Division of the World Among the "Great" Slave-owning Powers

	Colonies				Metropolises		Total	
	1876		1914		1914			
"Great" Powers	Square kilometres	Inhabitants	Square kilometres	Inhabitants	Square kilometres	Inhabitants	Square kilometres	Inhabitants
	millions		millions		millions		millions	
England	22.5	251.9	33.5	393.5	0.3	46.5	33.8	440.0
Russia	17.0	15.9	17.4	33.2	5.4	136.2	22.8	169.4
France	0.9	6.0	10.6	55.5	0.5	39.6	11.1	95.1
Germany	–	–	2.9	12.3	0.5	64.9	3.4	77.2
Japan	–	–	0.3	19.2	0.4	53.0	0.7	72.2
United States of America	–	–	0.3	9.7	9.4	97.0	9.7	106.7
Six "great" powers	40.4	273.8	65.0	523.4	16.5	437.2	81.5	960.6
Colonies belonging *not* to great powers (but to Belgium, Holland and other states)			9.9	45.3			9.9	45.3
Three "semi-colonial" countries (Turkey, China and Persia)							14.5	361.2
						Total	105.9	1,367.1
Other states and countries							28.0	289.9
Entire globe (without Polar regions)							133.9	1,657.0

But Germany is fighting not for the liberation, but for the oppression of nations. It is not the business of Socialists to help the younger and stronger robber (Germany) to rob the older and overgorged robbers. Socialists must take advantage of the struggle between the robbers to overthrow them all.

To be able to do this, the Socialists must first of all tell the people the truth, namely, that this war is in a treble sense a war between slaveowners to fortify slavery. This is a war firstly, to fortify the enslavement of the colonies by means of a "fairer" distribution and subsequent more "concerted exploitation of them; secondly, to fortify the oppression of other nations within the "great" powers, for both Austria and Russia (Russia more and much worse than Austria) maintain their rule only by such oppression, intensifying it by means of war; and thirdly, to fortify and prolong wage slavery, for the proletariat is split up and suppressed, while the capitalists gain, making fortunes out of the war, aggravating national prejudices and intensifying reaction, which has raised its head in all countries. even in the freest and most republican.

"War is the Continuation of Politics by Other" (i.e., Violent) "Means"

This famous aphorism was uttered by one of the profoundest writers on the problems of war, Clausewitz. Marxists have always rightly regarded this thesis as the theoretical basis of views concerning the significance of every given war. It was precisely from this viewpoint that Marx and Engels always regarded different wars.

Apply this view to the present war. You will see that for decades, for almost half a century, the governments and the ruling classes of England, and France, and Germany, and Italy, and Austria, and Russia, pursued a policy of, plundering colonies, of oppressing other nations, of suppressing the workingclass movement. It is this, and only this policy that is being continued in the present war. In particular, the policy of both Austria and Russia peacetime as well as in war, is a policy of enslaving and not of liberating nations. In China, Persia. India and other dependent countries, on the contrary, we have seen during the past decades a policy of rousing tens and hundreds of millions of people to national life, of liberating them from the oppression of the reactionary "great" powers. A war on such a historical ground can even today be a bourgeoisprogressive, nationalliberation war.

It is sufficient to glance at the present war from the viewpoint that it is a continuation of the politics of the great powers, and of the principal classes within them, to see at once the howling antihistoricalness, falsity and hypocrisy of the view that the "defence of the fatherland" idea can be justified in the present war.

THE EXAMPLE OF BELGIUM

The favourite plea of the socialchauvinist triple (now quadruple) entente (in Russia. Plekhanov and Co.), is the example of Belgium. But this example goes against them. The German imperialists shamelessly violated the neutrality of Belgium, as belligerent states have done always and everywhere, trampling upon all treaties and obligations if necessary. Let us suppose that all the states interested in the observation of international treaties declared war on Germany with the demand for the liberation and indemnification of Belgium. In such a case, the sympathies of Socialists would, of course, be on the side of Germany's enemies. But the whole point is that the "triple (and quadruple) entente" is waging war not over Belgium this is perfectly well known, and only hypocrites conceal this. England is grabbing Germany's colonies and Turkey; Russia is grabbing Galicia and Turkey, France wants AlsaceLorraine and even the left hank of the Rhine; a treaty has been concluded with Italy for the division of the spoils (Albania, Asia Minor); bargaining is going on with Bulgaria and Rumania, also for the division of the spoils. In the present war waged by the present governments it is impossible to help Belgium without helping to strangle Austria or Turkey, etc.! How does "defence of the fatherland" come in here? Herein, precisely, lies the specific feature of imperialist war, war between reactionarybourgeois, historically obsolete governments, waged for the purpose of oppressing other nations. Whoever justifies participation in the present war perpetuates imperialist oppression of nations. Whoever advocates taking advantage of the present embarrassments of the governments to fight for the social revolution champions the real freedom of really all nations, which is possible only under Socialism.

WHAT IS RUSSIA FIGHTING FOR?

In Russia, capitalist imperialism of the latest type has fully revealed itself in the policy of tsarism towards Persia, Manchuria and Mongolia; but, in general, military and feudal imperialism predominates in Russia. In no country in the world is the majority of the population oppressed so much as it is in Russia; Great Russians constitute only 43 per cent of the population, he., less than half; all the rest are denied rights as aliens, Of the 170 million inhabitants of Russia, about 100 million are oppressed and denied rights. Tsarism is waging war to seize Galicia and finally to crush the liberties of the Ukrainians, to seize Armenia, Constantinople, etc. Tsarism regards the war as a means of diverting attention from the growth of discontent within the country and of suppressing the growing revolutionary movement. At the present time, for every two Great Russians in Russia there are from two to three rightless "aliens": tsarism is striving by means of the war to increase the number of nations oppressed by Russia, to perpetuate this oppression and thereby undermine the struggle for freedom which the Great Russians themselves are waging. The possibility of oppressing and robbing other nations perpetuates economic stagnation, because, often, the source of income is not the development of productive forces, but the semifeudal exploitation of "aliens". Thus, on the part of Russia, the war is distinguished for its profoundly reactionary and antiliberating character.

SOCIAL CHAUVINISM

Socialchauvinism is advocacy of the idea of "defence of the fatherland" in the present war. Further, this idea logically leads to the abandonment of the class struggle during the war, to voting war credits, etc. Actually, the socialchauvinists are pursuing an antiproletarian, bourgeois policy; for actually, they are championing not "defence of the fatherland" in the sense of fighting foreign oppression, but the "right" of one or other of the "great" powers to plunder colonies and to oppress other nations. The socialchauvinists repeat the bourgeois deception of the people that the war is being waged to protect the freedom and existence of nations, and thereby they go over to the side of the bourgeoisie against the proletariat. In the category of socialchauvinists are those who justify and embellish the governments and bourgeoisie of one of the belligerent groups of powers, as well as those who, like Kautsky, argue that the Socialists of all the belligerent powers have an equal right to "defend the fatherland". Socialchauvinism, being actually defence of the privileges, advantages, robbery and violence of one's "own" (or every) imperialist bourgeoisie, is the utter betrayal of all socialist convictions and of the decision of the Basle International Socialist Congress.

THE BASLE MANIFESTO

The manifesto on war that was unanimously adopted in Basle in 1911 had in view the very war between England and Germany and their present allies that broke out in 1914 The manifesto openly declares that no plea of the interests of the people can justify such a war, waged "for the sake of the profits of the capitalists" and "the ambitions of dynasties" on the basis of the imperialist, predatory policy of the great powers. The manifesto openly declares that war is dangerous "for the governments" (all without exception), notes their fear of "a proletarian revolution", and very definitely points to the example of the Commune of 1871, and of OctoberDecember 1905, i.e., to the examples of revolution and civil war. Thus, the Basle Manifesto lays down, precisely for the present war, the tactics of revolutionary struggle by the workers on an international scale against their governments, the tactics of proletarian revolution. The Basle Manifesto repeats the statement in the Stuttgart resolution that, in the event of war breaking out, Socialists must take advantage of the "economic and political crisis" it will cause, to "hasten the downfall of capitalism", i.e., to take advantage of the governments' embarrassments and the anger of the masses, caused by the war, for the socialist revolution.

The policy of the socialchauvinists, their justification of the war from the bourgeoisliberation standpoint, their sanctioning of "defence of the fatherland", voting credits, entering cabinets, and so on and so forth, is downright treachery to Socialism, which can be explained only, as we wilt see lower down, by the victory of opportunism and of the nationalliberal labour policy in the majority of European parties.

FALSE REFERENCES TO MARX AND ENGELS

The Russian socialchauvinists (headed by Plekhanov), refer to Marx's tactics in the war of 1870; the German (of the type of Lensch, David and Co.) to Engels' statement in 1891 that in the event of war against Russia and France together, it would be the duty of the German Socialists to defend their fatherland; and lastly, the socialchauvinists of the Kautsky type, who want to reconcile and legitimatize international chauvinism, refer to the fact that Marx and Engels, while condemning war, nevertheless, constantly, from to 18701871 and 18761877, took the side of one or another belligerent state once war had broken out

All these references are outrageous distortions of the views of Marx and Engels in the interest of the bourgeoisie and the opportunists, in just the same way as the writings of the Anarchists Guillaume and Co. distort the views of Marx and Engels in justification of anarchism.

The war of 18701871 was a historically progressive war on the part of Germany until Napoleon III was defeated; for the latter, together with the tsar, had oppressed Germany for many years, keeping her in a state of feudal disintegration. But as soon as the war developed into the plunder of France (the annexation of Alsace and Lorraine), Marx and Engels emphatically condemned the Germans. And even at the beginning of that war Marx and Engels approved of the refusal of Bebel and Liebknecht to vote for credits and advised the SocialDemocrats not to merge with the bourgeoisie, but to uphold the independent class interests of the proletariat. To apply the appraisal of this bourgeoisprogressive and nationalliberating war to the present imperialist war means mocking at truth. The same applies with still greater force to the war of 18541855, and to all the wars of the nineteenth century, when there was no modern imperialism, no ripe objective conditions f or Socialism, and no mass Socialist parties in any of the belligerent countries, i.e., none of the conditions from which the Basle Manifesto deduced the tactics of "proletarian revolution" in connection with a war between the great powers.

Whoever refers today to Marx's attitude towards the wars of the epoch of the progressive bourgeoisie and forgets Man's statement that "the workers have no fatherland", a statement that applies precisely to the epoch of the reactionary, obsolete bourgeoisie, to the epoch of the socialist revolution. shamelessly distorts Marx and substitute, the bourgeois for the socialist point of view.

THE COLLAPSE OF THE SECOND INTERNATIONAL

The Socialists of all the world solemnly declared in Basle, in 1912, that they regarded the impending war in Europe as the "criminal" and most reactionary affair of all the governments, which must hasten the downfall of capitalism by inevitably calling forth a revolution against it. The war came, the crisis came. Instead of revolutionary tactics, the majority of the SocialDemocratic parties conducted reactionary tactics, went over to the side of their respective governments and bourgeoisie. This betrayal of Socialism signifies the collapse of the Second (18891914) International, and we must understand what caused this collapse, what brought socialchauvinism into being what gave it strength.

SOCIALCHAUVINISM IS CONSUMMATED OPPORTUNISM

During the whole epoch of the Second International, a struggle raged everywhere in the SocialDemocratic parties between the revolutionary and the opportunist wings. In a number of countries a split has taken place along this line (England, Italy, Holland, Bulgaria). Not a single Marxist has any doubt that opportunism expresses bourgeois policy within the workingclass movement, expresses the interests of the petty bourgeoisie and the alliance of a tiny section of bourgeoisified workers with "their" bourgeoisie against the interests of the proletarian masses, the oppressed masses.

The objective conditions of the end of the nineteenth century exceptionally intensified opportunism, converted the utilization of bourgeois legality into subservience to it, created a tiny stratum of bureaucrats and aristocrats within the working class, and drew into the ranks of the SocialDemocratic parties numerous pettybourgeois "fellow travellers".

The war accelerated this development and transformed opportunism into socialchauvinism, transformed the secret alliance between the opportunists and the bourgeoisie into an open one. Simultaneously, the military authorities everywhere have introduced martial law and have muzzled the mass of the workers, whose old leaders have nearly all gone over to the bourgeoisie.

Opportunism and socialchauvinism have the same economic basis: the interests of a tiny stratum of privileged workers and of the petty bourgeoisie who are defending their privileged position, their "right" to crumbs of the profits "their" national bourgeoisie obtain from robbing other nations, from the advantages of their position as the ruling nation, etc.

Opportunism and socialchauvinism have the same ideologicalpolitical content: collaboration of classes instead of class struggle, renunciation of revolutionary methods of struggle, helping one's "own" government in its embarrassed situation instead of taking advantage of these embarrassments for revolution. If we take all the European countries as a whole, if we pay attention not to individuals (even the most authoritative), we will find that it is the opportunist trend that has become the chief bulwark of socialchauvinism, whereas from the camp of the revolutionaries, more or less consistent protests against it are heard nearly everywhere. And if we take, for example, the grouping of trends at the Stuttgart International Socialist Congress in 1907, we will find that international Marxism was opposed to imperialism, while international opportunism was in favour of it already at that time.

Unity with the Opportunists

In the past epoch, before the war, although opportunism was often regarded as a "deviationist", "extremist" part of the

SocialDemocratic Party, it was nevertheless regarded as a legitimate part. The war has shown that this cannot be so in future. Opportunism has "matured", is now playing to the full its role as emissary of the bourgeois in the workingclass movement. Unity with the opportunists has become sheer hypocrisy, an example of which we see in the German SocialDemocratic Party. On all important occasions (for example, the voting on August 4), the opportunists come forward with an ultimatum, which they carry out with the aid of their numerous connections with the bourgeoisie, of their majority on the executives of the trade unions, etc. Unity with the opportunists actually means today, subordinating the working class to "its" national bourgeoisie, alliance with it for the purpose of oppressing other nations and of fighting for greatpower privileges, it means splitting the revolutionary proletariat in all countries.

Hard as the struggle may be, in individual cases, against the opportunists who predominate in many organisations, peculiar as the process of purging the workers' parties of opportunists may be in individual countries, this process is inevitable and fruitful. Reformist Socialism is dying; regenerated Socialism "will be revolutionary, uncompromising and insurrectionary", to use the apt expression of the French Socialist Paul Golay.

"Kautskyism"

Kautsky, the biggest authority in the Second International, gives us a highly typical and glaring example of how the verbal recognition of Marxism has led actually to its conversion into "Struveism", or into "Brentanoism". We see this also from the example of Plekhanov. By means of obvious sophistry they rob Marxism of its revolutionary living spirit; they recognise everything in Marxism except revolutionary methods of struggle, the preaching of and preparation for such methods, and the training of the masses precisely in this direction. Kautsky, in an unprincipled fashion, "reconciles" the fundamental idea of socialchauvinism, recognition of defence of the fatherland in the present war, with a diplomatic, sham concession to the Lefts it, the shape of abstaining from voting credits, the verbal claim of being in the opposition, etc. Kautsky, who in 1909 wrote a whole book on the approaching epoch of revolutions and on the connection between war and revolutions, Kautsky, who in 1912 signed the Basle Manifesto on taking revolutionary advantage of the impending war, is now, in every way, justifying and embellishing socialchauvinism and, like Plekhanov, joins the bourgeoisie iii ridiculing all thought of revolution, all steps towards direct revolutionary struggle.

The working class cannot play its worldrevolutionary role unless it wages a ruthless struggle against this renegacy. spinelessness, subservience to opportunism and unexampled vulgarization of the theories of Marxism. Kautskyism is not fortuity, but a social product of the contradictions within the Second International, a combination of loyalty to Marxism in words and subordination to opportunism in deeds.

This fundamental falseness of "Kautskyism" manifests itself in different ways in different countries. In Holland, RolandHolst while rejecting the idea of defending the fatherland, defends unity with the opportunists' party. In Russia Trotsky, while also rejecting this idea, also defends unity with the opportunist and chauvinist Nasha Zarya group. In Rumania, Rakovsky, while declaring war on opportunism as being responsible for the collapse of the International, is at the same time ready to recognise the legitimacy of the idea of defending the fatherland. All this is a manifestation of the evil which the Dutch Marxists (Gorter and Pannekoek) have called "passive radicalism", and which amounts to substituting for Marxism eclecticism in theory and servility to, or impotence in the face of, opportunism in practice.

The Marxists' Slogan is the Slogan of Revolutionary SocialDemocracy

The war has undoubtedly created a most acute crisis and has increased the distress of the masses to an incredible degree. The reactionary character of this war, and the shameless lies told by the bourgeoisie of all countries in covering up their predatory aims with "national" ideology, are inevitably creating, on the basis of an objectively revolutionary situation, revolutionary moods among the masses. It is our duty to help the masses to become conscious of these moods, to deepen and formulate them. This task is correctly expressed only by the slogan: convert the imperialist war into civil war; and all consistently waged class struggles during the war, all seriously conducted "mass action" tactics inevitably lead to this. It is impossible to foretell whether a powerful revolutionary movement will flare up during the first or the second war of the great powers, whether during or after it; in any case, our bounden duty is systematically and undeviatingly to work precisely in this direction.

The Basle Manifesto refers directly to the example set by the Paris Commune, i.e., to the conversion of a war between governments into civil war. Half a century ago, the proletariat was too weak; the objective conditions for Socialism had not yet ripened; there could be no coordination and cooperation between the revolutionary movements in all the belligerent countries; the "national ideology" (the traditions of 1792), with which a section of the Parisian workers were imbued, was their pettybourgeois weakness, which Marx noted at the time, and was one of the causes of the fall of the Commune. Half a century after it, the conditions that weakened the revolution at that time have passed away, and it is unpardonable for a Socialist at the present time to resign himself to the abandonment of activities precisely in the spirit of the Paris Communards.

The Example Shown by the Fraternisation in the Trenches

The bourgeois newspapers of all the belligerent countries have reported cases of fraternisation between the soldiers of the belligerent nations even in the trenches. And the issue by the military authorities (of Germany, England) of draconic orders against such fraternisation proved that the governments and the bourgeoisie attached grave importance to it. He fact that such cases of fraternisation have been possible even when opportunism reigns supreme in the top ranks of the SocialDemocratic parties of Western Europe, and when socialchauvinism is supported by the entire SocialDemocratic press and by all the authorities of the Second International, shows us how possible it would be to shorten the present criminal, reactionary and slaveowners' war and to organise a revolutionary international movement if systematic work were conducted in this direction, if only by the Leftwing Socialists in all the belligerent countries.

THE IMPORTANCE OF AN UNDERGROUND ORGANISATION

The most prominent Anarchists all over the world, no less than the opportunists, have disgraced themselves with socialchauvinism (in the spirit of Plekhanov and Kautsky) in this war. One of the useful results of this war will undoubtedly be that it will kill both anarchism and opportunism.

While under no circumstances or conditions refraining from utilizing all legal possibilities, however small, for the purpose of organizing the masses and of preaching Socialism, the SocialDemocratic parties must break with subservience to legality. "You shoot first, Messieurs the Bourgeoisie," wrote Engels, hinting precisely at civil war and at the necessity of our violating legality after the bourgeoisie had violated it. The crisis has shown that the bourgeoisie violate it in all countries, even the freest, and that it is impossible to lead the masses to revolution unless an underground organisation is set up for the purpose of advocating, discussing, appraising and preparing revolutionary methods of struggle. In Germany, for example, all the honest things that Socialists are doing, are being done in spite of despicable opportunism and hypocritical "Kautskyism", and are being done secretly. In England, people are sent to penal servitude for printing appeals against joining the army.

To regard the repudiation of underground methods of propaganda, and ridiculing the latter in the legally published press, as being compatible with membership of the SocialDemocratic Patty is treachery to Socialism.

Concerning Defeat of "One's Own" Government in the Imperialist War

Both the advocates of victory for their governments in the present war and the advocates of the slogan "neither victory not defeat", equally take the standpoint of socialchauvinism. A revolutionary class cannot but wish for the defeat of its government in a reactionary war, cannot fail to see that its military reverses facilitate its overthrow.

Only a bourgeois who believes that a war started by the governments must necessarily end as a war between governments and wants it to end as such, can regard as "ridiculous" and "absurd" the idea that the Socialists of all the belligerent countries should wish for the defeat of all "their" governments and express this wish. On the contrary, it is precisely a statement of this kind that would conform to the cherished thoughts of every classconscious worker, and would be in line with our activities towards converting the imperialist war into civil war.

Undoubtedly, the serious antiwar agitation that is being conducted by a section of the British, German and Russian Socialists has "weakened the military power" of the respective governments, but such agitation stands to the credit of the Socialists. Socialists must explain to the masses that they have no other road of salvation except the revolutionary overthrow of "their" governments, and that advantage must be taken of these governments' embarrassments in the present war precisely for this purpose.

Pacifism and the Peace Slogan

The sentiments of the masses in favour of peace often express incipient protest, anger and consciousness of the reactionary character of the war. It is the duty of all SocialDemocrats to utilise these sentiments. They will take a most ardent pan in every movement and in every demonstration on this ground; but they will not deceive the people by conceding the idea that peace without annexations, without the oppression of nations, without plunder, without the germs of new wars among the present governments and ruling classes is possible in the absence of a revolutionary movement. Such a deception of the people would merely play into the hands of the secret diplomacy of the belligerent governments and facilitate their counter revolutionary plans. Whoever wants a lasting and democratic peace must be in favour of civil war against the governments and the bourgeoisie.

THE RIGHT OF NATIONS TO SELF-DETERMINATION

The most widespread deception of the people perpetrated by the bourgeoisie it, the present war is the concealment of its predatory aims with "nationalliberation" ideology. The English promise the liberation of Belgium, the Germans of Poland, etc. Actually, as we have seen, this is a war waged by the oppressors of the majority of the nations of the world for the purpose of fortifying and expanding such oppression.

Socialists cannot achieve their great aim without fighting against all oppression of nations. Therefore, they must without fail demand that the SocialDemocratic parties of oppressing countries (especially of the socalled "great" powers) should recognise and champion the right of oppressed nations to self-determination, precisely in the political sense of the term, i.e., the tight to political secession. The Socialist of a ruling or colonyowning nation who fails to champion this right is a chauvinist.

The championing of this right, far from encouraging the formation of small states, leads, on the contrary, to the freer, fearless and therefore wider and mote widespread formation of very big states and federations of states, which are more beneficial for the masses and more fully in keeping with economic development.

The Socialists of oppressed nations must, in their turn, unfailingly fight for the complete (including organisational) unity of the workers of the oppressed and oppressing nationalities. The idea of the juridical separation of one nation from another (socalled "culturalnational autonomy" advocated by Bauer and Renner) is reactionary.

Imperialism is the epoch of the constantly increasing oppression of the nations of the world by a handful of "great" powers and, therefore, it is impossible to fight for the socialist international revolution against imperialism unless the right of nations to self-determination is recognized. "No nation can be free if it oppresses other nations" (Marx and Engels). A proletariat that tolerates the slightest violence by "its" nation against other nations cannot be a socialist proletariat.

CLASSES AND PARTIES IN RUSSIA

The Bourgeoisie and the War

To one respect, the Russian government has not lagged behind its European confrères; like them, it has succeeded in deceiving "its" people on a grand scale. A huge, monstrous machine of falsehood sod cunning was set going in Russia too for the purpose of infecting the masses with chauvinism, of creating the impression that the tsarist government is waging a "just" war, that it is disinterestedly defending its "brother Slavs", etc.

The landlord class and the upper stratum of the commercial and industrial bourgeoisie ardently supported the tsarist government's bellicose policy. They are rightly expecting enormous material gains and privileges for themselves out of the partition of the Turkish and the Austrian legacy. A whole series of their congresses already have a foretaste of the profits that would flow into their pockets if the tsarist army were victorious. Moreover, the reactionaries are very well ante that if anything can postpone the downfall of the Romanov monarchy and delay the new revolution in Russia, it can only be a foreign war that ends in victory for the tsar.

Broad strata of the urban "middle" bourgeoisie, of the bourgeois intelligentsia, professional people, etc., were also infected with chauvinismat all events at the beginning of the war. The Cadetsthe party of the Russian liberal bourgeoisiewholly and unreservedly supported the tsarist government. In the sphere of foreign policy the Cadets have long been a government party. PanSlavismwith the aid of which tsarist diplomacy has more than once carried out its grand political swindleshas become the official ideology of the Cadets. Russian liberalism has degenerated into national liberalism. It is vying in "patriotism" with the Black Hundreds; it always willingly votes for militarism, navaliant etc. In the camp of Russia liberalism, approximately the same thing is observed as was seen in the 70s in Germany when "freethinking" liberalism decayed and from it arose a nationalliberal party. The Russian liberal bourgeoisie has definitely taken the path of counterrevolution. The point of view of the R.S.D.L.P. on this question has been fully confirmed. Life has shattered the view held by our opportunists that Russian liberalism is still a motive force of the revolution in Russia.

Among the peasantry, the ruling clique, with the aid of the bourgeois press, the clergy, etc., also succeeded in rousing chauvinist sentiments. But, as the soldiers return from the field of slaughter, sentiment in the rural districts will undoubtedly turn against the tsarist monarchy. The bourgeoisdemocratic parties that come in contact with the peasantry failed to withstand the chauvinist wave. The Trudovik party in the State Duma refused to vote for war credits; but through the mouth of its leader Kerensky it made a "patriotic" declaration which played extremely well into the hands of the monarchy. The entire legally published press of the "Narodniks" in general, trailed behind the liberals. Even the Leftwing of bourgeois democracythe socalled SocialistRevolutionary Party, which is affiliated to the International Socialist Bureaufloated in the same stream. Mr. Rubanovich. that party's representative on the I.S.B., comes out as an open socialchauvinist. Half of this party's delegates at the London Conference of "Entente" Socialists voted for a chauvinist resolution (while the other half abstained from voting).

In the illegally published press of the Socialist Revolutionaries (the newspaper = Novosti and others) chauvinists predominate. The revolutionaries "from bourgeois circles", i.e., the bourgeois revolutionaries not connected with the working class, have suffered utter bankruptcy in this war. The sad fate of Kropotkin, Burtsev and Rubanovich is extremely significant.

THE WORKING CLASS AND THE WAR

The only class in Russia that they did not succeed in infecting with chauvinism is the proletariat. Only the most ignorant strata of the workers were involved in the few excesses that occurred at the beginning of the war. The part played by workers in the Moscow antiGerman riots was greatly exaggerated. In general, and on the whole, the working class of Russia proved to be immune to chauvinism.

This is to be explained by the revolutionary situation in the country and by the general conditions of life of the Russian proletariat. The years 19121914 marked the beginning of a new, grand revolutionary upswing in Russia. We again witnessed a great strike movement such as the world has not known. The number involved in the mass revolutionary strike in 1913 was, at the very lowest estimation, one and a half million, and it, 1914 it rose above two million and drew near to the level of 1905. On the eve of the war, in St. Petersburg, things had already developed to the first barricade battles.

The underground Russian SocialDemocratic Labour Party performed its duty to the International to the full. The banner of internationalism did not falter in its hands. Our Party had broken organisationally with the opportunist groups and elements long ago; its feet were not weighted with the fetters of opportunism and of "legalism at any price", and this circumstance helped it to perform its revolutionary dutyjust as the breakaway from Bissolati's opportunist party helped the Italian comrades too.

The general situation in our country is inimical to the efflorescence of "socialist" opportunism among the masses of the workers. In Russia we see a whole series of shades of opportunism and reformism among the intelligentsia, the petty bourgeoisie, etc.; but it constitutes an insignificant minority among the politically active strata of the workers. The privileged stratum of workers and office employees in our country is very weak. The fetishism of legality could not be created here. The Liquidators (the party of the opportunists led by Axelrod, Potressov, Cherevanin, Maslov, and others) found no serious support among the masses of the workers before the war.

The elections to the Fourth State Duma resulted in the return of all the six antiliquidator worker deputies. The circulation of and collection of funds for the legally published workers' press in Petrograd and Moscow have proved irrefutably that fourfifths of the classconscious workers are opposed to opportunism and liquidationism.

Since the beginning of the war the tsarist government has arrested and exiled thousands and thousands of advanced workers, members of our underground R.S.D.L.P. This circumstance, together with the introduction of martial law in the country, the suppression of our newspapers, and so forth, has retarded the movement. But for all that, out Party is continuing its underground revolutionary activities. In Petrograd, the committee of our Party is publishing the underground newspaper Protetarsky = Golos.

Articles from the Central Organ SotsialDemokrat, published abroad, are reprinted in Petrograd and sent out to the provinces. Manifestoes are secretly printed and circulated even in soldiers' barracks. In various secluded places outside the city, secret workers' meetings ate held. Lately big strikes of metal workers have begun in Petrograd. In connection with these strikes our Petrograd Committee has issued several appeals to the workers.

The Russian SocialDemocratic Labour Group in the State Duma and the War

In 1913 a split occurred among the SocialDemocratic deputies in the State Duma. On one side were the seven supporters of opportunism led by Chkheidze. They were elected for the seven nonproletarian gubernias where the workers numbered 214,000. On the other side were six deputies, all from workers' curiae, elected for the most industrialised centres in Russia, in which the workers numbered 1,008,000.

The chief issue in the split was: the tactics of revolutionary Marxism or the tactics of opportunist reformism? In practice, the disagreement manifested itself mainly in the sphere of work outside of parliament among the masses. It Russia this work had to be conducted secretly if those conducting it wanted to remain on revolutionary ground. The Chkheidze group remained a faithful ally of the Liquidators who repudiated underground work, and defended them in all talks with the workers, at all meetings. Hence the split. the six deputies formed the R.S.D.L. group. The year's work has shown irrefutably that this is the group that the overwhelming majority of the Russian workers supports.

On the outbreak of the war the disagreement stood out in glaring relief. he Chkheidze group confined itself to parliamentary action. It did not vote for credits, for had it done so it would have roused against itself a storm of indignation among the workers. (We have seen that in Russia even the pettybourgeois Trudoviki did not vote for credits); but it did not utter a protest against socialchauvinism either.

The R.S.D.L. group, expressing the political line of our. Party, acted differently. It carried into the very depths of the working class a protest against the war; it conducted antiimperialist propaganda among the broad masses of the Russian proletarians.

And it met with a very sympathetic response among the workerswhich frightened the government and compelled it, in flagrant violation of its own laws, to arrest our comrades, the deputies, and to sentence them to lifelong exile it, Siberia. In its very first official announcement of the arrest of our comrades the tsarist government wrote:

> *An entirely exceptional position in this respect was taken by some members of SocialDemocratic societies, the object of whose activities was to shake the military might of Russia by agitating against the war by means of underground appeals and verbal propaganda.*

In response to Vandervelde's wellknown appeal "temporarily" to stop the struggle against tsarismit has now become known from the evidence of Prince Kudashev, the tsar's envoy in Belgium, that Vandervelde did not draw up this appeal alone, but in collaboration with the abovementioned tsar's envoyonly our Party, through its Central Committee, replied in the negative. The guiding centre of the Liquidators agreed with Vandervelde and officially stated in the press that "in its activities it will not counteract the war."

The tsarist government's primary charge against out comrades, the deputies, was that they propagated this negative answer to Vandervelde among the workers.

At the trial, the tsarist Prosecutor, Mr. Nenarokomov, set up the German and French Socialists as examples for our comrades. "The German SocialDemocrats," he said, "voted for the war credits and proved to be the friends of the government. That is how the German SocialDemocrats acted, but the dismal knights of Russian SocialDemocracy did not act in this way... The Socialists of Belgium and France unanimously forgot their quarrels with other classes, forgot party strife and unhesitatingly tallied round the flag." But the members of the R.S.D.L. group, obeying the instructions of the Central Committee of the Party, did not act in this way, he said...

The trial unfolded an imposing picture of the extensive, underground andwar agitation our Party was conducting among the masses of the proletariat. It goes without saying that the tsarist court did not by a very long way reveal all the activities our comrades were conducting in this sphere; but even what was revealed showed how mud, had boa, done within the short space of a few months.

At the trial the secret manifestoes issued by our groups and committees against the war and for international tactics were read. Threads stretched from the classconscious workers all over Russia to the members of the R.S.D.L. group, and the latter did all in its power to help the workers to appraise the war from the standpoint of Marxism.

Comrade Muranov, the deputy of the workers of the Kharkov Gubernia, said at the trial:

> *"Understanding that the people did not send me into the State Duma for the purpose of wearing out the seat of a Duma armchair, I travelled about the country to ascertain the mood of the working class." He admitted at the trial that he took upon himself the function of a secret agitator of our Party, that in the Urals he organised a workers' committee at the Verkhneisetsky Works, and in other places. The trial showed that after the war broke out members of the R.S.D.L. group travelled through almost the whole of Russia for propaganda purposes, that Muranov, Petrovsky. Badayev and others arranged numerous workers' meetings, at which antiwar resolutions were passed, and so forth.*

The tsarist government threatened the accused with capital punishment. Owing to this, not all of them behaved at the actual trial as bravely as Comrade Muranov. They tried to make it difficult for the tsarist prosecutors to secure their conviction. The Russian socialchauvinists are now meanly utilising this to obscure the essence of the question: what kind of parliamentarism does the working class need?

Parliamentarism is recognized by Südekum and Heine, Sembat and Valiant, Bissolati and Mussolini, Chkheidze and Plekhanov, and parliamentarism is recognised by our comrades in the R.S.D.L. Duma group; it is recognised by the Bulgarian and Italian comrades who have broken with the chauvinists. There are different kinds of parliamentarism. Some utilise the parliamentary arena in order to win the favour of their governments, or, at best, to wash their hands of everything, like the Chkheidze group. Others utilise parliamentarism in order to remain revolutionary to the end, to perform their duty as Socialists and internationalists even under the most difficult circumstances. The parliamentary activities of some bring them into ministerial seats; the parliamentary activities of others bring themto prison, to exile, to penal servitude. Some serve the bourgeoisie, othersthe proletariat. Some are socialimperialists. Others are revolutionary Marxists.

THE RESTORATION

How should the International be restored? But first, a few words about how the International should not be restored.

The method of the socialchauvinists and of the "centre"

Oh, the socialchauvinists of all countries are big "internationalists"! Since the very beginning of the war they have been burdened with care for the International. On the one hand, they assure us that the talk about the collapse of the International is "exaggerated". Actually, nothing exceptional has occurred. Listen to Kautsky: simply, the International is a "peacetime instrument"; naturally, this instrument was found to be somewhat not up to the mark in wartime. On the other hand, the socialchauvinists of all countries have found a very simpleand chiefly, an internationalway out of the situation that has arisen. A simple way out: it is only necessary to wait until the war ends; but until the war ends the Socialists of each country must defend their fatherland and support "their" government; when the war endsmutual "amnesty", admission that everybody was right, that in peacetime we live like brothers, but in wartime weon the basis of such and such resolutionscall upon the German workers to exterminate their French brothers, and vice versa.

On this Kautsky and Plekhanov and Victor Adler and Heine are equally agreed. Victor Adler writes that "when we have passed through this hard time, out first duty will be to refrain from pointing to the mote in each other's eye." Kautsky asserts that "up till now no voices of serious Socialists have been heard from any side that rouse apprehensions" concerning the fate of the International. Plekhanov says that "it is unpleasant to grasp the hands" (of the German SocialDemocrats) "that reek of the blood of the innocently killed." But he at once goes on to propose an "amnesty": "here it will be quite appropriate," he writes, "to subordinate the heart to the mind. For the sake of the great cause, the International will have to take into consideration even belated remorse." Heine in Sozialistische Monatshefte describes Vandervelde's behaviour as "courageous and proud", and sets him upan example for the German Lefts.

In short, whet the war ends, appoint, commission consisting of Kautsky and Plekhanov, Vandervelde and Adler and a "unanimous" resolution in the spirit of mutual amnesty will be drawn up in a trice. The dispute will be safely covered up. Instead of helping the workers to understand what has occurred, they will deceive them with sham, paper "unity". The amalgamation of the socialchauvinists and hypocrites of all countries will be described as the restoration of the International.

We must not conceal from ourselves the fact that the danger of such a "restoration is very great. The socialchauvinists of all countries are equally interested in it All of them are equally unwilling that the masses of the workers themselves should try to grasp the issue: Socialism or nationalism? All of them are equally interested in coveting up each other's sins. None of them is able to propose anything except what is proposed by that virtuoso in "international" hypocrisy, Kautsky.

And yet, this danger is scarcely realised. During the year

of war we have witnessed a number of attempts to restore international connections. We will not speak of the conferences in London and Vienna, at which downright chauvinists assembled to help the General Staffs and the bourgeoisie of their "fatherlands". We have in mind the conferences in Lugano and Copenhagen , the International Women's = Conference and the International Youth Conference. These assemblies were inspired by the best wishes. But they totally failed to see the abovementioned danger. They did not lay down a fighting line for internationalists. They did not point out to the proletariat the danger that threatens it from the socialchauvinists' method of "restoring" the International. At best, they confined themselves to repeating the old resolutions without indicating to the workers that unless a struggle is waged against the socialchauvinists, the cause of Socialism is hopeless. At best they marked time.

THE STATE OF AFFAIRS AMONG THE OPPOSITION

There can be no doubt whatever that what interests all internationalists most is the state of affairs among the German SocialDemocratic opposition. Official German SocialDemocracy, which was the strongest and the leading party in the Second International, struck the heaviest blow at the international workers' organisation. But at the same time, it was in German SocialDemocracy that the strongest opposition was found. Of all the big European patties, it was in the German party that the loud voice of protest of the comrades who have remained loyal to the banner of Socialism was first raised. It was with joy that we read the magazines Lichtstrahlen and Die Internationale. With still greater joy we learned of the distribution in Germany of secretly printed manifestoes, as for example the manifesto entitled: The Chief Enemy Is at Home. This showed that the spirit of Socialism is alive among the German workers, That there are still people in Germany capable of upholding revolutionary Marxism.

The split in the presentday socialist movement has been most strikingly revealed within German SocialDemocracy. Here we very distinctly see three trends: the opportunistchauvinists, who have nowhere sunk to such a degree of renegacy as they have in Germany; the Kautskyan "Centre", which has here proved to be incapable of playing any other role than that of servitors of the opportunists; and the Leftwho are the only SocialDemocrats in Germany.

Naturally, what interests us most of all is the state of affairs among the German Left. In it we see our comrades, the hope of all the internationalist elements.

What is the State of Affairs in it?

The magazine Die Internationale was quite right when it wrote that the German Left was still in a state of ferment, that considerable regroupings still lie ahead in it, that there are more resolute and less resolute elements within it.

We Russian internationalists do not in the least, of course, claim the right to interfere in the internal affairs of our comrades the German Lefts. We are aware that they alone are fully competent to determine their methods of fighting the opportunists in conformity with the conditions of time and place. Only, we deem it our tight and duty frankly to express our opinion on the state of affairs.

We are convinced that the author of the leading article in the magazine Die Internationale was profoundly right when he asserted that the Kautskyan "Centre" is doing more harm to Marxism than avowed socialchauvinism. Whoever now obscures disagreements, whoever now, in the guise of Marxism, preaches to the workers what Kautskyism is preaching, is lulling the workers, is more harmful than the Südekums and Heines, who put the question bluntly and compel the workers to try to grasp the issue.

The fact that Kautsky and Haase are permitting themselves lately to demur against the "official bodies" should mislead nobody. The disagreements between them and the Scheidemanns are not on fundamentals. he former believe that Hindenburg and Mackensen are already victorious and that they can already permit themselves the luxury of protesting against annexations. The latter believe that Hindenburg and Mackensen are not yet victorious and that, therefore, it is necessary "to bold out to the end".

Kautskyism is waging only a sham fight against the "official bodies" precisely in order to be able, after the war, to obscure the fundamental dispute for the workers and to gloss the matter over with the 1,001st puffy resolution couched in a vaguely "Leftist" spirit, in the drafting of which the diplomats of the Second International are such masters.

It is quite understandable that in their arduous struggle against the "official bodies" the German opposition should also make use of this unprincipled opposition raised by Kautskyism. But what must remain the touchstone for every interntionalist ishostility towards neoKautskyism. Only he is a genuine internationalist who fights Kautskyism, who understands that, fundamentally, the "Centre", even after the sham turn taken by its leaders, remains an ally of the chauvinists and opportunists.

Of enormous importance is our attitude towards the wavering elements in the International in general. These elementsmainly Socialists of the pacifist shadeare to be found both in the neutral countries and in some of the belligerent countries (in England, for example, the Independent Labour Party). These elements can be our fellow travellers. Rapprochement with them in opposition to the socialchauvinists is necessary. But it must be borne in mind that they are only fellow travellers, that on the chief and fundamental issues, with the restoration of the International, these elements will go not with us, but against us, they will go with Kautsky, Scheidemann, Vandervelde and Sembat. At international conferences we must not limit out programme to what is acceptable to these elements. If we do, we will become the captives of the wavering pacifists. This is what happened, for example, at the International Women's Conference in Berne. The German delegation, which supported Comrade Clara Zetkin's point of view, actually played the part of the "Centre" at this conference. The Women's Conference said only what was acceptable to the delegates from the opportunist Dutch party led by Troelstra, and to the delegates of the Independent Labour Party, whichwe will not forget thisat the London conference of "Entente" chauvinists voted for Vandervelde's resolution. We express our greatest respect for the I.L.P. for the brave struggle it has been waging against the British government during the war. But we know that this party has not adopted the Marxist stand. We, however, are of the opinion that the chief task of the SocialDemocratic opposition at the present moment is to raise the banner of revolutionary Marxism, to tell the workers firmly and definitely how we regard imperialist wars, to issue the watchword of mass revolutionary action, i.e., transform the epoch of imperialist wars into the beginning of the epoch of civil wars.

In spite of everything, there are revolutionary SocialDemocratic elements in many countries. They are to be found in Germany, and in Russia, and in Scandinavia (the influential trend of which Comrade Höglund is the representative), and in the Balkans (the party of the Bulgarian = "Tesnyaki"), and in Italy, and in England (a section of the British Socialist Party), and in France (Vaillant himself has admitted in L'Humanité that he has received letters of protest from internationalists, but he has not published one of them in full), and in Holland (the Tribunists), etc. To rally these Marxist elementshowever small their numbers may be at the beginningto recall in their name the now forgotten words of genuine Socialism, to call upon the workers of all countries to break with the chauvinists and to come under the old banner of Marxismsuch is the task of the day.

Conferences with socalled programmes of "action" have amounted up till now only to the proclamation, more or less fully, of the programme of simple pacifism. Marxism is not pacifism. It is necessary, of course, to fight for the speediest termination of the war. But only if a revolutionary struggle is called for does the demand for "peace acquire proletarian meaning. Without a series of revolutions, socalled democratic peace is a philistine utopia. The purpose of a teal programme of action would be served only by a Marxian programme, which gave the masses a full and clear explanation of what has occurred, which explained what imperialism is and how to combat it, which openly stated that it was opportunism that led to the collapse of the Second International, which openly called for the building of a Marxist International without and against the opportunists. Only. such a programme as would show that we have confidence in ourselves, confidence in Marxism, that we proclaim a lifeanddeath struggle against opportunism would sooner or later ensure for us the sympathy of the genuine proletarian masses.

THE RUSSIAN SOCIALDEMOCRATIC LABOUR PARTY AND THE THIRD INTERNATIONAL

The Russian SocialDemocratic Labour Party split away from its opportunists long ago. The Russian opportunists have now, in addition, become chauvinists. This only strengthens our opinion that a split from them in the interests of Socialism is essential. We are convinced that the SocialDemocrats' present disagreements with the socialchauvinists are in no way less wide that the Socialists' disagreements with the Anarchists when the SocialDemocrats split away from the latter. The opportunist Monitor rightly said in Preussische Jahrbücher that the present unity was to the advantage of the opportunists and the bourgeoisie because it compelled the Lefts to submit to the chauvinists and prevents the workers from grasping the issue and from forming their own genuinely workers', genuinely socialist party. We are most firmly convinced that in the present state of affairs, a split from the opportunists and chauvinists is the primary duty of the revolutionaryjust as a split from the yellows, the antiSemites, the liberal workers' unions, etc., was essential precisely in the interests of the speediest enlightenment of the backward workers and of drawing them into the ranks of the SocialDemocratic Party.

In our opinion, the Third International should be built on precisely such a revolutionary basis. For our Party, the question as to whether it is expedient to break with the socialchauvinists does not exist. Pot it, this question has been irrevocably settled. The only question that exists for our Party is whether this can be achieved in the nearest future on an international scale.

It is quite understandable that to bring about an international Marxist organisation, there must be a readiness to form independent Marxist parties in different countries.

Germany, being the country with the oldest and strongest workingclass movement, is of decisive importance he immediate future will show whether conditions have already ripened for the formation of a new, Marxist International.

If they have, our Party will gladly join such a Third International that will be purged of opportunism and chauvinism. If they have not, it will show that a more or less prolonged evolution is needed for this purging. In that case, our Party will be the extreme opposition within the old Internationaluntil a base is formed in different countries for an international working men's association that stands on the basis of revolutionary Marxism.

We do not, nor can we, know, what developments will take place in the international arena within the next few years. But there is one thing we know for certain, and of which we are unshakably convinced, namely, that our Party, in our country, among our proletariat, will work tirelessly in the abovementioned direction, and by all its daily activities will build up the Russian section of the Marxist International.

In Russia too we have no lack of avowed socialchauvinists and "Centre" groups. These people will fight against the formation of a Marxist International. We know that Plekhanov, in principle, stands on the same ground as Südekum and is already stretching out a hand to him. We know that the socalled "Organisation Committee" led by Axelrod is preaching Kautskyism on Russian soil. In the guise of workingclass unity, these people are preaching unity with the opportunists and, through them, with the bourgeoisie. But everything we know about the present workingclass movement in Russia fully convinces us that the classconscious proletariat in Russia will, as hitherto, remain with our Party.

DIVISION OF THE WORLD AMONG THE GREAT POWERS

In his book, on "the territorial development of the European colonies", A. Supan, the geographer, gives the following brief summary of this development at the end of the nineteenth century:

PERCENTAGE OF TERRITORY BELONGING TO THE EUROPEAN COLONIAL POWERS
(Including the United States)

	1876	1900	Increase or decrease
Africa..........	10.8	90.4	+79.6
Polynesia....	56.8	98.9	+42.1
Asia............	51.5	56.6	+5.1
Australia.....	100.0	100.0	
America......	27.5	27.2	0.3

"The characteristic feature of this period," he concludes, "is, therefore, the division of Africa and Polynesia." As there are no unoccupied territoriesthat is, territories that do not belong to any state in Asia and America, it is necessary to amplify Supan's conclusion and say that the characteristic feature of the period under review is the final partitioning of the globefinal, not in the sense that repartition is impossible; on the contrary, repartitions are possible and inevitablebut in the sense that the colonial policy of the capitalist countries has completed the seizure of the unoccupied territories on our planet. For the first time the world is completely divided up, so that in the future only redivision is possible, i.e., territories can only pass from one "owner" to another, instead of passing as ownerless territory to an owner. Hence, we are living in a peculiar epoch of world colonial policy, which is most closely connected with the "latest stage in the development of capitalism", with finance capital. For this reason, it is essential first of all to deal in greater detail with the facts, in order to ascertain as exactly as possible what distinguishes this epoch from those preceding it, and what the present situation is. In the first place, two questions of fact arise here: is an intensification of colonial policy, a sharpening of the struggle for colonies, observed precisely in the epoch of finance capital? And how, in this respect, is the world divided at the present time?

The American writer, Morris, in his book on the history of colonisation, made an attempt to sum up the data on the colonial possessions of Great Britain, France and Germany during different periods of the nineteenth century. The following is a brief summary of the results he has obtained:

COLONIAL POSSESSIONS						
Year	Great Britain		France		Germany	
	Area (000,000 sq. m.)	Pop. (000,000)	Area (000,000 sq. m.)	Pop. (000,000)	Area (000,000 sq. m.)	Pop. (000,000)
1815-30	?	126.4	0.02	0.5	—	—
1860	2.5	145.1	0.2	3.4	—	—
1880	7.7	267.9	0.7	7.5	—	—
1899	9.3	309.0	3.7	56.4	1.0	14.7

For Great Britain, the period of the enormous expansion of colonial conquests was that between 1860 and 1880, and it was also very considerable in the last twenty years of the nineteenth century. For France and Germany this period falls precisely in these twenty years. We saw above that the development of premonopoly capitalism, of capitalism in which free competition was predominant, reached its limit in the 1860s and 1870s. We now see that it is precisely after that period that the tremendous "boom" in colonial conquests begins, and that the struggle for the territorial division of the world becomes extraordinarily sharp. It is beyond doubt, therefore, that capitalism's transition to the stage of monopoly capitalism, to finance capital, is connected with the intensification of the struggle for the partitioning of the world.

Hobson, in his work on imperialism, marks the years 18841900 as the epoch of intensified "expansion" of the chief European states. According to his estimate, Great Britain during these years acquired 3,700,000 square miles of territory with 57,000,000 inhabitants; France, 3,600,000 square miles with 36,500,000; Germany, 1,000,000 square miles with 14,700,000; Belgium, 900,000 square miles with 30,000,000; Portugal, 800,000 square miles with 9,000,000 inhabitants. The scramble for colonies by all the capitalist states at the end of the nineteenth century and particularly since the 1880s is a commonly known fact in the history of diplomacy and of foreign policy.

In the most flourishing period of free competition in Great Britain, i.e., between 1840 and 1860, the leading British bourgeois politicians were opposed to colonial policy and were of the opinion that the liberation of the colonies, their complete separation from Britain, was inevitable and desirable. M. Beer, in an article, "Modern British Imperialism", published in 1898, shows that in 1852, Disraeli, a statesman who was generally inclined towards imperialism, declared: "The colonies are millstones round our necks." But at the end of the nineteenth century the British heroes of the hour were Cecil Rhodes and Joseph Chamberlain, who openly advocated imperialism and applied the imperialist policy in the most cynical manner!

It is not without interest to observe that even then these leading British bourgeois politicians saw the connection between what might be called the purely economic and the sociopolitical roots of modern imperialism. Chamberlain advocated imperialism as a "true, wise and economical policy", and pointed particularly to the German, American and Belgian competition which Great Britain was encountering in the world market. Salvation lies in monopoly, said the capitalists as they formed cartels, syndicates and trusts.

Salvation lies in monopoly, echoed the political leaders of the bourgeoisie, hastening to appropriate the parts of the world not yet shared out. And Cecil Rhodes, we are informed by his intimate friend, the journalist Stead, expressed his imperialist views to him in 1895 in the following terms: "I was in the East End of London (a workingclass quarter) yesterday and attended a meeting of the unemployed. I listened to the wild speeches, which were just a cry for 'bread! bread!' and on my way home I pondered over the scene and I became more than ever convinced of the importance of imperialism.... My cherished idea is a solution for the social problem, i.e., in order to save the 40,000,000 inhabitants of the United Kingdom from a bloody civil war, we colonial statesmen must acquire new lands to settle the surplus population, to provide new markets for the goods produced in the factories and mines. The Empire, as I have always said, is a bread and butter question. If you want to avoid civil war, you must become imperialists.

That was said in 1895 by Cecil Rhodes, millionaire, a king of finance, the man who was mainly responsible for the

AngloBoer War. True, his defence of imperialism is crude and cynical, but in substance it does not differ from the "theory" advocated by Messrs. Maslov, Südekum, Potresov, David, the founder of Russian Marxism and others. Cecil Rhodes was a somewhat more honest socialchauvinist....

To present as precise a picture as possible of the territorial division of the world and of the changes which have occurred during the last decades in this respect, I shall utilise the data furnished by Supan in the work already quoted on the colonial possessions of all the powers of the world. Supan takes the years 1876 and 1900; I shall take the year 1876a year very aptly selected, for it is precisely by that time that the premonopolist stage of development of WestEuropean capitalism can be said to have been, in the main, completedand the year 1914, and instead of Supan's figures I shall quote the more recent statistics of Hübner's Geographical and Statistical Tables. Supan gives figures only for colonies; I think it useful, in order to present a complete picture of the division of the world, to add brief data on noncolonial and semicolonial countries, in which category I place Persia, China and Turkey: the first of these countries is already almost completely a colony, the second and third are becoming such.

We thus get the following result:

COLONIAL POSSESSIONS OF THE GREAT POWERS
(000,000 square kilometers and 000,000 inhabitants)

	Colonies				Metropolitan countries		Total	
	1876		1914		1914		1914	
	Area	Pop.	Area	Pop.	Area	Pop.	Area	Pop.
Great Britain	22.5	251.9	33.5	393.5	0.3	46.5	33.8	444.0
Russia	17.0	15.9	17.4	33.2	5.4	136.2	22.8	169.4
France	0.9	6.0	10.6	55.5	0.5	39.6	11.1	95.1
Germany	—	—	2.9	12.3	0.5	64.9	3.4	77.2
United States	—	—	0.3	9.7	9.4	97.0	9.7	106.7
Japan	—	—	0.3	19.2	0.4	53.0	0.7	72.2
Total for 6 Great Powers	40.4	273.8	65.0	523.4	16.5	437.2	81.5	960.6

Colonies of other powers (Belgium, Holland, etc.)	9.9	45.3
Semi-colonial countries (Persia, China, Turkey)	14.5	361.2
Other countries	28.0	289.9
Total for the world	133.9	1,657.0

We clearly see from these figures how "complete" was the partition of the world at the turn of the twentieth century. After 1876 colonial possessions increased to enormous dimensions, by more than fifty per cent, from 40,000,000 to 65,000,000 square kilometres for the six biggest powers; the increase amounts to 25,000,000 square kilometres, fifty per cent more than the area of the metropolitan countries (16,500,000 square kilometres). In 1876 three powers had no colonies, and a fourth, France, had scarcely any. By 1914 these four powers had acquired colonies with an area of 14,100,000 square kilometres, i.e., about half as much again as the area of Europe, with a population of nearly 100,000,000. The unevenness in the rate of expansion of colonial possessions is very great. If, for instance, we compare France, Germany and Japan, which do not differ very much in area and population, we see that the first has acquired almost three times as much colonial territory as the other two combined. In regard to finance capital, France, at the beginning of the period we are considering, was also, perhaps, several times richer than Germany and Japan put together.

In addition to, and on the basis of, purely economic conditions, geographical and other conditions also affect the dimensions of colonial possessions. However strong the process of levelling the world, of levelling the economic and living conditions in different countries, may have been in the past decades as a result of the pressure of largescale industry, exchange and finance capital, considerable differences still remain; and among the six countries mentioned we see, firstly, young capitalist countries (America, Germany, Japan) whose progress has been extraordinarily rapid; secondly, countries with an old capitalist development (France and Great Britain), whose progress lately has been much slower than that of the previously mentioned countries, and thirdly, a country most backward economically (Russia), where modern capitalist imperialism is enmeshed, so to speak, in a particularly close network of precapitalist relations.

Alongside the colonial possessions of the Great Powers, we have placed the small colonies of the small states, which are, so to speak, the next objects of a possible and probable "redivision" of colonies. These small states mostly retain their colonies only because the big powers are torn by conflicting interests, friction, etc., which prevent them from coming to an agreement on the division of the spoils. As to the "semicolonial" states, they provide an example of the transitional forms which are to be found in all spheres of nature and society. Finance capital is such a great, such a decisive, you might say, force in all economic and in all international relations, that it is capable of subjecting, and actually does subject, to itself even states enjoying the fullest political independence; we shall shortly see examples of this. Of course, finance capital finds most "convenient", and derives the greatest profit from, a form of subjection which involves the loss of the political independence of the subjected countries and peoples. In this respect, the semicolonial countries provide a typical example of the "middle stage". It is natural that the struggle for these semidependent countries should have become particularly bitter in the epoch of finance capital, when the rest of the world has already been divided up.

Colonial policy and imperialism existed before the latest stage of capitalism, and even before capitalism. Rome, founded on slavery, pursued a colonial policy and practised imperialism. But "general" disquisitions on imperialism, which ignore, or put into the background, the fundamental difference between socioeconomic formations, inevitably turn into the most vapid banality or bragging, like the comparison: "Greater Rome and Greater Britain." Even the capitalist colonial policy of previous stages of capitalism is essentially different from the colonial policy of finance capital.

The principal feature of the latest stage of capitalism is the domination of monopolist associations of big employers. These monopolies are most firmly established when all the sources of raw materials are captured by one group, and we have seen with what zeal the international capitalist associations exert every effort to deprive their rivals of all opportunity of competing, to buy up, for example, ironfields, oilfields, etc. Colonial possession alone gives the monopolies complete guarantee against all contingencies in the struggle against competitors, including the case of the adversary wanting to be protected by a law establishing a state monopoly. The more capitalism is developed, the more strongly the shortage of raw materials is felt, the more intense the competition and the hunt for sources of raw materials throughout the whole world, the more desperate the struggle for the acquisition of colonies.

"It may be asserted," writes Schilder, "although it may sound paradoxical to some, that in the more or less foreseeable future the growth of the urban and industrial population is more likely to be hindered by a shortage of raw materials for industry than by a shortage of food." For example, there is a growing shortage of timberthe price of which is steadily risingof leather, and of raw materials for the textile industry. "Associations of manufacturers are making efforts to create an equilibrium between agriculture and industry in the whole of world economy; as an example of this we might mention the International Federation of Cotton Spinners' Associations in several of the most important industrial countries, founded in 1904, and the European Federation of Flax Spinners' Associations, founded on the same model in 1910."

Of course, the bourgeois reformists, and among them particularly the presentday adherents of Kautsky, try to belittle the importance of facts of this kind by arguing that raw materials "could be" obtained in the open market without a "costly and dangerous" colonial policy; and that the supply of raw materials "could be" increased enormously by "simply" improving conditions in agriculture in general. But such arguments become an apology for imperialism, an attempt to paint it in bright colours, because they ignore the principal feature of the latest stage of capitalism: monopolies. The free market is becoming more and more a thing of the past; monopolist syndicates and trusts are restricting it with every passing day, and "simply" improving conditions in agriculture means improving the conditions of the masses, raising wages and reducing profits. Where, except in the imagination of sentimental reformists, are there any trusts capable of concerning themselves with the condition of the masses instead of the conquest of colonies?

Finance capital is interested not only in the already discovered sources of raw materials but also in potential sources, because presentday technical development is extremely rapid, and land which is useless today may be improved tomorrow if new methods are devised (to this end a big bank can equip a special expedition of engineers, agricultural experts, etc.), and if large amounts of capital are invested. This also applies to prospecting for minerals, to new methods of processing up and utilising raw materials, etc., etc. Hence, the inevitable striving of finance capital to enlarge its spheres of influence and even its actual territory. In the same way that the trusts capitalise their property at two or three times its value, taking into account its "potential" (and not actual) profits and the further results of monopoly, so finance capital in general strives to seize the largest possible amount of land of all kinds in all places, and by every means, taking into account potential sources of raw materials and fearing to be left behind in the fierce struggle for the last remnants of independent territory, or for the repartition of those territories that have been already divided.

The British capitalists are exerting every effort to develop cotton growing in their colony, Egypt (in 1904, out of 2,300,000 hectares of land under cultivation, 600,000, or more than onefourth, were under cotton); the Russians are doing the same in their colony, Turkestan, because in this way they will be in a better position to defeat their foreign competitors, to monopolise the sources of raw materials and form a more economical and profitable textile trust in which all the processes of cotton production and manufacturing will be "combined" and concentrated in the hands of one set of owners.

The interests pursued in exporting capital also give an impetus to the conquest of colonies, for in the colonial market it is easier to employ monopoly methods (and sometimes they are the only methods that can be employed) to eliminate competition, to ensure supplies, to secure the necessary "connections", etc.

The noneconomic superstructure which grows up on the basis of finance capital, its politics and its ideology, stimulates the striving for colonial conquest. "Finance capital does not want liberty, it wants domination," as Hilferding very truly says. And a French bourgeois writer, developing and supplementing, as it were, the ideas of Cecil Rhodes quoted above, writes that social causes should be added to the economic causes of modern colonial policy: "Owing to the growing complexities of life and the difficulties which weigh not only on the masses of the workers, but also on the middle classes, 'impatience, irritation and hatred are accumulating in all the countries of the old civilisation and are becoming a menace to public order; the energy which is being hurled out of the definite class channel must be given employment abroad in order to avert an explosion at home'."

Since we are speaking of colonial policy in the epoch of capitalist imperialism, it must be observed that finance capital and its foreign policy, which is the struggle of the great powers for the economic and political division of the world, give rise to a number of transitional forms of state dependence. Not only are the two main groups of countries, those owning colonies, and the colonies themselves, but also the diverse forms of dependent countries which, politically, are formally independent, but in fact, are enmeshed in the net of financial and diplomatic dependence, typical of this epoch. We have already referred to one form of dependencethe semicolony. An example of another is provided by Argentina.

"South America, and especially Argentina," writes SchulzeGaevernitz in his work on British imperialism, "is so dependent financially on London that it ought to be described as almost a British commercial colony." Basing himself on the reports of the AustroHungarian Consul at Buenos Aires for 1909, Schilder estimated the amount of British capital invested in Argentina at 8,750 million francs. It is not difficult to imagine what strong connections British finance capital (and its faithful "friend", diplomacy) thereby acquires with the Argentine bourgeoisie, with the circles that control the whole of that country's economic and political life.

A somewhat different form of financial and diplomatic dependence, accompanied by political independence, is presented by Portugal. Portugal is an independent sovereign state, but actually, for more than two hundred years, since the war of the Spanish Succession (170114), it has been a British protectorate. Great Britain has protected Portugal and her colonies in order to fortify her own positions in the fight against her rivals, Spain and France. In return Great Britain has received commercial privileges, preferential conditions for importing goods and especially capital into Portugal and the Portuguese colonies, the right to use the ports and islands of Portugal, her telegraph cables, etc., etc. Relations of this kind have always existed between big and little states, but in the epoch of capitalist imperialism they become a general system, they form part of the sum total of "divide the world" relations and become links in the chain of operations of world finance capital.

In order to finish with the question of the division of the world, I must make the following additional observation. This question was raised quite openly and definitely not only in American literature after the SpanishAmerican War, and in English literature after the AngloBoer War, at the very end of the nineteenth century and the beginning of the twentieth; not only has German literature, which has "most jealously" watched "British imperialism", systematically given its appraisal of this fact. This question has also been raised in French bourgeois literature as definitely and broadly as is thinkable from the bourgeois point of view. Let me quote Driault, the historian, who, in his book, Political and Social Problems at the End of the Nineteenth Century, in the chapter "The Great Powers and the Division of the World", wrote the following: "During the past few years, all the free territory of the globe, with the exception of China, has been occupied by the powers of Europe and North America.

This has already brought about several conflicts and shifts of spheres of influence, and these foreshadow more terrible upheavals in the near future. For it is necessary to make haste. The nations which have not yet made provision for themselves run the risk of never receiving their share and never participating in the tremendous exploitation of the globe which will be one of the most essential features of the next century (i.e., the twentieth). That is why all Europe and America have lately been afflicted with the fever of colonial expansion, of 'imperialism', that most noteworthy feature of the end of the nineteenth century." And the author added: "In this partition of the world, in this furious hunt for the treasures and the big markets of the globe, the relative strength of the empires founded in this nineteenth century is totally out of proportion to the place occupied in Europe by the nations which founded them. The dominant powers in Europe, the arbiters of her destiny, are not equally preponderant in the whole world. And, as colonial might, the hope of controlling as yet unassessed wealth, will evidently react upon the relative strength of the European powers, the colonial question"imperialism", if you willwhich has already modified the political conditions of Europe itself, will modify them more and more."

7

STRATEGIES OF ANNIHILATION

According to Russell F. Weigley's The American Way of War (1977), the United States' approach to military strategy has long rested on what is called total war. In a nutshell, total warriors make war on an enemy's entire societywhat the anthropologists might call its material culturethat is, on the enemy's resources, food and other economic production, and on anything which might sustain the enemy's ability to keep military forces in the field. Such war is not exclusively modern, but looks backward towards ancient warfare, which often entailed the slaughter of all enemy males, enslavement of enemy women and children, and eradication of the enemy's whole existence as an independent political society. Rome's triumph over Carthage comes to mind.

Over the centuriesfrom St. Augustine forwardmany Christian churchmen and writers sought to lessen the horrors of war by means of Just War theory. Their goal was to leave society in general, that is, civilians, as untouched as possible by conflicts set off by the quarrels of the political classes. This aim was not always realized. According to historian John U. Nef, it was the prosperous bourgeois citystates of Renaissance Italy which implemented the practice of limited warfare, which came fairly close to the just war model.

The rise of large territorial monarchies, from the late 1400s onward, broadened the scale of warfare, and the costly and bitter wars following upon the Reformation were a setback for the notion of "civilized warfare." It may indeed have been the sheer destructiveness of the socalled wars of religion, which led, over time, to greater acceptance of limits on warmaking.

Wars were "bad for business," and the growing importance of bourgeois enterprise in Europe gave added weight to arguments against largescale war. The 18th and 19th centuries saw increased adherence to a code of civilized war.

It is true enough that rules were not followed very strictly in wars involving different civilizations or cultures. There is little to recommend the conduct of European powers in their overseas empires. But in Europe at least, as HansHermann Hoppe argues in Democracy: The God That Failed, territorial monarchs had institutional incentives both to limit the causes over which they fought their rivals and to restrict the costs and scope of such wars. In British North America, colonial frontier wars, or "Indian" wars, often took on the character of wars for survival. Weigley believes that such wars gave American warmaking an early push towards the psychology of total war. Likewise, Americans tended to conceive of the French presence in North America as a total problem. Here an inherited English antiCatholicism played its role, as it did later with regard to the Spanish Empire, or its successor states like Mexico.

In the American Revolution, destruction of British political control was the key to victory. In regions with numerous "Tories" the war resembled civil war and, accordingly, did approach total war. Still, partisan warfare by local forces seeking to drive out invaders need not become total war, if only because the enemy did not bring his own civilians with him to serve as targets. The Americans prevailed on the basis of a protracted war but without developing a doctrine of total war.

THE FRENCH PRECEDENT

The wars set off by the French Revolution provided a longrun threat to the persistence of civilized, rulebound warfare. Able to conscript hundreds of thousands of ideologically motivated republican citizens, the new French state put colossal armies in the field. Napoleon Bonaparte, an evil genius of sorts, showed how to use such mass armies, and other powers struggled to catch up. In Prussia, Karl von Clausewitz sought to draw theoretical lessons from these developments in On War (Vom Kriege).

Wars had become colossal exercises in logistics and maneuver, drawing more and more of a nation's population into their maw. In the early 20th century, the German strategic writer Hans Delbrück attempted to sum up matters thus far. He held that there were at bottom two kinds of war strategy: that of Niederwerfung, "suppression," and that of Ermattung, "attrition." It should be added that these kinds of war could conceivably obtain between actual combatants, leaving society relatively unscathed. The steady upward ratcheting of the scale and costs of wars had farther to go before unalloyed total war could stand forth in fullness.

THE UNIONSAVERS' EXPEDIENTS

It was in North America that the new model was first perfected. The old union faltered in 1861. The ensuing war presented serious problems to those who wished to "save" the union. Under the existing rules of warfare, the defending Confederate States had a number of natural advantages. To counter those, total war entered into Union strategy from at least 1862. The oldschool generals sacked for being "ineffective" were precisely those who drew back from the new philosophy of war put into practice by Generals like Pope, Sherman, and Sheridan.

Northern policymakers soon theorized their practice. Here Francis Lieber has pride of place. Lieber, a German immigrant who had fought in the wars against Napoleon, wasout of some combination of liberalism, romanticism, and nationalismextremely sentimental about the state (which Nietzsche, by contrast, called the coldest of cold monsters). Thus Lieber could write in 1838 that "the state stands incalculably above the individual, is worthy of every sacrifice, of life, and goods, of wife and children, for it is the society of societies, the sacred union by which the creator leads man to civilization, the bond, the pacifier, the humanizer, of men, the protector of all undertakings...."

Out of this pseudoHegelian waffle comes the notion that freedom can be realized only within the modern abstract state; in the US, this meant the allegedly indestructible union. Along with this perilous modification of liberalism came, in practice, a legalpositivist approach to the laws of war, embodied in General Orders No. 100, which Lieber wrote for Lincoln's War Department.

Section 15 of these Orders reads: "Military necessity admits of all direct destruction of life or limb of armed enemies, and other persons whose destruction is incidentally unavoidable in the armed contests of war....." Naturally, the decision as to which persons it was "whose destruction is incidentally unavoidable" was best left to commanders in the field, or their superiors.

A cynic might well say that this "code" allowed for the afterthefact justification of anything a commander might claim had been "necessary" to achieve military objectives. One such cynic was James Seddon, Confederate Secretary of War, who commented: "[I]n this code of military necessity... the acts of atrocity and violence which have been committed by the officers of the United States and have shocked the moral sense of civilized nations are to find an apology and defense." Further, "a military commander under this code may pursue a line of conduct in accordance with principles of justice, faith, and honor, or he may justify conduct correspondent with the warfare of the barbarous hordes who overran the Roman Empire...."

In 1915, historian John Bigelow characterized the war thus: "Depredation and spoliation, especially in the latter part of the war were the general policy of Lincoln's government; and as a matter of fact Eastern Virginia and other parts of the South were swept clearer than the Shenandoah Valley of everything useful to man and beast." And historian Charles Royster observed in 1991 that the "Civil War, as practiced by the belligerents and characterized by Sherman, implemented two propositions which later wars took much further: that the nation and the nation's professed ideals admit no necessary limit in their fight to prevail; that the methods of waging war do not differ categorically if at all between the belligerent whose cause is labeled just and the belligerent whose cause is labeled unjust. Neither of these propositions commands universal assent, yet modern belligerents have acted as if they were true."

Given the assumption of a right to win, the property and even the lives of enemy civilians began to weigh much less than they had in the older rules of war. Faced with such matters, Lincoln apologists typically resort to what historian Jeffrey Rogers Hummel calls the HitlerStalinMao test. Clearly, Sherman's March falls far short of that.

For one such historian, the fact that Northern soldiers did not directly shoot civilians is a sufficient proof of the humanity of the war. This is all well and good, but one would like an explanation for the roughly 50,000 missing Southern civilians of all colors and creeds. They seem to have perished from causes attendant on the war, once it became a war against property and economic resources.

In July 1862, Lincoln rather typically told Southern unionists, who were complaining of Northern seizures of property that "broken eggs cannot be mended"a statement which puts him directly in the line of JacobinBolshevik political ruthlessness. As a result of all this, Lincoln has become "famed for his compassion," in historian James M. McPherson's words. It would appear that Lincoln's myth has long since outrun the facts.

So why dwell on that war? One dwells there precisely because that war became the template, the ideological framework, within which policies were made and within which all respectable discussions took place ever after. To be very brief, General Grant showed what could be done with grand Napoleonic battles of annihilation (or "combats" in Weigley's terms) undertaken with cheap conscripts. Confederate commanders obliged him by doing much the same. This was very costly in manpower, and more importantly, politically. Northern war weariness threatened to bring about peace before salvation of the union had been achieved. The Southern States had only to remain unconquered.

To break out of this box, the Northern leadership turned Sherman, Sheridan, and others loose on Southern society as such. By living off the resources of the enemy, Sherman could ignore problems of supply while "making Georgia howl," as he delicately put it. Of $100 million dollars in property damage inflicted on his famous march, Sherman bragged that just $20 million had a real military purpose and the remaining $80 million was "simple waste and destruction."

Thus the preferred strategy became one of making war on the enemy's society generally, to undermine his armies in the field. Having led to victory, Lincoln's policies are now taken as sacred text, precedent, and proof that all later actions of a like kind are rightful and just, without anyone ever offering proof that the original acts were rightful and just. For the moment, we may chalk this up to an ineradicable American pragmatism, and go on. After all, Lincoln's generals won, and this carries great moral weight in some circles.

A military technician, ignoring questions raised by oldfashioned morality, could easily consider Sherman's strategy a brilliant shortcut. Such was the judgment, for example, of Captain B. H. LiddellHart, British military theorist and historian. Defenders of total war make much of the way in which it allegedly "saves lives" by shortening the war. It seems likely that total war distributes deaths differently between the belligerents than would otherwise happenand at higher total numbers.

PLAINS INDIANS

Before drawing any conclusions, we must continue our cook's tour of US wars. The connection between total war and Indian Wars has already been mooted. It is probably no accident that General Sherman had seen service in the Second Seminole War in the early 1840s. He hated being attacked by mobile opponents able to disappear, and called for total eradication of the Seminole people.

As for General Sheridan, he told his subordinates about to engage western Indians, "I want you to be bold, enterprising, and at all times full of energy, when you begin, let it be a campaign of annihilation, obliteration and complete destruction...." In these little wars, wanton destruction of buffalo herds was aimed at eliminating the enemy's food source. Pained by criticism of his total war tactics against Indians, Sheridanin a letter to his old comrade Shermanasked rhetorically, "Did we cease to throw shells into Vicksburg or Atlanta because women and children were there?" Of course they had not.

Present at Prussian Headquarters as an observer during the FrancoPrussian War (18701871), Sheridan espoused the gospel of total war. "The people must be left nothing but their eyes to weep with over the war," he told the Prussians. The New World thus enlightened the Old.

SPANISHAMERICAN WAR AND PHILIPPINE "INSURRECTION"

The SpanishAmerican War (1898) was too brief to offer much in the way of advances in total war. It is mainly interesting as the beginning of US overseas empire, formal and informal. What is interesting is the sequel, the socalled Philippine Insurrection (18991902).

To make good the real estate deal with Spain, which brought the Philippine Islands under US sovereignty, a costly counterinsurgency was fought. General Orders No. 100 were allegedly still in force, but proved flexible enough to permit the deaths of some 200,000 Filipinos, mostly noncombatants, before the US was able to claim victory and begin administering its newfound "India."

Historians keen on finding ironies might turn their attention from the American South for a few minutes and savor these: The US, having denounced Spanish "atrocities" in Cuba from 18951898, adopted the same tactics to subdue the Filipinos. The US was simply more effective. By a wonderful coincidence, Britain was in these same years waging a counterinsurgency in South Africa against the Afrikaner people. The AngloAmerican relationship thrived on the shared experience, and the two governments conspicuously refrained from criticizing one another's tactics in dealing with "rebels."

WORLD WAR I

World War I took the Napoleonic model of colossal combats, which sacrificed big mobs of conscripted cannon fodder, to new heights. Millions could take part. Now, Europeans experienced the costly sort of war undertaken by Grant and Lee. In an effort to find a way out, short of calling the damned thing off (that would never do), the powers looked around for previously unlawful means of punishing the enemy's society.

Britain undertook a starvation blockade of Germany. Germany responded with submarine warfare against neutral shipping. The latter helped bring the US into the war with a mixed bag of sordid mercantilist goals and high idealism.

All across the board, the old rules of war gave wayin the direction of total war. The most that can be said is that the settlement was in some ways worse than the war itself, setting the stage for the next European civil war as well as for the present excitement in the Middle East. Finally, interesting experiments with aircraft seemed to herald even better ways of making war on the enemy's entire society.

AIR POWER BIDS FAIR TO SOLVE ALL TECHNICAL PROBLEMS

In the wake of World War I, Italian General Guido Douhet theorized that aerial bombardment would be the key to winning future wars. Intimidation of civilian populations would cause them to make their governments yield to an enemy's will. It was British and American strategists who took up the theme and tailored their air forces to the task of saturation bombing, unlike such powers as Germany and Soviet Russia.

In 1925, Captain Elbridge Colby, US Army, helped formulate the US attitude towards air power as an instrument of total war. He wrote that a "belligerent will not wish to risk his planes and pilots, expend his gasoline, or waste his munitions, on any objectives except those of military importance." This was already problematic, given the US tradition of defining "military targets" rather broadly.

Colby went on to say that everyone knows that bombing is highly inaccurate. "Innocent people are bound to be struck," he says, even if the bomber's intention is to strike a genuinely military target [my italics]. He surveyed standing legal doctrine and concluded, rather predictably, that since adherence to the rules would virtually outlaw bombing, it was the rules, not the bombing, which must yield. No one, he said, could possibly be expected to forego wielding such a convenient and useful weapon. Interestingly, he cites British bombing of Afghanistan in May 1919 as telling precedent.

WORLD WAR II AND THE FULFILMENT OF TOTAL WAR

World War II was the apotheosis of total war. This may explain its lasting popularity with proponents of political management of human life. Deliberate carpetbombing of cities to kill civilians as such came into its own. The most that one can say is that in Europe it was mainly the British who insisted on targeting cities per se, while the Americans stuck to targets of military significance, albeit under their rather broad and careless definitions. In the Far East, US air forces firebombed Japanese cities and civilians with great abandon. Hundreds of thousands of civilians died in both theatres.

Historian David M. Kennedy writes: "[T]he great nuclear blast that obliterated Hiroshima hardly represented a moral novelty by this date in the conflict. The moral rules that had long stayed the warriors' hands from taking up weapons of mass destruction against civilian populations had long since been violently breached...."

Of the bombings of Japan, General Curtis LeMay said: "You've got to kill people, and when you've killed enough, they stop fighting." This goes beyond even General Sherman's wildest rhetoricand actionbut states a proposition widely accepted as selfevident truth by contemporary Americans. Nuclear bombs fulfilled the total warrior's dream, but had the odd sideeffect of making major wars so potentially costly as to be unthinkable for the foreseeable future.

HOT WARS WITHIN THE COLD WAR

In the Korean War, the US doctrine of total war and hysterically broad use of overwhelming firepower got further exercise. General Emmett O'Donnell commented: "I would say that the entire, almost the entire, Korean peninsula, is just a terrible mess. Everything is destroyed. There is nothing standing worthy of the name.... Just before the Chinese came in we were grounded. There were no more targets in Korea."

Even Churchill, never bombshy when it came to Germany, objected to US use of napalm in Korea. (2,300 gallons were used in one attack on Pyongyang.) To quote the jovial Curtis LeMay again: "We burned down just about every city in North and South Korea both.... We killed off over a million civilian Koreans and drove several million more from their homes." Given such a mode of waging war, one might think that even those allegedly being "protected" by these exercises would begin to have their doubts.

Of Vietnam, I shall say very little. Only those who have been asleep will be unaware that civilian deaths in Southeast Asia resulting from the US mode of warfare match, or exceed those in Korea, especially when other parts of IndoChina are taken into account.

It does not change such facts to point at other ruthless forces, such as the Khmer Rouge. In any case, consistency on the part of those doing the pointing would require them to explain why such a public enemy as Pol Pot could later be the recipient of US support after his colorful career as murderer "of his own people."

Perhaps the only novelty in Vietnam was the highflown social scientific theorizing attached to the bombing campaign. This was an interesting application of behaviorist ratpsychology, which, however, cast more doubt on the methodology than on the putative rats. As in World War II, bombing did not have the desired and predicted effect on enemy popular morale. Such unhappy outcomes have never made believers in air power lose heart.

We must note, in passing, extensive US bombing of irrigation dams in North Vietnam in late 1972, intended to destroy rice crops on which the population depended.

This was a real Nuremburg War Crimes Trial item, but no one ever appeared in court. Noam Chomsky heroically brought these matters, both theory and practice, to public attention many years ago, which may account for his skepticism about subsequent US crusades. For this wellearned scepticism he is currently being pilloried by the neoconservatives.

TOTAL WAR WITH A HUMAN FACE

In the postCold War period, we have begun to see a repackaging of US public doctrine into a new system of discourse or representations of how wars are actually conducted. Bombs and rockets are now much friendlier. Civilians are no longer harmed "unnecessarily," given the unspeakable accuracy and precision of the new, improved weaponry.

The spin is that no one who knows the deep moral rectitude of US statesmen could now dream that civilians are ever targeted on purpose. Naturally, there is some slippage in warfare, they say, but one has to expect that. Even so, the deaths of some 600 Iraqi civilians in the Amiriya bomb shelter during the Gulf War did require some fancy footwork from the spokespersons, even granting the generous US notion of "target."

But what were the "targets" in Iraq? They were precisely what applied total war doctrine says they should be: everything that supports the enemy's societywater systems, electrical production, bridges, roads,but the point is made. If these things can be destroyed without directly killing large numbers of civilians, so much the better in the new, kindlier total war.

The PR flacks may reinvent total war all they wish, with ribbons and bows, but the old concerns still peek out. Thus, an essay in the Marine Corps Gazette (October 1989), written by five officers, sketches out a theory of "fourth generation" warfare to deal with changing conditions abroad. In this brave new world, "tactical and strategic levels will blend as the opponent's political infrastructure and civilian society become battlefield[!] targets" [my italics]. Elsewhere, this gets a friendlier face as "a goal of collapsing the enemy internally rather than physically destroying him [a distinction with not much of a difference?]. Targets will include such things as the population's support for the war and the enemy's culture [my italics]. Correct identification of enemy strategic centers of gravity will be highly important."

This sounds pretty total to me. Of course they also warn that we must watch out for reprisals on American soil. Yes, one might wish to allow for that.

The public attention span is short. If a half million Iraqi civilians (or more) die from lack of civilized infrastructure, combined with a blockade poorly hidden behind the weasel word "sanctions," the public may never notice. This is the sheer genius of the present transformation of total war. The new total war is indirect and subtle and, therefore, less likely to arouse concerns about its costs, much less its morality. Hence the effort to disguise each new effortIraq, Kosovo, or the present illdefined "war'with the fig leaf of the UN, NATO, or some other coalition of the Good against the Bad.

What we see is an effort to achieve global hegemony on the cheap. It is especially important that it be cheap politicallyat home. If it costs a large amount of money, that can be discounted as imperial overhead, particularly if costs can be shifted onto some of the overseas provinces. As selflicensed counterfeiters to the world, US leaders can achieve some of this through routine monetary inflation. And why should allied foreign power elites get a free ride, anyway?

THE STATE OF PLAY AT THE BEGINNING OF THE THIRD MILLENNIUM

Of collateral damage, i.e., dead civilians, in the present campaign against the Fuzzy Wuzzies, British Secretary of State for Defense Geoff Hoon has lately opined: "There is always going to be a risk that cannot be avoided." Not for him, one imagines. This suggests that even having an air force adds up to an intention to commit war crimes. Time was when one could tell a power's air strategy by the kinds of aircraft built. US total warriors have ruined even this test by turning fighter jets into virtual bombers by means of those much advertised rockets.

But consider the phrase, "collateral damage." It has almost become an embarrassment because of overuse during the Gulf War. Nonetheless, it is organically linked to the doctrine of Good Intentions. The US never intends to harm civilians. Therefore, any actual harming of civilians is unintentional, accidental, and morally neutral. The mere fact that, empirically, a broad notion of targeting and seemingly endless munitions lead to rather sloppy results is not felt as refutation of the foregoing. One might ask the several hundred Panamanians citizens of a friendly nation with whom the US was not at warkilled during the comic opera "arrest" of Manuel Noriega, about that.

By now, we are back to Lincoln and the classic doctrine. As it now stands, US total war doctrine holds that as long as one's heart is pure, one's goalshowever impossibleare "humanitarian," and one's domestic political system is democratic, one may do literally anything to defeat a proclaimed enemy society. This represents a projection of the trauma of 18611865, as experienced by the Northern leadership, onto the entire globe. Glory, glory, hallelujah, untruths go marching on. This is why Lincoln is so heavily drawn on, in these moments, as precedent, justification, and inspirational (if depressive) genius and patron saint of all US wars.

There have been many examples of the "if Lincoln did it, it must be right" genre lately. Every leftist, liberal, centrist, and neoconservative defender of empire has weighed in just such terms, mainly in aid of increased surveillance and new inroads on civil liberties. In his useful book, Crusade: The Untold Story of the Gulf War (1993), Rick Atkinson played this card to rationalize the famous "turkey shoot," i.e., the mass slaughter by UScoalition forces of tens of thousands of retreating Iraqi conscripts. Those defeated forces in no way endangered allied forces, unless the US coalition really intended to occupy and reinvent Iraq. Nonetheless, allied forces simply massacred them because it was in their power to do so. Little of the warrior ethic was on display there.

But Atkinson brings the ultimate argument to bear: "The law of warthe orders signed by Abraham Lincoln before Gettysburg were an examplepermitted an attack on enemy combatants, whether advancing, retreating, or standing still." Further: "The prevalent American military philosophy since the Civil War had embraced a 'strategy of annihilation,' the relentless bludgeoning of an enemy to destroy his armed forces and ability to wage war."

It is time, then, for a discussion of ends and means in relation to war and peace. Clever fellows like Jonah Goldberg like to deconstruct the popular saying, "The end doesn't justify the means." Quite so. Means do justify ends. The question is whether or not particular ends hallow any and every old means one could come up with.

The total warriors have had their say about this for nearly a century and a half. Their later theorizings, most notably during the High Cold War at the hands of such worthies as Hermann Kahn, Henry Kissinger, and the like, amounted to a gross distortion of Just War theory. They sought to focus all attention on jus ad bellum, i.e., whether or not a particular cause was just. It cannot be said that they did a strikingly good job on this front or that their efforts had much to do with actually existing US foreign policy.

Of jus in bello, i.e., what means were morally supportable in war, they said rather little. The Good Intentions took care of that. This goodness radiated outwards, enveloping all US military practicesand indeed all conceivable US military practiceswith the all the finality of a newly discovered 14th Amendment "penumbra" wiping out a longstanding constitutional interpretation. The Good could do no Bad. Conversely, the Bad could do no Good. No weapon, however massively destructive, was immoral or frightening in the hands of the Good, just as no weapon, however modest or plausibly related to selfdefense, could be suffered in the hands of the Bad.

Under this genial doctrine, there are entirely good nations, whose every act, of whatever kind, against certified entirely bad nations must needs be rightful and true. Doubters are told to gird themselves up with a pseudoStoicism which holds that "broken eggs cannot be mended." Things just happen, you know, when just crusades are afoot.

One begins to wonder if this construction is not as crazy and unlimited, in its own way, as Soviet MarxismLeninism ever was. A look at the recent rash of neoconservative writings on the present crisis suggests that only an explanation in terms of mistaken theology will suffice. This brings us to the decayed Puritanism of the "savers" and refounders of the Union (the Founders having been mainly Southerners). Historian William Appleman Williams writes of the New England Puritans that their externalization of evil onto their opponents "not only distorted the Puritans' own doctrine, it inclined them toward a solution which involved the extension of their system over others.".

This world outlook, decayed or otherwise, still partly animates the ongoing US crusade. Matters are even worse in that US leaders have the resources to pursue their postProtestant "vision of omnipotence" (to quote Williams again), since the American economy still functions fairly well, in contrast to the late Soviet economy. They have in hand the means to pursue their Faustian dream. And yet, despite all the expensive "defense" they provide us with, we seem increasingly unsafe.

What Might be the Alternative?

But let us return to the strategic front. Weigley observes that already in 1926, a writer in the Naval Institute Proceedings, William Howard Gardner, had spotted a flaw in the US leaders' ambitions:

> *"There is great importance in the fact that in a war between the United States and an Asiatic power the latter's aims would seem distinctly 'limited' to many Americans, whereas, in order to maintain our position in Asiatic affairs, we might have to aim at 'unlimited' reduction of the enemy's country, though not necessarily by invasion in force. In other words, the geographic distribution of interests is such that the inauguration of a 'limited' war by an Asiatic power would be likely to compel us to carry through an 'unlimited' war to victory as the only alternative to accepting defeat. Consequently, the enemy's combativeness would be aroused to the utmost while some among us probably would rather yield than continue the war."*

It is interesting that Weigley refers to this as "the American problem" [my italics]. It certainly is that, provided US leaders insist on world hegemony. One has to believe in quite a lot of highflown and farfetched worldland theory in the tradition of Mackinder and Haushofer to buy that project. I shall soon undertake a web search to see if Zbigniew Brzezinksi, an architect of our "successful" Afghan caper of the 1980s, has written much on whether or not the moon is made of ice.

Our only hope of deliverance from our pending transformation into an ersatz British Empire lies in adopting a different conception of American foreign policy. This would mean giving up Lincoln's idea of America as the "last best hope" of mankind, and his successors' program of exporting our blessings by force. This would mean a final, fond farewell to the civic religion forged in the fires of Atlanta and Columbia.

While Russell Weigley has been a good guide to the United States' philosophy of war, he has said little about the necessity or merits of those wars. For this, we turn to Williams, whose work was a singleminded, radical critique of the US Empire and its Open Door ideology. To this we add the free market economics of Murray Rothbard, which shows us how to disaggregate, or unpack, the ideological categories of the prevailing system.

In those quasiHegelian categories, the empire is the only possible "realm of freedom." Freedom is, in fact, precisely that which the empire allows or commands. All else is anarchy or oppression. Rothbard starts with the simplest lesson of all: the state is not the nation, the state is not the people, and the state is not society. See especially, Murray N. Rothbard, "War, Peace, and the State" in Egalitarianism as a Revolt Against Nature and Other Essays (2000), pp. 115132, for the wideranging consequences of this simple insight.

I have no space here to dwell on how war invariably strengthens the state. I take that as given. With empire, we have far too many opportunities for war, and therefore for state aggrandizement. Americans need to decide whether they wish to regain their freedoms. If they do not, they can sign up for the "national greatness" and imperialism offered by the neoconservatives.

One of the burdens Americans will bear, if they choose the latter path, will be the costsin life, liberty, property, and social moralityof total war. The point of this essay has not been to make anyone feel guilty about the methods used in past wars. I know no one, personally, who burned Atlanta or bombed

Dresden. It is just that, given the track record of the strategists we have had, if we stay on the imperial highway, sooner or later some of us will be asked to undertake, or acquiesce in, the inglorious deeds of total war, however sanitized and repackaged they may be. I don't know if we should really want that for our children or our grandchildren.

What is needed is an historically formed understanding of the pattern of US wars; how certain kinds of challenge, and not others, call forth an armed response; how pretended "negotiations" always break down, systematically; how loveable, local revolutionary "allies" are always shoved to one side while the US appropriates their cause, from 1898 on; how war immediately becomes total war; how the proper authorities always demand Unconditional Surrender, as if such a demand were normal; how widespread destruction gives way, after victory, to sentimental but profitable "reconstruction" of the chastened foe. In short, what we need is the historical vision we never got in high school.

A FINAL OBSERVATION

In his exhaustive account of US military practice, Weigley remarks that America has produced only one gifted practitioner of the war of attrition (partisan war), General Nathaniel Greene. I ask, Why might that be? I answer that it is because the Revolution was in most respects a just war of defense, and not a war for empire. It has been a long time since we fought a war which was clearly of that character.

8

THIRTY SIX STRATEGIES OF WAR

Without proper rendering support, you may see question marks, boxes, or other symbols instead of Chinese characters.

The ThirtySix Stratagems is a collection of 36 Chinese proverbs used to illustrate stratagems used in politics as well as in civil interaction. They were first published in the western world by Harro von Senger from Switzerland, whose Chinese translation of his books also started a boom about the 36 stratagems in China; after hearing the proverb "Of the ThirtySix Stratagems, fleeing is best" in Taipei University, he began to inquire about those "36 plans".

Note that they are often misnamed as strategies; however, stratagem (synonymous to ruse) has nothing to do with strategy (being a longterm plan or outline).

THE TERM "STRATAGEM"

"Stratagem" is a rather ancient word for a ruse. Harro von Senger used the word "stratagem" in his translation of the 36 stratagems to differentiate them from the negative connotation of "ruse".

In the German "Duden" dictionary, "List" (ruse) is defined as " a means of reaching a goal unorthodoxically by deceiving somebody " a means of reaching a goal unorthodoxically.

As "ruse" is normally associated with deception, damage and harm, Senger used "stratagem" as a more neutral word to clarify that the second meaning, to reach a goal unorthodoxically, mostly by masquerading the intent and doing the unexpected, is meant.

Relevance in the West and the East

Senger notes that as ruses were mostly condemned as "the last means of the incapable when all other has failed" (Clausewitz) and unChristian, there is no culture of applying and discovering stratagems in the west. This leads to:

* ruses that are applied normally are executed dilettantish and badly planned,
* ruses applied by the more stratagemcompetent fareastern world are not discovered and countered,
* while the expertise of stratagems allows somebody to plan and evaluate his ruses ethically, western ruses normally are applied unplanned and ruthlessly,
* in communication with fareastern instances, it frequently leads to misunderstandings as westerners do not have stratagem expertise, while all they communicate is analyzed stratagemically. Senger explains that this was particularly true for the frequent references to human rights by western politicians. Senger brings examples how Chinese politicians wittily win battles of words when confronted directly, and explains that many Chinese come to the conclusion that the west itself uses the subject as a ruse to weaken the evolving China as a future economic and global power and stage it mainly as a show for their own voters.

Senger cites a Chinese newspaper article discussing whether stratagem expertise should be imparted in children's education, that comes to the conclusion that this was not a question of "if", but of "how". ("Die Kunst der List", 2001).

He states that there are two modes of stratagem usage:

1. Activeto apply stratagems to reach one's own goals
2. Passiveto analyze actions and statements of others with regard to stratagem usage.

This view, however, is not completely valid. For example, the surviving Roman and Byzantine manuals list several stratagems, many found in the list below, and political thinkers, such as Niccolo Macchiavelli see ruses as perfectly good means of politics and warfare. Clausewitz actually encourages the use of stratagems when at disadvantaged position; he doesn't advocate them as silver bullets since they usually are more likely to fail than succeed and attempting them may divert resources off where they are needed (as happened with the Japanese in the Battle of Midway). Many of the stratagems listed in the 36 strategies have been carried out successfully in the West just as well.

Ethics and Stratagems

Ethics and stratagems are one of his major subjects; while he states that the use of ruses was not despised by Christian teachings (he cites Matthew 10,16: I am sending you out like sheep among wolves. Therefore be as shrewd as snakes and as innocent as doves. (NIV)), he divides stratagem usage into four categories:

1. Stratagem usage to inflict damage
2. Stratagem usage to serve a goal
3. Stratagem usage to make a prank
4. Ethically ambivalent stratagem usage.

Apart from to be able to use stratagems competently, stratagem expertise was important to discover stratagems used by others to damage oneself.

Stratagem Categories

Senger divides stratagems into seven categories:

1. Simulation or Masking: 1, 3, 6, 8, 10, 24, 25,
2. Dissimulation or Feint: 7, 27, 29, 32, 34
3. Information or Disclosure: 13, 26,
4. Exploiting, taking Advantage: 2, 4, 5, 12, 14, 15, 16, 17, 18, 19, 20, 22, 23, 28, 30, 31, 33
5. Linking more than one stratagem: 35
6. Flight Stratagems: 9, 11, 21, 36

Cungen GE, a Chinese researcher of 36 Stratagems from the perspective of modern business competition, supports the readymade six groups of classification of these stratagems in the book of Thirtysix Stratagems (The Secret of War):

1. The Stratagems of Winning;
2. The Stratagems of Defending;
3. The Stratagems of Attacking;
4. The Stratagems of Scuffling;
5. The Stratagems of Merging;
6. The Stratagems of Losing.

Origin

The name of the collection comes from the Book of Qi, in its seventh biographical volume, Biography of Wáng Jìngzé. Wáng was a general who had served Southern Qi since the first Emperor Gao of the dynasty. When Emperor Ming came to power and executed many members of the court and royal family for fear that they would threaten his reign, Wáng believed that he would be targeted next and rebelled.

When Wáng received news that Xiao Baojuan, son and crown prince of Emperor Ming, had escaped in haste after learning of the rebellion, he commented that, which can be translated literally as "of the thirtysix stratagems of Lord Tán, retreat was his best, you father and son should run for sure". Lord Tán here refers to general Tan Daoji of the Liu Song Dynasty, who was forced to retreat after his failed attack on Northern Wei, and Wáng mentioned his name in contempt as an example of cowardice.

It should be noted that the number thirtysix was used by Wáng as a figure of speech in this context, and is meant to denote numerous stratagems instead of any specific number. Wáng's choice of this term was in reference to the I Ching, where six is the number of Yin that shared many characteristics with the dark schemes involved in military strategy. As thirtysix is the square of six, it therefore acted as a metaphor for numerous strategies. Since Wáng was not referring to any thirtysix specific stratagems however, the thirtysix proverbs and their connection to military strategies and tactics are likely to have been created after the fact, with the collection only borrowing its name from Wáng's saying.

The ThirtySix Stratagems have variably been attributed to Sun Tzu from the Spring and Autumn Period of China, or Zhuge Liang of the Three Kingdoms period, but neither are regarded as the true author by historians. Instead, the prevailing view is that the ThirtySix Stratagems may have originated in both written and oral history, with many different versions compiled by different authors throughout Chinese history. NOTE: Some stratagems reference occurrences in the time of Sun Bin, approx. 150 years after Sun Wu's death..

The original handcopied paperback that is the basis of the current version was believed to have been discovered in China's Shaanxi province, of an unknown date and author, and put into print by a local publisher in 1941. The ThirtySix Stratagems only came to the public's attention after a review of it was published in the Chinese Communist Party's Guangming Daily newspaper on September 16th, 1961. It was subsequently reprinted and distributed with growing popularity.

CUNGEN GE

The ThirtySix Stratagems are divided into a preface, six chapters containing six stratagems each, and an afterword that was incomplete with missing text. The first three chapters generally describe tactics for use in advantageous situations, whereas the last three chapters contain stratagems that are more suitable for disadvantageous situations. The original text of the ThirtySix Stratagems has a laconic style that is common to Classical Chinese. Each proverb is accompanied by a short comment, no longer than a sentence or two, that explains how said proverb is applicable to military tactics. These 36 Chinese proverbs are related to 36 battle scenarios in Chinese history and folklore, predominantly of the Warring States Period and the Three Kingdoms Period.

Winning Stratagems

1. *Deceive the heavens to cross the ocean*

The stratagem references an episode when Tang emperor Tang Gaozong balked from crossing the sea to a campaign against Koguryo. His General brought him the invitation of a wealthy peasant to supper. As the emperor entered this house, it began to shakethe General had deceivedly lured the emperor onto a ship! Upon discovering this, the emperor decided to carry on and later finished the successful campaign.

This stratagem means that you mask your real goals, thus deceiving even the emperor / heavens itself with a fake goal, until they are confronted with finished facts. Harro von Senger notes in the GermanLanguage "Die List" that to grasp the full meaning, it would be something like "to deceive the holy virgin Mary" in the western hemisphere.

Usage

This strategy made use of the human weakness that, people eventually become unaware of common everyday activities, or events that keeps repeating itself. When this happens, it is the best moment carry out one's previously hidden true objective.

- In the Second World War, Hitler spread misinformation about a planned date for the Invasion of France, but later delayed the date. This was repeated many times, and eventually France and England grew used to the false information, and regarded all Germany planned invasions as hoaxes. Then one day, Germany invaded France with lighting speed, conquering France.
- In the Second World War, the Allies' Operation Quicksilver created a phantom army in Kent complete with fake radio chatter that diverted German attentions from real Allied armies and their intended objective of Normandy.

2. *Besiege Wèi to rescue Zhào*

When the enemy is too strong to be attacked directly, then attack something he holds dear. Know that he cannot be superior in all things. Somewhere there is a gap in the armour, a weakness that can be attacked instead.

The origins of this proverb is from the Warring States Period. The state of Wèi attacked Zhao and laid siege to its capital Handan. Zhào turned to Qí for help, but the Qí general Sun Bin determined it would be unwise to meet the army of

Wèi head on, so he instead attacked their capital at Daliang. The army of Wèi retreated in haste, and the tired troops were ambushed and defeated at the Battle of Guiling, with the Wèi general Pang Juan slain on the field. Note that this campaign is also described explicitly in the Art of War of Master Sun Bin the younger.

Usage

The idea here is to avoid a head on battle with a strong enemy, and instead strike at his weakness elsewhere. This will force the strong enemy to retreat in order to support his weakness. Battling against the now tired and lowmorale enemy will give a much higher chance of success.

- o In the Second Punic War at the Battle of Zama Scipio Africanus was able to defeat Hannibal's army in Italy not by facing him in the field but by destroying his power base in Spain and menacing his home city of Carthage

3. *Kill with a borrowed knife*

Attack using the strength of another (in a situation where using one's own strength is not favourable). Trick an ally into attacking him, bribe an official to turn traitor, or use the enemy's own strength against him.

Usage

The idea here is to cause damage to the enemy, by getting a 3rd party to do the deed.

oDuring the Three Kingdoms era, Guan Yu, one of the head generals of the Kingdom of Shu, was engaged in the Battle of Fancheng against Cao Cao. Cao Cao sent an advisor to Sun Quan to encourage him to attack and capture Jing Province. Cao Cao promised that all lands south of Yangtze River will be Sun Quan's after this act. Several weeks thereafter, the Kingdom of Wu (Sun Quan), which had secretly allied itself with the Kingdom Wei ((Cao Cao)), attacked Guan Yu's army at Jiangling. Sun Quan, a previous ally of the Kingdom of Shu, surprised and defeated the Shu forces there, forcing Guan Yu to lift the siege on Fancheng and retreat. During his retreat, Guan Yu was captured by Sun Quan's forces and was executed.

This caused great hatred between Liu Bei and Sun Quan, and eventually the hatred led to many battles between the two states.

Although Cao Cao did not live to see it, these conflicts eventually allowed the Kingdom of Wei (Cao Cao) to conquer the Kingdom of Shu Liu Bei and the Kingdom of Wu Sun Quan, allowing the Kingdom of Wei (Cao Cao) to conquer China and unify it under the rule of the Kingdom of Wei (Cao Cao).

In 1936, Stalin began to second guess his most trusted advisors and generals. Hitler made a list of the most dangerous generals within Russia, and created an underground report regarding them selling Russian information to Germany.

Many false mails between them were also made. Russian spies got hold of this detailed list of the Russian generals and the mails they had allegedly sent to Germany. 8 generals were immediately imprisoned. After a 30 minute trial, all of the generals were judged guilty of treason, and all were executed within 12 hours. When Germany and Russia engaged in combat later on, Russia had to fight without some of its best generals.

4. *Substitute leisure for labour*

It is an advantage to choose the time and place for battle. In this way you know when and where the battle will take place, while your enemy does not. Encourage your enemy to expend his energy in futile quests while you conserve your strength. When he is exhausted and confused, you attack with energy and purpose.

Usage

The idea is to have your troops wellprepared for battle, in the same time that the enemy is rushing to fight against you. This will give your troops a huge advantage in the upcoming battle, of which you will get to select the time and place.

In the Battle of Maling, Wei had both the number and morale advantage over the Qi troops. Sun Bin ordered his Qi troops to retreat, while encouraging the Wei troops to pursue them with haste. The end result was that the Qi forces were well prepared and well located for an ambush, while the Wei forces were tired from the speedy march. The battle was really one sided due to this difference.

5. *Loot a house on fire.*

When a country is beset by internal conflicts, when disease and famine ravage the population, when corruption and crime are rampant, then it will be unable to deal with an outside threat. This is the time to attack.

Usage

Keep gathering internal information about an enemy. If the enemy is currently in its weakest state ever, attack it without mercy and totally destroy it to prevent future troubles.

Before the Battle of Gaixia, both Chu and Han forces were tired from a long lasting siege. After a peace treaty, the tired Chu troops began retreating out of Han territory. Han Xin and Zhang Liang both advised to Liu Bang :"We already control half of the empire. Even within Chu, many governors favour us being the ruler, and will not give Xiang Yu support unless forced to.

The Chu troops are currently tired and face serious food stortages. The heavens have decided to end Xiang Yu 's power. If we let Xiang Yu escape, it will be like keeping a tiger alive only to kill its owner later. We must strike now and end this threat." After some thinking, Liu Bang gave the order to attack Xiang Yu, and eventually ended Chu.

6. *Make a sound in the east, then strike in the west.*

In any battle the element of surprise can provide an overwhelming advantage. Even when face to face with an enemy, surprise can still be employed by attacking where he least expects it. To do this you must create an expectation in the enemy's mind through the use of a feint.

Usage

The idea here is to get the enemy to focus his forces in a location, and then you attack elsewhere which would be weakly defended.

In 1798, Napoleon Bonaparte had planned an invasion of Egypt. But in order for his ground troops to be transported into Egypt, he would have to get through the powerful British Navy. Napoleon decided to avoid a direct confrontation during the transportation, since a defeat here would cost many lives. Napoleon informed his Mediterranean fleet that they were to join up with the fleet in the north, and attack Ireland. As a result of this news, Horatio Nelson stationed his fleet in the west of the Mediterranean, in order to block the French fleet from moving up north.

Napoleon then quickly crdered his Mediterranean fleet to transport ground troops into Egypt. By the time Horatio discovered Napoleon 's plans, about 3 weeks had passed and a large French army had gathered in Egypt. Although the French Mediterranean fleet was eventually destroyed in the Battle of the Nile, Napoleon was able to conquer Egypt with his ground troops.

In the 1991 Gulf War the coalition through Military deception was able to convince the Iraqis that the coalition intended an amphibious attack into Kuwait and was able to fix Iraqi forces in positions that could play no effective part when the real attack came.

ENEMY DEALING STRATAGEMS

7. *Create something from nothing*

A plain lie. Make somebody believe there was something when there is in fact nothing.

Usage

One method of using this strategy is to create an illusion of something 's existence, while it does not exist. Another method is to create an illusion that something does not exist, while it does.

- o During the Battle of Fei River, Former Qin had an overwhelming manpower over Jin. But instead of backing down to defend, Jin attacked Former Qin forces early and formed wide formations, giving an illusion that Jin had the manpower to match Former Qin 's forces.

Fu Jian began planning his moves in fear, and later on ordered his vast forces to back out from the river banks. The low morale Former Qin troops went into chaos, and Jin came out of the battle victorious.

- o During the Battles of Yongqiu and Suiyang, the Tang soldiers in Yongqiu were running out of arrows. Zhang Xun ordered about 1,000 scarecrows be made. At night, soldiers put their own armor onto the scarecrows, and hung them down from the Castle walls. Yan forces saw this and shot many arrows at the scarecrows, since they thought they were Tang soldiers. By the time the Yan forces found out what happened, the Tang troops had already received about 200,000 arrows. When this happened again later, Yan soldiers did not shoot one single arrow at them. But these dark figures were real Tang soldiers, who quickly attacked the sleeping Yan ranks. The vast Yin forces were forced to retreat from their position.
- o In Advance fee frauds, victims are lured by making them believe there was awaiting a large amount of money for them ("Something") while there is in fact "Nothing".

8. *Openly repair the gallery roads, but sneak through the passage of Chencang*

Deceive the enemy with an obvious approach that will take a very long time, while surprising him by taking a shortcut and sneak up to him. As the enemy concentrates on the decoy, he will miss you sneaking up to him.

The phrase originated from the ChuHan contention, where Liu Bang retreated to the lands of Sichuan to prepare for a confrontation with Xiang Yu. Once he was fully prepared, Liu Bang sent men to openly repair the gallery roads he had destroyed earlier, while secretly moving his troops towards Guanzhong through the small town of Chencang instead.

When Xiang Yu received news of Liu Bang repairing the gallery roads, he dismissed the threat since he knew the repairs would take years to complete. This allowed Liu Bang to retake

Guanzhong by surprise, and eventually led to his victory over Xiang Yu and the birth of the Han Dynasty.

Usage

This tactic is an extension of the "Make a sound in the east, then strike in the west" tactic. But instead of simply spreading misinformation to draw the enemy 's attention, physical baits are used to increase the enemy 's certainty on the misinformation. These baits must be easily seen by the enemy, to ensure that they draw the enemy 's attention. At the same time, the baits must act as if what they meant to do what they were falsely doing, to avoid drawing the enemy 's suspection.

- In 263 during the Three Kingdoms era, Deng Ai was facing off against Jiang Wei in one of the many battles between the two. Jiang Wei 's goal was to take one of the Wei fortresses. Deng Ai engaged Jiang Wei 's forces and was able to win a few early battles, and Jiang Wei retreated for a short distance before making camp. Deng Ai order his troops to set up defences along a river, since the nearby Jiang Wei forces would certainly return. After 3 days, Jiang Wei 's forces did indeed return. But they simply camped and did not prepare to cross the river. Deng Ai sensed that Jiang Wei 's main forces had gone around the river to take the fortress directly. So he ordered all forces to retreat back to the fortress to defend. Everything was just as Deng Ai had predicted, and due to his prior preparations, Jiang Wei 's siege at the fortress ended in a failure. Jiang Wei had used the tactic wrongly, because his forces at the river did not draw enough enemy attention to cause them to stay at the river.
- Prior to the Battle of Normandy, the Allies wanted to draw the Axis attention away from Normandy. An entirely fictitious First U.S. Army Group ("FUSAG"), was created for this purpose. Dummy tanks, trucks, planes and camps were made. They were placed in an area which led Germany to believe that the actual large

scale invasion would take place in Pas de Calais. The air defense in this area was at a minimum, to allow Luftwaffe to photograph them easily. Allied naval bombardment was focused on Pas de Calais instead of Normandy. Dummy paratroopers were also used to create further uncertainty on the Germany side regarding the actual location of the invasion. This led the German defense forces into disorder, and allowed the Normandy operation to be carried out with "relative" ease.

9. Watch the fires burning across the river

Delay entering the field of battle until all the other players have become exhausted fighting amongst themselves. Then go in full strength and pick up the pieces.

10. *Hide a knife behind a smile*

Charm and ingratiate yourself to your enemy. When you have gained his trust, you move against him in secret.

11. *Sacrifices the plum tree to preserve the peach tree*

There are circumstances in which you must sacrifice shortterm objectives in order to gain the longterm goal. This is the scapegoat strategy whereby someone else suffers the consequences so that the rest do not.

Cao Cao of the Three Kingdoms Period demonstrated this strategy. During a siege, Cao supplies ran low so he called in the supply captain and told him to dilute the rice with water to save grains. When the soldiers started to complain, Cao ordered for the captain to be killed. He would explain to his troops that the captain has been selling supplies to the enemy. This raises the army morale and they were victorious in a few more days.

12. *Take the opportunity to pilfer a goat (traditional Chinese*

While carrying out your plans be flexible enough to take advantage of any opportunity that presents itself, however small, and avail yourself of any profit, however slight.

ATTACKING STRATAGEMS

13. *Startle the snake by hitting the grass around it.*

Do something unaimed, but spectacular ("hitting the grass") to provoke a response of the enemy ("startle the snake"), thereby giving away his plans or position, or just taunt him. Do something unusual, strange, and unexpected as this will arouse the enemy's suspicion and disrupt his thinking. More widely used as "[Do not] startle the snake by hitting the grass". An imprudent act will give your position or intentions away to the enemy.

14. *Borrow a corpse to resurrect the soul*

Take an institution, a technology, or a method that has been forgotten or discarded and appropriate it for your own purpose. Revive something from the past by giving it a new purpose or bring to life old ideas, customs, or traditions and reinterpret them to fit your purposes.

15. *Entice the tiger to leave its mountain lair*

Never directly attack an opponent whose advantage is derived from its position. Instead lure him away from his position thus separating him from his source of strength. At the Battle of Hastings the Normans were initially unable to break the Saxon shield wall placed at the top of a hill, however by feigning retreat they were able to entice some of the Saxons to break ranks and opened a gap that allowed them to scatter the Saxon army.

16. *In order to capture, one must let loose*

Cornered prey will often mount a final desperate attack. To prevent this you let the enemy believe he still has a chance for freedom. His will to fight is thus dampened by his desire to escape. When in the end the freedom is proven a falsehood the enemy's morale will be defeated and he will surrender without a fight.

17. *Tossing out a brick to get a jade gem*

Bait someone by making him believe he gains something or just make him react to it ("toss out a brick") and obtain something valuable from him in return ("get a jade gem"). This proverb is based on a story involving two famous poets of the Tang Dynasty. There was a great poet named Zhao Gu and another lesser poet by the name of Chang Jian. While Chang

Jian was traveling in Suzhou, he heard news that Zhao Gu would be visiting a temple in the area.

Chang Jian wished to learn from the master poet, so he devised a plan and went to the temple in advance, then wrote a poem on the temple walls with only two of the four lines completed, hoping Zhao Gu would see it and finish the poem. Zhao Gu acted as Chang Jian forsaw, and from this story came the proverb.

- o Often, China lures foreign investors with the prospect of astronomical returns; in China, they discover that the figures were grossly overestimated and face technology transfer treaties or suffer from industrial espionage. (After von Senger)
- o Advance fee fraud targets this belief in the victims: They are made believe they will make sizable gains ("get a jade gem"), but first must make down payments ("toss a brick"). As the initiators did "Create something from Nothing" (strategem no. 7), the victims lose their payments.

18. *Defeat the enemy by capturing their chief*

If the enemy's army is strong but is allied to the commander only by money or threats, then take aim at the leader. If the commander falls the rest of the army will disperse or come over to your side. If, however, they are allied to the leader through loyalty then beware, the army can continue to fight on after his death out of vengeance.

CHAOS STRATAGEMS

19. *Remove the firewood under the cooking pot*

Take out the leading argument or asset of someone; "steal someone's thunder".

20. *Catch a fish while the water is disturbed*

Create confusion and use this confusion to further your own goals.

21. *Slough off the cicada's golden shell*

Mask yourself. Either leave flamboyant traits behind, thus

going incognito; or just masquerade yourself and create an illusion to fit your goals and distract others.

With the Battle of Gallipoli evacuation the British and Anzac forces were able to retreat without being routed by creating the illusion that their trenches remained occupied.

22. *Shut the door to catch the thief*

If you have the chance to completely capture the enemy then you should do so thereby bringing the battle or war to a quick and lasting conclusion.

To allow your enemy to escape plants the seeds for future conflict. But if they succeed in escaping, be wary of giving chase.

23. *Befriend a distant state while attacking a neighbour*

It is known that nations that border each other become enemies while nations separated by distance and obstacles make better allies.

When you are the strongest in one field, your greatest threat is from the second strongest in your field, not the strongest from another field. Otto von Bismarck made the League of the Three Emperors and treaties with the British Empire and Italy in order to isolate France, from which he feared an attack.

24. *Obtain safe passage to conquer the State of Guo*

Borrow the resources of an ally to attack a common enemy. Once the enemy is defeated, use those resources to turn on the ally that lent you them in the first place. The Peninsular War started when Napoleon attempted to conquer Spain by stealth, under the guise of friendship and forming an alliance against Britain and Portugal.

PROXIMATE STRATAGEMS

25. *Replace the beams with rotten timbers.*

Disrupt the enemy's formations, interfere with their methods of operations, change the rules in which they are used to following, go contrary to their standard training. In this way you remove the supporting pillar, the common link that makes a group of men an effective fighting force.

26. *Point at the mulberry tree while cursing the locust tree.*

To discipline, control, or warn others whose status or position excludes them from direct confrontation; use analogy and innuendo. Without directly naming names, those accused cannot retaliate without revealing their complicity.

27. *Feign madness but keep your balance.*

Hide behind the mask of a fool, a drunk, or a madman to create confusion about your intentions and motivations. Lure your opponent into underestimating your ability until, overconfident, he drops his guard. Then you may attack. Lucius Junius Brutus feigned idiocy for many years while he secretly prepared to depose Tarquinius Superbus, the last King of Rome.

28. *Remove the ladder when the enemy has ascended to the roof.*

With baits and deceptions lure your enemy into treacherous terrain. Then cut off his lines of communication and avenue of escape. To save himself he must fight both your own forces and the elements of nature. The Grande Armee was destroyed in the 1812 invasion of Russia by a combination of the Russian winter, a scorched earth strategy and the Russian army. Napoleon had been spurred on by the prize of capturing Moscow and with it the defeat of Russia; however all he found was a burnt out and empty city, and found his forces cut off in hostile terrain and weather with no supplies.

29. *Deck the tree with false blossoms.*

Tying silk blossoms on a dead tree gives the illusion that the tree is healthy. Through the use of artifice and disguise make something of no value appear valuable; of no threat appear dangerous; of no use appear useful.

30. *Make the host and the guest exchange roles.*

Usurp leadership in a situation where you are normally subordinate. Infiltrate your target.

DEFEAT STRATAGEMS

31. *The beauty trap (honey trap).*

Send your enemy beautiful women to cause discord within his camp. This strategy can work on three levels. First, the ruler becomes so enamoured with the beauty that he neglects his duties and allows his vigilance to wane. Second, other males at court will begin to display aggressive behaviour that inflames minor differences hindering cooperation and destroying morale.

Third, other females at court, motivated by jealousy and envy, begin to plot intrigues further exacerbating the situation. Even though this has been done many times, perhaps the most famous historical example is Xi Shi who was sent to the State of Wu during the Spring and Autumn Period.

32. *The empty fort strategy.*

When the enemy is superior in numbers and your situation is such that you expect to be overrun at any moment, then drop all pretence of military preparedness and act casually. Unless the enemy has an accurate description of your situation this unusual behaviour will arouse suspicions. With luck he will be dissuaded from attacking.

33. *Let the enemy's own spy sow discord in the enemy camp.*

Undermine your enemy's ability to fight by secretly causing discord between him and his friends, allies, advisors, family, commanders, soldiers, and population. While he is preoccupied settling internal disputes his ability to attack or defend, is compromised.

During the Second World War the German intelligence agency the Abwehr under Wilhelm Canaris actively colluded with the Allies to undermine the Nazi regime.

34. *Inflict injury on one's self to win the enemy's trust.*

Pretending to be injured has two possible applications. In the first, the enemy is lulled into relaxing his guard since he no longer considers you to be an immediate threat.

The second is a way of ingratiating yourself to your enemy by pretending the injury was caused by a mutual enemy. This strategy was perhaps best demonstrated during the Spring and Autumn Period.

After his defeat by King Fuchai of Wu, King Goujian of Yue pretended to go to Wu to become a servant of Fuchai. After gaining Fuchai's trust, Guo Jian was allow back to Yue. There he strengthen his military and in 482 BC while Fuchai was trying to gain hegemony, he attacked and conquered the capital. Some years later in 478 BC, he annexed Wu and forced Fuchai to commit suicide.

35. *Chain stratagems.*

In important matters one should use several stratagems applied simultaneously after another, as in a chain of stratagems. Keep different plans operating in an overall scheme; however, in this manner if any one strategy fails the chain breaks and the whole scheme fails.

36. *If everything else fails, retreat.*

If it becomes obvious that your current course of action will lead to defeat then retreat and regroup. When your side is losing there are only three choices remaining: surrender, compromise, or escape. Surrender is complete defeat, compromise is half defeat, but escape is not defeat. As long as you are not defeated, you still have a chance.

9

THE ART OF WAR

The beginning of The Art of War, in a "classical" bamboo book from the reign of the Qianlong Emperor.

The Art of War is a Chinese military treatise written during the 6th century BC by Sun Tzu. Composed of 13 chapters, each of which is devoted to one aspect of warfare, it has long been praised as the definitive work on military strategies and tactics of its time.

The Art of War is one of the oldest books on military strategy in the world. Like a work of mathematics or science, much of the work is dedicated to defining its concepts in what has been described as a series of formulas. It is the first and one of the most successful works on strategy and has had a huge influence on Eastern and Western military thinking, business tactics, and beyond. Sun Tzu was the first to recognize the importance of positioning in strategy and that position is affected both by objective conditions in the physical environment and the subjective opinions of competitive actors in that environment. He taught that strategy was not planning in the sense of working through a todo list, instead it requires quickly responding appropriately to changing conditions. Planning works in a controlled environment, but in a competitive environment, competing plans collide creating situations that no one plans.

The book was first translated into a European language in 1782 by French Jesuit Jean Joseph Marie Amiot, and had possibly influenced Napoleon, and even the planning of Operation Desert Storm. Leaders as diverse as Mao Zedong, General Pervez Musharraf, Vo Nguyen Giap, and General

Douglas MacArthur have claimed to have drawn inspiration from the work.

The Art of War has also been applied, with much success, to business and managerial strategies.

THE 13 CHAPTERS

Chapter titles from Lionel Giles' 1910 translation

I. Laying Plans

II. Waging War

III. Attack by Stratagem

IV. Tactical Dispositions

V. Energy

VI. Weak Points and Strong

VII. Manœuvering

VIII. Variation in Tactics

IX. The Army on the March

X. Terrain

XI. The Nine Situations

XII. The Attack by Fire

XIII. The Use of Spies

Chapter titles from ChowHou Wee's 2003 translation

I. Detail Assessment and Planning

II. Waging War

III. Strategic Attack

IV. Disposition of the Army

V. Forces

VI. Weaknesses and Strengths

VII. Military Manoeuvres

VIII. Variations and Adaptability

IX. Movement and Development of Troops

X. Terrain

XI. The Nine Battlegrounds

XII. Attacking with Fire

XIII. Intelligence and Espionage

Chapter titles from R.L. Wing's 1988 translation

I. The Calculations

II. The Challenge

III. The Plan of Attack

IV. Positioning

V. Directing

VI. Illusion and Reality

VII. Engaging The Force

VIII. The Nine Variations

IX. Moving The Force

X. Situational Positioning

XI. The Nine Situations

XII. The Fiery Attack

XIII. The Use of Intelligence

- The first chapter, "Planning," explores the five key elements that define competitive position (mission, climate, ground, leadership, and methods) and how to evaluate your competitive strengths against your competition.
- "Going to War" explains the economic nature of competition and how success requires making winning pay, which in turn, requires limiting the cost of competition and conflict.
- "Planning the Attack" defines the source of strength as unity, not size, and the five ingredients that you need to succeed in any competitive situation.
- "Positioning" explains the importance of defending existing positions until you can advance them and how you must recognize opportunities, not try to create them.
- "Force" explores the use of creativity and timing to build your competitive momentum.
- "Weakness and Strength" explains how your opportunities come from the openings in the environment

caused by the relative weakness of your competitors in a given area.

- "Armed Conflict" explains the dangers of direct conflict and how to win those confrontations when they are forced upon you.
- "Adapting to the Situation" focuses on the need for flexibility in your responses. It explains how to respond to shifting circumstances successfully.
- "Armed March" describes the different situations in which you find yourselves as you move into new competitive arenas and how to respond to them. Much of it focuses on evaluating the intentions of others.
- "Field Position" looks the three general areas of resistance (distance, dangers, and barriers) and the a six types of ground positions that arise from them. Each of these six field positions offers certain advantages and disadvantages.
- "Nine Terrain" describes nine common situations (or stages) in a competitive campaign, from scattering to deadly, and the specific focus you need to successfully navigate each of them.
- "Attacking with Fire" explains the use of weapons generally and the use of the environment as a weapon specifically. It examines the five targets for attack, the five types of environmental attack, and the appropriate responses to such attack.
- "Using Spies" focuses on the importance of developing good information sources, specifically the five types of sources and how to manage them.

ANNOTATIONS

Before the bamboo scroll version was discovered by archaeologists in April 1972, the most cited version of The Art of War was the Annotation of Sun Tzu's Strategies by Cao Cao, the founder of the Kingdom of Wei. In the preface, he wrote that previous annotations were not focused on the essential ideas. Other annotations cited in official history books include

Shen You (176204)'s Sun Tzu's Military Strategy, Jia Xu's Copy of Sun Tzu's Military Strategy, Cao Cao and Wang Ling's Sun Tzu's Military Strategy.

The Book of Sui documented seven books named after Sun Tzu. An annotation by Du Mu also includes Cao Cao's annotation. Li Jing's The Art of War is said to be a revision of Sun Tzu's strategies. Annotations by Cao Cao, Du Mu and Li Quan were translated into Tangut language before 1040 AD.

After the movable type printer was invented, The Art of War (with Cao Cao's annotations) was published as a military text book, known as Seven Military Classics with six other strategy books. A book named Ten Schools of The Art of War Annotations was published before 1161 AD.

As a required reading military textbook since the Song Dynasty, Seven Military Classics (????) has many annotations. More than 30 differently annotated versions of this book exist today.

Vernacular Chinese became increasingly popular in the late 1920s. Annotations in Vernacular Chinese began to appear after this time. Some of these works were translated from other languages, such as Japanese.

The two most common traditional Chinese versions of the Art of War, (the Complete Specialist Focus and Military Bible versions) were the sources for early translation into English and other languages. It was not until the 1970s that these works were compiled with more recent archeological discoveries into a single more complete version in Taipei. The resulting work is known as the Complete Version of Sun Tzu's Art of War for the National Defense Research Investigation Office has been the source for more recent and complete translations.

Quotations

Verses from the book occur in modern daily Chinese idioms and phrases, such as the last verse of Chapter 3:

So it is said that if you know your enemies and know yourself, you will fight without danger in battles.

If you only know yourself, but not your opponent, you may win or may lose.

If you know neither yourself nor your enemy, you will always endanger yourself. This has been more tersely interpreted and condensed into the modern proverb:

If you know both yourself and your enemy, you can come out of hundreds of battles without danger.

Many people interpret this sentence as 'If you know both sides, you will win a hundred times in one hundred battles. This translation is incorrect. The word '?' in Chinese means 'danger'. '?' in this sentence is better interpreted as 'numerous' rather than 'hundred'.

Furthermore, knowing both sides doesn't guarantee winning. Since in the beginning paragraph of chapter four, Sun Tsu wrote 'Hence, we can well predict who would win but there is no strategy guaranteeing winning'. The reason of the uncertainty is quite simple. How about dealing with the opponent who knows both sides better than you do?

Similar verses have also been borrowedin a manner construing skillfulness as victory "without fighting"for example:

Therefore one hundred victories in one hundred battles is not the most skillful. Seizing the enemy without fighting is the most skillful.

And, the most famous quotation (chapter 1, paragraph 18):

All warfare is based on deception.

Military Applications

In many East Asian countries, The Art of War was part of the syllabus for potential candidates of military service examinations. Various translations are available.

During the Sengoku era in Japan, a daimyo named Takeda Shingen (15211573) is said to have become almost invincible in all battles without relying on guns, because he studied The Art of War. The book even gave him the inspiration for his famous battle standard "Furinkazan" (Wind, Forest, Fire and Mountain), meaning fast as the wind, silent as a forest, ferocious as fire and immovable as a mountain.

The translator Samuel B. Griffith offers a chapter on "Sun Tzu and Mao TseTung" where The Art of War is cited as influencing Mao's On Guerilla Warfare, On the Protracted War, and Strategic Problems of China's Revolutionary War and includes Mao's quote: "We must not belittle the saying in the book of Sun Wu Tzu, the great military expert of ancient China, 'Know your enemy and know yourself and you can fight a thousand battles without disaster.'"

During the Vietnam War, some Vietcong officers studied The Art of War, and reportedly could recite entire passages from memory.

The Department of the Army in the United States, through its Command and General Staff College, has directed all units to maintain libraries within their respective headquarters for the continuing education of personnel in the art of war. The Art of War is specifically mentioned by name as an example of works to be maintained at each individual unit, and staff duty officers are obliged to prepare short papers for presentation to other officers on their readings.

Applicability Outside the Military

Since at least the 1980s, The Art of War has been applied to fields well outside the military. Much of the text is about how to fight wars without actually having to do battle: it gives tips on how to outsmart one's opponent so that physical battle is not necessary. As such, it has found application as a training guide for many competitive endeavors that do not involve actual combat.

The book has gained popularity in corporate culture; there have been a variety of business books written applying its lessons to "office politics" and corporate strategy. Many Japanese companies make the book required reading for their key executives. The book is also popular among Western business management, who have turned to it for inspiration and advice on how to succeed in competitive business situations.

The Art of War has also been the subject of various law books and legal articles on the trial process, including negotiation tactics and trial strategy.

It has also crept its way into sport: Australian cricket coach John Buchanan handed out excerpts from the book to his players before a match against England in 2001, and the book is allegedly a favorite of University of South Carolina football head coach Steve Spurrier.

Former Brazilian football coach, and current coach of the Portuguese national football team Luiz Felipe Scolari uses the book to plot his football strategy. In the 2002 FIFA World Cup he gave each of his players copies. In the recent 2006 FIFA World Cup in Germany he used the book to plan his team's win against England.

On the popular reality television show Survivor: China, participants were given copies as a source of strategy and advice.

It has found use in political campaigning as well; Republican election strategist Lee Atwater claimed he travelled everywhere with it.

Some have also interpreted The Art of War as providing methods for developing social strategies, such as social relationships, maintaining romantic relationships, and seduction. The book stresses subtlety and always making it appear like one is trying to achieve something other than one's actual intention.

The use of individual quotations from the book as a source of fortune cookielike proverbs and not seeing the general coherence of the text has been criticized by many scholars of Chinese history.

The book has also gained influence among players of strategy games, including TCGs, collectible miniatures games, and realtime strategy games.

10

MODERN WAR MILITARY STRATEGY

Military strategy is a collective name for planning the conduct of warfare. Derived from the Greek strategos, strategy was seen as the "art of the general". Military strategy deals with the planning and conduct of campaigns, the movement and disposition of forces, and the deception of the enemy. The father of modern strategic study, Carl von Clausewitz, defined military strategy as "the employment of battles to gain the end of war." Liddell Hart's definition put less emphasis on battles, defining strategy as "the art of distributing and applying military means to fulfill the ends of policy" Hence, both gave the preeminence to political aims over military goals, ensuring civilian control of the military. Military strategy was one of a triumvirate of "arts" or "sciences" that govern the conduct of warfare; the others being tactics, the execution of plans and manœuvering of forces in battle, and logistics, the maintenance of an army. The border line between strategy and tactics is blurred and sometimes categorisation of a decision is a matter of almost personal opinion.

FUNDAMENTALS OF MILITARY STRATEGY

Strategy and tactics are closely related. Both deal with distance, time and force but strategy is large scale while tactics are small scale. Originally strategy was understood to govern the prelude to a battle while tactics controlled its execution. However, in the world wars of the 20th century, the distinction between maneuver and battle, strategy and tactics, became blurred. Tactics that were once the province of a company of cavalry would be applied to a panzer army. It is often said that the art of strategies defines the goals to achieve in a military campaign, while tactics defines the methods to achieve these goals.

Strategic goals could be "We want to conquer area X", or "We want to stop country Y's expansion in world trade in commodity Z"; while tactical decisions range from "We're going to do this by a naval invasion of the North of country X", "We're going to blockade the ports of country Y", all the way down to "C Platoon will attack while D platoon provides fire cover".

In its purest form, strategy dealt solely with military issues. In earlier societies, a king or political leader was often the same person as the military leader. If he was not, the distance of communication between the political and the military leader was small.

But as the need of a professional army grew, the bounds between the politicians and the military came to be recognized. In many cases, it was decided that there was a need for a separation. As French statesman Georges Clemenceau said, "war is too important a business to be left to soldiers." This gave rise to the concept of the grand strategy which encompasses the management of the resources of an entire nation in the conduct of warfare.

In the environment of the grand strategy, the military component is largely reduced to operational strategythe planning and control of large military units such as corps and divisions. As the size and number of the armies grew and the technology to communicate and control improved, the difference between "military strategy" and "grand strategy" shrank.

Fundamental to grand strategy is the diplomacy through which a nation might forge alliances or pressure another nation into compliance, thereby achieving victory without resorting to combat. Another element of grand strategy is the management of the postwar peace. As Clausewitz stated, a successful military strategy may be a means to an end, but it is not an end in itself. There are numerous examples in history where victory on the battlefield has not translated into long term peace, security or tranquility.

PRINCIPLES OF MILITARY STRATEGY

Many military strategists have attempted to encapsulate a successful strategy in a set of principles. Sun Tzu defined 13 principles in his The Art of War while Napoleon listed 115 maxims. American Civil War General Nathan Bedford Forrest required only one: "to git thar furst with the most men". The fundamental concepts common to most lists of principles are:

1. The Objective
2. Offense
3. Cooperation
4. Concentration (Mass)
5. Economy
6. Manoeuvre
7. Surprise
8. Security
9. Simplicity

Which are reflected in the United States Army's United States Army Field Manual (FM3) of Military Operations (sections 432 to 439) as:

1. Objective (Direct every military operation towards a clearly defined, decisive, and attainable objective)
2. Offensive (Seize, retain, and exploit the initiative)
3. Mass (Concentrate combat power at the decisive place and time)
4. Economy of Force (Allocate minimum essential combat power to secondary efforts)
5. Maneuver (Place the enemy in a disadvantageous position through the flexible application of combat power)
6. Unity of Command (For every objective, ensure unity of effort under one responsible commander)
7. Security (Never permit the enemy to acquire an unexpected advantage)

8. Surprise (Strike the enemy at a time, at a place, or in a manner for which he is unprepared)
9. Simplicity (Prepare clear, uncomplicated plans and clear, concise orders to ensure thorough understanding)

Some strategists assert that adhering to the fundamental principles guarantees victory while others claim war is unpredictable and the general must be flexible in formulating a strategy. Field Marshal Count Helmuth von Moltke expressed strategy as a system of "ad hoc expedients" by which a general must take action while under pressure. These underlying principles of strategy have survived relatively unscathed as the technology of warfare has developed.

Strategy (and tactics) must constantly evolve in response to technological advances. A successful strategy from one era tends to remain in favor long after new developments in military weaponry and matériel have rendered it obsolete. World War I, and to a great extent the American Civil War, saw Napoleonic tactics of "offense at all costs" pitted against the defensive power of the trench, machine gun and barbed wire. As a reaction to her WWI experience, France entered World War II with a purely defensive doctrine, epitomized by the "impregnable" Maginot Line, but only to be completely circumvented by the German blitzkrieg.

DEVELOPMENT OF MILITARY STRATEGY

Early Military Strategy

The principles of military strategy can be found as far back as 500 BC in the works of Sun Tzu and Chanakya. The campaigns of Alexander the Great, Chandragupta Maurya, Hannibal, Qin Shi Huang, Julius Cæsar, Zhuge Liang, and Khalid ibn alWalid demonstrate strategic planning and movement. Mahan describes in the preface to The Influence of Sea Power upon History how the Romans used their sea power to effectively block the sea lines of communication of Hannibal with Carthage; and so via a maritime strategy achieved Hannibal's removal from Italy, despite never beating him there with their legions.

In 1520 Niccolò Machiavelli's Dell'arte della guerra (Art of War) dealt with the relationship between civil and military matters and the formation of the grand strategy. In the Thirty Years' War, Gustavus Adolphus of Sweden demonstrated advanced operational strategy that led to victories in Holy Roman Empire area.

It was not until the 18th century that military strategy was subjected to serious study. In the Seven Years' War (17561763), Frederick the Great improvised a "strategy of exhaustion" (see Attrition warfare) to hold off his opponents and conserve his Prussian forces. Assailed from all sides by France, Austria, Russia and Sweden, Frederick exploited his central position which enabled him to move his army along interior lines and concentrate against one opponent at a time. Unable to achieve victory, he was able to stave off defeat until a diplomatic solution was reached. Frederick's "victory" led to great significance being placed on "geometric strategy" which emphasized lines of manoeuvre, awareness of terrain and possession of critical strongpoints.

Genghis Khan and the Mongols

As a counterpoint to European developments in the strategic art, the Mongol Emperor Genghis Khan provides a useful example. Genghis' successes, and those of his successors, were based upon manoeuvre and terror. The point of Genghis' strategic assault was nothing less than the psychology of the opposing population. By a steady and meticulous implementation of this strategy, Genghis and his descendants were able to conquer most of Eurasia.

The building blocks of Genghis' army and his strategy were his tribal levies of mounted archers and (just as important) the vast horseherds of Mongolia. Each archer had at least one extra horse; (it was an average five horses per man) thus the entire army could move with incredible rapidity. Moreover since horse milk and horse blood were the staples of the Mongolian diet, Genghis' horseherds functioned not just as his means of movement but also as his logistical tail. All other necessities could be foraged and plundered. It was not until well into the 20th century that any army was able to match the rapidity of deployment of Genghis' armies. Compared to the armies of Genghis, all other armies were heavy and comparatively immobile. Through manoeuver and continuous assault, Chinese, Persian, Arab and Eastern European armies could be stressed until they broke, and then annihilated in pursuit.

When confronted with a fortified city, the Mongol imperatives of manoeuver and speed required that it be quickly subdued. Here the fear engendered by the awful reputation of the Mongolians helped. So too did primitive biological warfare. A trebuchet or other type of ballista weapon would be used to launch dead animals and corpses into a barricaded city, spreading disease and death among the inhabitants. If a particular town or city displeased the Mongolian Khan, everyone in the city would be killed to set an example for all other cities. This could be called a form of psychological warfare.

Note that of the above list of strategic terms, even this elementary summary indicates that the Mongols strategy was directed towards an objective (that schwerpunkt (main focus) being nothing less than the psychology of the opposing population) achieved through the offensive; the offensive was characterized by concentration of forces, manoeuvre, surprise and simplicity.

Napoleonic Strategy

The French Revolution and the Napoleonic Wars that followed revolutionized military strategy. The impact of this period was still to be felt in the American Civil War and the early phases of World War I. With the advent of cheap small arms and the rise of the drafted citizen soldier, armies grew rapidly in size to become massed formations. This necessitated dividing the army first into divisions and later into corps. Along with divisions came divisional artillery; lightweight, mobile and with great range and firepower. The rigid formations of pikemen and musketeers firing massed volleys gave way to light infantry fighting in skirmish lines.

Napoleon I of France took advantage of these developments to pursue a brutally effective "strategy of annihilation" that cared little for the mathematical perfection of the geometric strategy. Napoleon invariably sought to achieve decision in battle, with the sole aim of utterly destroying his opponent, usually achieving success through superior manouevre. As ruler and general he dealt with the grand strategy as well as the operational strategy, making use of political and economic measures.

While not the originator of the methods he used, Napoleon very effectively combined the maneuver and battle stages into one event. Before this, General Officer had considered the approach to battle a separate event. However, Napoleon used the maneuver to battle to dictate how and where the battle would progress. The Battle of Austerlitz was a perfect example of this maneuver. Napoleon withdrew from a strong position to draw his opponent forward and tempt him into a flank attack, weakening his center. This allowed the French army to split the allied army and gain victory.

Napoleon used two primary strategies for the approach to battle. His "Maneuver De Derrière" was intended to place the French Army across the enemy's lines of communications. This forced the opponent to either march to battle with Napoleon or attempt to find an escape route around the army. By placing his army into the rear, his opponents supplies and communications would be cut. This had a negative effect on enemy morale. Once joined, the battle would be one in which his opponent could not afford defeat. This also allowed Napoleon to select multiple march routes into a battle site. Initially, the lack of force concentration helped with foraging for food and sought to confuse the enemy as to his real location and intentions. This strategy, along with the use of forced marches created a morale bonus that played heavily in his favor.

The "indirect" approach into battle also allowed Napoleon to disrupt the linear formations used by the allied armies. As the battle progressed enemy committed their reserves to stabilize the situation, Napoleon would suddenly release the flanking formation to attack the enemy. His opponents, being suddenly confronted with a new threat and with little reserves, had no choice but to weaken the area closest to the flanking formation and draw up a battle line at a right angle in an attempt to stop this new threat. Once this had occurred, Napoleon would mass his reserves at the hinge of that right angle and launch a heavy attack to break the lines. The rupture in the enemy lines allowed Napoleon's cavalry to flank both lines and roll them up leaving his opponent no choice but to surrender or flee.

The second strategy used by Napoleon I of France when confronted with two or more enemy armies was the use of the central position. This allowed Napoleon to drive a wedge to separate the enemy armies. He would then use part of his force to mask one army while the larger portion overwhelmed and defeated the second army quickly. He would then march on the second army leaving a portion to pursue the first army and repeat the operations. This was designed to achieve the highest concentration of men into the primary battle while limiting the enemy's ability to reinforce the critical battle. The central position had a weakness in that the full power of the pursuit of the enemy could not be achieved because the second army needed attention. So overall the preferred method of attack was the flank march to cross the enemies logistics. Napoleon used the central position strategy during the Battle of Waterloo Hundred Days. Napoleon masked Arthur Wellesley, 1st Duke of Wellington and massed against the Prussian army, and then after the Ligny battle was won, Napoleon attempted to do the same to the Allied/English army located just to the south of Waterloo. His subordinate was unable to mask the defeated Prussian army, who reinforced the Waterloo battle in time to defeat Napoleon and end his domination of Europe. It can be said that the Prussian Army under Gebhard Leberecht von Blücher used the "maneuver de derrière" against Napoleon who was suddenly placed in a position of reacting to a new enemy threat.

Napoleon's practical strategic triumphs, repeatedly leading smaller forces to defeat larger ones, inspired a whole new field of study into military strategy. In particular, his opponents were keen to develop a body of knowledge in this area to allow them to counteract a masterful individual with a highly competent group of officers, a General Staff. The two most significant students of his work were Carl von Clausewitz, a

Prussian with a background in philosophy, and AntoineHenri Jomini, who had been one of Napoleon's staff officers. Clausewitz's On War has become the bible of strategy, dealing with political, as well as military, leadership. His most famous assertion being:

> *"War is not merely a political act, but also a real political instrument, a continuation of policy carried out by other means."*

Clausewitz dismissed "geometry" as an insignificant factor in strategy, believing instead in the Napoleonic concept of victory through battle and destruction of the opposing force, at any cost. However, he also recognized that limited warfare could influence policy by wearing down the opposition through a "strategy of attrition".

In contrast to Clausewitz, AntoineHenri Jomini dealt mainly with operational strategy, planning & intelligence, the conduct of the campaign, and "generalship" rather than "statesmanship". He proposed that victory could be achieved by occupying the enemy's territory rather than destroying his army. As such, geometric considerations were prominent in his theory of strategy. Jomini's two basic principles of strategy were to concentrate against fractions of the enemy force at a time and to strike at the most decisive objective.

One notable exception to Napoleon's strategy of annihilation and a precursor to trench warfare were the Lines of Torres Vedras during the Peninsular campaign. French Armies lived off the land and when they were confronted by a line of fortifications which they could not out flank, they were unable to continue the advance and were forced to retreat once they had consumed all the provisions of the region in front of the lines.

The Peninsular campaign was notable for the development of another method of warfare which went largely unnoticed at the time, but would become far more common in the 20th century. That was the aid and encouragement the British gave to the Spanish to harass the French behind their lines which led them to squander most of the assets of their Iberian army in protecting the army's line of communications. This was a very cost effective move for the British, because it cost far less to aid Spanish insurgents than it did to equip and pay regular British army units to engage the same number of French troops. As the British army could be correspondingly smaller it was able to supply its troops by sea and land without having to live off the land as was the norm at the time. Further, because they did not have to forage they did not antagonise the locals and so did not have to garrison their lines of communications to the same extent as the French did. So the strategy of aiding their Spanish civilian allies in their guerrilla or 'small war' benefited the British in many ways, not all of which were immediately obvious.

STRATEGY IN THE INDUSTRIAL AGE

The evolution of military strategy continued in the American Civil War (186165). The practice of strategy was advanced by generals such as Robert E. Lee, Ulysses S. Grant and William Tecumseh Sherman, all of whom had been influenced by the feats of Napoleon (Thomas "Stonewall" Jackson was said to have carried a book of Napoleon's maxims with him). However, the adherence to the Napoleonic principles in the face of technological advances such as the longrange infantry rifle generally led to disastrous consequences. The time and space in which war was waged changed as well. Railroads enabled swift movement of large forces but the manoeuvring was constrained to narrow, vulnerable corridors. Steam power and ironclads changed transport and combat at sea.

There was still room for triumphs of strategy of manoeuvre such as Sherman's March to the Sea in 1864, but these depended upon an enemy's unwillingness to entrench. Towards the end of the war, especially in defense of static targets as in the battles of Cold Harbor and Vicksburg, trenches between both sides grew to a World War I scale. Many of the lessons of the American Civil War were forgotten when in wars like the AustroPrussian War or the FrancoPrussian War manoeuvre won the day.

In the period preceding World War I, two of the most influential strategists were the Prussian generals, Helmuth von Moltke and Alfred von Schlieffen. Under Moltke the Prussian army achieved victory in the AustroPrussian War (1866) and the FrancoPrussian War (187071), the latter campaign being widely regarded as a classic example of the conception and execution of military strategy. In addition to exploiting railroads and highways for manoeuvre, Moltke harnessed the telegraph for control of large armies. He recognised the increasing need to delegate control to subordinate commanders and to issue directives rather than specific orders.

Moltke is most remembered as a strategist for his belief in the need for flexibility and that no plan, however well prepared, can be guaranteed to survive beyond the first encounter with the enemy.

Field Marshal Schlieffen succeeded Moltke and directed German planning in the lead up to World War I. He advocated the "strategy of annihilation" but was faced by a war on two fronts against numerically superior opposition. The strategy he formulated was the Schlieffen Plan, defending in the east while concentrating for a decisive victory in the west, after which the Germans would go on to the offensive in the east. Influenced by Hannibal's success at the Battle of Cannae, Schlieffen planned for a single great battle of encirclement, thereby annihilating his enemy.

Another German strategist of the period was Hans Delbrück who expanded on Clausewitz's concept of "limited warfare" to produce a theory on the "strategy of exhaustion". His theory defied popular military thinking of the time, which was strongly in favour of victory in battle, yet World War I would soon demonstrate the flaws of a mindless "strategy of annihilation".

At a time when industrialisation was reaping major advances in naval technology, one American strategist, Alfred Thayer Mahan, almost singlehandedly brought the field of naval strategy up to date. Influenced by Jomini's principles of strategy, he saw that in the coming wars, where economic strategy could be as important as military strategy, control of the sea granted the power to control the trade and resources needed to wage war. Mahan pushed the concept of the "big navy" and an expansionist view where defence was achieved by controlling the sea approaches rather than fortifying the coast. His theories contributed to the naval arms race between 1898 and 1914.

STRATEGY IN WORLD WAR I

At the start of World War I strategy was dominated by the offensive thinking that had been in vogue since 1870, despite the more recent experiences of the Second Boer War (18991902) and RussoJapanese War (190405), where the machine gun demonstrated its defensive capabilities. By the end of 1914, the Western Front was a stalemate and all ability to manoeuver strategically was lost. The combatants resorted to a "strategy of attrition". The German battle at Verdun, the British on the Somme and at Passchendaele were among the first widescale battles intended to wear down the enemy. Attrition was timeconsuming so the duration of World War I battles often stretched to weeks and months. The problem with attrition was that the use of fortified defenses in depth generally required a ratio of ten attackers to one defender, or a level of artillery support which was simply not feasible until late 1917, for any reasonable chance of victory. The ability of the defender to move troops using interior lines prevented the possibility of fully exploiting any breakthrough with the level of technology then attainable.

Perhaps the most controversial aspect of strategy in World War I was the difference among the British between the "Western" viewpoint (held by Field Marshal Haig) and the "Eastern"; the former being that all effort should be directed against the German Army, the latter that more useful work could be done by attacking Germany's allies. The term "Knocking away the props" was used, perhaps an unfortunate consequence of the fact that all of Germany's allies lay south of (i.e. 'beneath') her on the map. Apologists and defenders of the Western viewpoint make the valid point that Germany's allies were more than once rescued from disaster or rendered capable of holding their own or making substantial gains by the provision of German troops, arms or military advisers, whereas those allies did not at any time provide a similar function for Germany. That is, it was Germany which was the prop, and her allies (particularly Bulgaria and AustriaHungary) did not suffer significant reverses until Germany's ability to come to their aid was grossly impaired.

On other fronts, there was still room for the use of strategy of manoeuver. The Germans executed a perfect battle of annihilation against the Russians at the Battle of Tannenberg (1914). In 1915 Britain and France launched the wellintentioned but poorly conceived and ultimately fruitless Dardanelles Campaign, combining naval power and an amphibious landing, in an effort to aid their Russian ally and knock the Ottoman Empire out of the war. The Palestine campaign was dominated by cavalry, which flourished in the local terrain, and the British achieved two breakthrough victories at Gaza (1917) and Megiddo (1918). Colonel T.E. Lawrence and other British officers led Arab irregulars on a guerrilla campaign against the Ottomans, using strategy and tactics developed during the Boer Wars.

World War I saw armies on a scale never before experienced. The British, who had always relied on a strong navy and a small regular army, were forced to undertake a rapid expansion of the army. This outpaced the rate of training of generals and staff officers able to handle such a mammoth force, and overwhelmed the ability of British industry to equip it with the necessary weapons and adequate highquality munitions until late in the war. Technological advances also had a huge influence on strategy: aerial reconnaissance, artillery techniques, poison gas, the automobile and tank (though the latter was, even at the end of the war, still in its infancy), telephone and radio telegraphy.

More so than in previous wars, military strategy in World War I was directed by the grand strategy of a coalition of nations; the Entente on one side and the Central Powers on the other. Society and economy were mobilized for total war. Attacks on the enemy's economy included Britain's use of a naval blockade and Germany employing submarine warfare against merchant shipping.

Unity of command became a question when the various nation states began coordinating assaults and defenses. Under the pressure of horrendously destructive German attacks beginning on March 21, 1918, the Entente eventually settled under Field Marshal Foch. The Germans generally led the Central Powers, though German authority diminished and lines of command became confused at the end of the war.

WW1 strategy was dominated by the "Spirit of the Offensive" where generals resorted almost to mysticism in terms of a soldiers personal "attitude" in order to break the stalemate, this led to nothing but bloody slaughter as troops in close ranks charged machineguns. Each side developed an alternate thesis. The British under Churchill developed tank warfare with which they eventually won the war.

The Germans developed a "doctrine of autonomy" the forerunner of both blitzkrieg and modern infantry tactics using groups of Stormtroopers who would advance in small mutually covering groups from cover to cover with "autonomy" to exploit any weakness they discovered in enemy defenses. Almost all the blitzkrieg commanders of WWII, particularly Rommel were stormtroopers in World War 1. After the Treaty of BrestLitovsk Germany launched and almost succeeded in a final offensive, however the new tactics of autonomy revealed a weakness in terms of overall coordination and direction. The March offensive, intended to drive a wedge between the French and British armies, turn on the latter and destroy it, lost direction and became driven by its territorial gains, its original purpose neglected.

World War I ended when the ability of the German army to fight became so diminished that Germany asked for peace conditions. The German military, exhausted by the efforts of the March offensives and dispirited by their failure, was first seriously defeated during the battle of Amiens (811 August 1918) and the German homefront entered general revolt over a lack of food and destruction of the economy. Victory for the Entente was almost assured by that point, and the fact of Germany's military impotence was driven home in the following hundred days. In this time, the Entente reversed the gains the Germans had made in the first part of the year, and the British Army (spearheaded by the Canadians and Australians) finally broke the Hindenburg defensive system.

Though his methods are questioned, Britain's Field Marshal Haig was ultimately proved correct in his grand strategic vision: "We cannot hope to win until we have defeated the German Army." By the end of the war, the best German troops were dead and the remainder were under continuous pressure on all parts of the Western Front, a consequence in part of an almost endless supply of fresh American reinforcements (which the Germans were unable to match) and in part of industry at last supplying the weakened Entente armies with the firepower to replace the men they lacked (whilst Germany wanted for all sorts of materials thanks to the naval blockade). Interior lines thus became meaningless as Germany had nothing more to offer its allies. The props eventually fell, but only because they were themselves no longer supported.

The role of the tank in World War One strategy is often poorly understood. Its supporters saw it as the weapon of victory, and many observers since have accused the high commands (especially the British) of shortsightedness in this matter, particularly in view of what tanks have achieved since. Nevertheless, the World War I tank's limitations, imposed by the limits of contemporary engineering technology, have to be borne in mind.

They were slow (men could run, and frequently walk, faster); vulnerable (to artillery) due to their size, clumsiness and inability to carry armour against anything but rifle and machine gun ammunition; extremely uncomfortable (conditions inside them often incapacitating crews with engine fumes and heat, and driving some mad with noise); and often despicably unreliable (frequently failing to make it to their targets due to engine or track failures).

This was the factor behind the seemingly mindless retention of large bodies of cavalry, which even in 1918, with armies incompletely mechanised, were still the only armed force capable of moving significantly faster than an infantryman on foot. It was not until the relevant technology (in engineering and communications) matured between the wars that the tank and the airplane could be forged into the coordinated force needed to truly restore manoeuvre to warfare.

STRATEGY DEVELOPMENT BETWEEN WORLD WARS

In the years following World War I, two of the technologies that had been introduced during that conflict, the aircraft and the tank, became the subject of strategic study.

The leading theorist of air power was Italian general Giulio Douhet who believed that future wars would be won or lost in the air. The air force would carry the offensive and the role of the ground forces would be defensive only. Douhet's doctrine of strategic bombing meant striking at the enemy's heartlandhis cities, industry and communications. Air power would thereby reduce his willingness and capacity to fight. At this time the idea of the aircraft carrier and its capabilities also started to change thinking in those countries with large fleets, but nowhere as much as in Japan. The UK and USA seem to have seen the carrier as a defensive weapon and their designs mirrored this, the Japanese Imperial navy seem to have developed a new offensive strategy based around the power projection these made possible.

British general J. F. C. Fuller, architect of the first great tank battle at Cambrai, and his contemporary, B. H. Liddell Hart, were amongst the most prominent advocates of mechanization and motorization of the army in Britain. In Germany, study groups were set up by Von Seekt, commander of the Reichwehr Truppenamt, for 57 areas of strategy and tactics to learn from WW1 and to adapt strategy to avoid the stalemate and then defeat they had suffered. All seem to have seen the strategic shock value of mobility and the new possibilities made possible by motorised forces. Both saw that the armoured fighting vehicle demonstrated firepower, mobility and protection. The Germans seem to have seen more clearly the need to make all branches of the Army as mobile as possible to maximise the results of this strategy. It would negate the static defences of the trench and machine gun and restore the strategic principles of manoeuvre and offense. Nevertheless, it was the British Army which was the only one truly mechanised at the beginning of the Second World War, the Germans still relying on horse traction for a portion of their artillery.

The innovative German Major (later General) Heinz

Guderian developed the motorised part of this strategy as the head of one of the Truppenamt groups and may have incorporated Fuller's and Liddell Hart's ideas to amplify the groundbreaking Blitzkrieg effect that was seen used by Germany against Poland in 1939 and later against France in 1940. France, still committed to stationary World War I strategies, was completely surprised and summarily overwhelmed by Germany's mobile combined arms doctrine and Guderian's Panzer Corps.

Technological change had an enormous effect on strategy, but little effect on leadership. The use of telegraph and later radio, along with improved transport, enabled the rapid movement of large numbers of men. One of Germany's key enablers in mobile warfare was the use of radios, where these were put into every tank. However, the number of men that one officer could effectively control had, if anything, declined. The increases in the size of the armies led to an increase in the number of officers. Although the officer ranks in the US Army did swell, in the German army the ratio of officers to total men remained steady. See Van Creveld's "Fighting Power" for more on this topic.

STRATEGY IN WORLD WAR II

German Strategy

The German strategies of World War II were almost exclusively designed or condoned by Adolf Hitler himself. Though he was an amateur strategist at best, the initial successes of his unconventional and aggressive strategies, both military and political (e.g. Czechoslovakia, Poland, France), combined with the mythical attributes ascribed to him ("Führerprinzip"), led to wide support for his leadership, both among the German population and the traditional military.

The main point of Hitler's strategy was the accumulation of "Lebensraum" ("Living space") for the German race. He felt that the German borders were too contained to secure their appropriate position in the geopolitical world relations, and that he needed territories similar to the (British and French) colonies to secure enough economic resources to secure Germany's position as a major power. Furthermore, the current population of these territories needed to be enslaved, migrated, or exterminated, and repopulated by Germanic settlers. He felt that these areas could best be secured in the East (Poland, Ukraine, Russia) because he thought the races populating these territories were inferior.

The intended strategy to achieve these goals was a series of relatively short wars, employing "blitzkrieg" tactics, to defeat one opponent at a time, and thus securing more land step by step. These wars were to be intertwined with periods of peace, or stalemate, when the German army could resupply and accumulate force for the next war. The initial success of this strategy (the remilitarization of the Saarland, the Austrian Anschluss, and the occupation in two stages of Czechoslovakia) stifled critique and gave Hitler great prestige. Hitler didn't realize that the turning point had come with the invasion of Poland. Both France and Britain had frowned upon his expansion, and declared war on Germany on that occasion. Hitler believed that Britain could be appeased by the defeat of France, but he had underestimated the British determination. Even though Britain couldn't do much against Germany at first, a war of attrition had begunsomething that the "blitzkrieg" concept was never designed for.

In the later years of the war, Hitler's strategy became more and more based on intuition, flawed logic, and unrealistic assumptions. However, the strength of his hold on domestic policy remained so strong, that his "brilliance" was not questioned, or was quickly suppressed. In the final stages of the war, his actions and orders had turned into the rambling of a madman rather than any attempt to conduct a coherent strategy.

Anglo-American Strategy

Confronted with the rise of Hitler's power on the continent, and realizing the brutality of his regime, the British gradually turned to a fierce opposition and finally a war declaration over the invasion of Poland. Britain wasn't prepared for war, especially on land, and the initial years were a series of defeats, as they got thrown off the European continent everywhere (France, Norway, Greece). However, the sea ensured their survival, since Germany had no navy to speak of compared to the British. After air superiority over the Channel was secured in the battle of Britain, and the antisubmarine weapons were perfected to win the battle of the Atlantic, Britain itself was not threatened anymore. Strategic plans could turn to the offensive, especially with the USA leaning more and more to a war with Germany.

After the USA entered the war, Europe (as opposed to the Pacific) was chosen as the prime theater of operations by the formulation of the "Germany first" principle at the Arcadia Conference. However, their land armies wouldn't be capable of invading the mainland of Europe for years, even as Stalin pleaded for this to alleviate pressure on the Russian front. Instead, the Allies decided to take an indirect approach by invading Europe from the South. After cleansing North Africa of Axis forces (the invasion of French NorthAfrica and El Alamein), Sicily and southern Italy were invaded, effectively knocking Italy out of the war. Given that the terrain circumstances in this area were unviable to turn this route into the main thrust on Germany itself, the main purpose of these operations weren't mainly territorial, but focused on tying up as many German forces in southern Europe as possible, thereby alleviating pressure from the Soviets as well as thinning the garrison forces in France, where the main Allied force was still planned to invade.

In the air war, superiority was gained pretty early. After that, the Allies launched a strategic bombing campaign against Germany. After initial emphasis on economic targets (factories, infrastructure, etc), the Allies turned more and more towards terror bombing of German cities.

Soviet Strategy

Early Soviet strategy intended to avoid war for as long as possible. After the cleansing of the Red Army officer corps, the army was seen as unfit to conduct any kind of serious war, and this proved to be true by the Finnish winter war. With the signing of the MolotovRibbentrop pact, Joseph Stalin believed he had secured peace for as long as he needed to rebuild the Soviet military force.

The Barbarossa campaign of 1941 came as a complete surprise to the Soviets. Nevertheless, they reacted swiftly, particularly in the civilian aspect. As the army was being defeated and gave ground at an amazing speed, a gigantic operation was staged to move the economic capacity from the Western areas that were about to be overrun, to Eastern regions that were out of reach for the Germans, like the Ural. Entire factories, including their labour force, were simply moved out of reach from the Germans, and what couldn't be taken was destroyed ("Scorched earth"). Thus, even though huge territories were captured by the Germans, the production potential was relatively unharmed, and the factories shifted to mass production of military equipment quickly, outproducing the German economy soon.

After achieving numerical superiority, the Soviets were still qualitatively inferior. To compensate this, they emphasized on gaining an even larger quantitative edge. The later offensive Soviet campaigns all saw a massive employment of manpower, often resulting in extremely bloody battles. It wasn't unusual that Soviet "victories" inflicted far larger casualties on themselves than on the Germans. However, the total national manpower pool was so much larger than the German one, that this still led to success.

Japanese Strategy

Japanese World War II strategy was driven by two factors: the desire to expand their territories on the mainland of Asia (China and Manchuria), and the need to secure the supply of raw resources that they didn't have themselves, particularly oil. Since their quest after the former (conquest of Chinese provinces) endangered the latter (an oil boycott by the USA and its Allies), the Japanese government saw no other option than to conquer the oil sources in SouthEast Asia. Since these were controlled by American allies, war with the USA was also inevitable; and given that fact, they decided it would be best to deal a big blow to them first. This was executed in the Pearl Harbor strike, crippling the American battle fleet.

Japan hoped that it would take America so long to rebuild, that by the time they were back in force in the Pacific, they would consider the new balance of power a "fait accompli", and barter for peace. They had underestimated the psychological effect of the Pearl Harbor strike; the USA wouldn't negotiate with an enemy that had struck them in this way. Even though SouthEast Asia was quickly conquered (Philippines, Indochina, Malaya, Dutch East Indies), the early sea battles in the Pacific were tied. After the vital aircraft carrier force was destroyed in the Battle of Midway, the Japanese had to revert to a stiff defense that they kept up for three years after that.

American Pacific Strategy

Since the American economic force was much larger than the Japanese, even considering their effort in the European theatre, the numerical inferior US forces remaining in the area after Pearl Harbor weren't afraid to battle the Japanese; they knew they could replace battle losses faster than the Japanese. In several aircraft carrier battles, the initiative was taken from the Japanese, and after the Battle of Midway, the Japanese navy was rendered helpless, effectively giving the Americans the possibility to sail wherever they wanted.

As the Japanese offensive died down in the second half of 1942, the Americans saw themselves confronted with an endless amount of fortified garrisons on small islands in the ocean. They decided on a strategy of "leapfrogging", leaving the strongest garrisons alone, just cutting their supply, and securing bases of operation on the lightly defended isles instead. They kept up this strategy until they were in the Japanese waters themselves, allowing the aerial bombing of the Japanese mainland.

Australian Strategy

Australia's historical ties with Britain meant that with the commencement of World War II her armies were sent overseas to contribute to battles in Europe. Fear from the north was so understated that at the outbreak of open warfare with Japan, Australia itself was extremely vulnerable to invasion (possible invasion plans were considered by the Japanese high command). Australia's policy became based entirely on domestic defense following the attacks on Pearl Habour and British assets in the

South Pacific. Defying strong British opposition, Australian Prime Minister John Curtin recalled most troops from the European conflict for the defense of the nation.

Australia's defensive doctrine saw a fierce campaign being fought along the Kokoda track in New Guinea, which was the first land defeat upon the Japanese in the Pacific Theatre. This policy sought to further stretch Japanese supply lines, preventing the invasion of the Australian mainland until the arrival of fresh American troops and the return of seasoned Australian soldiers from Europe. This can be seen as a variant of the war of attrition strategy, where the defenderout of necessityhad to hold the aggressor at a semistatic defensive line, rather than falling back in the face of superior numbers. This method is in stark contrast to the Russian scorched earth policy against Napoleon in 1812, where the defenders yielded home territory in favour of avoiding open battle. In both cases the lack of supplies was successful in blunting the assaults, following exhaustive defensive efforts.

Cold War Strategy

The Cold War was the last time period dominated by the threat of total world annihilation through the use of nuclear weapons, a policy known as mutually assured destruction. As a consequence it was also a war in which attacks were not exchanged between the two main rivals, the United States and the Soviet Union. Instead, the war was fought through proxies. Instead of mainly being confined to Europe or the Pacific, the entire world was the battlefield, with countries rather than armies acting as main players. The only constant rule was that troops of the Soviet Union and the United States could not overtly fight with each other.

The difference between tactics, strategy and grand strategy began to melt during the Cold War as command and communication technologies improved to a greater extent, in first world armed forces. The third world armed forces controlled by the two superpowers found that grand strategy, strategy and tactics, if anything, moved further apart as the command of the armies fell under the control of super power leaders.

American cold warriors like Dean Acheson and George C. Marshall quickly recognized that the key to victory was the economic defeat of the Soviet Union.

The Soviet Union had adopted an aggressive posture of Communist expansionism following the end of World War II, with the United States and its strong navy quickly finding that it had to aggressively defend much of the world from the Soviet Union and the spread of communism.

Strategies during the Cold War also dealt with nuclear attack and retaliation. The United States maintained a policy of limited first strike throughout the Cold War. In the event of a Soviet attack on the Western Front, resulting in a breakthrough, the United States would use tactical nuclear weapons to stop the attack.

The view from Moscow was to adapt to the prevailing changes in the NATO strategic policies that are divided by periods as:

- Strategy of massive retaliation (1950s)
- Strategy of flexible reaction (1960s)
- Strategies of realistic threat and containment (1970s)
- Strategy of direct confrontation (1980s) one of the elements of which became the new highly effective highprecision targeting weapons.
- Strategic Defense Initiative (also known as "Star Wars") during its 1980s development which became a core part of the strategic doctrine based on Defense containment.

Soviet Union responded by adopting a policy of no first use, involving massive retaliation resulting in mutual assured destruction. So, if the Warsaw Pact attacked using conventional weapons, NATO would use tactical nukes.

The Soviet Union would respond with an all out nuclear attack, resulting in a similar attack from the United States, with all the consequences the exchange would entail. This did not happen. The United States continues to maintain a policy of limited first strike to the present (October 2006).

Post Cold War Strategy

Strategy in the post Cold War has come to be defined by the hyperpower status of the United States.

It is increasingly relying on advanced technology to minimize casualties and improve efficiency. The technological quantum leaps brought by the Digital Revolution are essential for this strategy. See: Networkcentric warfare.

The gap in strategy today (from a western viewpoint) is in what the Americans call "asymmetric warfare": the battle against guerrilla forces by conventional national armed forces. The classical strategic triumvirate of politics/military/populace is very weak against protracted warfare of paramilitary forces such as the Provisional Irish Republican Army, Hezbollah, ETA, and AlQaeda.

The ability of conventional forces to deliver utility (effect) from their hugely powerful forces is largely nullified by the difficulties of distinguishing and separating combatants from the civilian populace in whose company they hide. The use of the military by the politicians to police areas seen as bases for these guerrillas leads to them becoming targets themselves which eventually undermines the support of the populace from whom they come and whose values they represent.

The primary effect of insurgent elements upon conventional force strategy is realized in the twofold exploitation of the inherent violence of military operations. Conventional armies face political attrition for each action they take. Insurgent forces can cause harm and create chaos, whereby the conventional army suffers a loss of confidence and esteem; or they can drive the conventional elements into an attack which further exacerbates the civilian condition.

The militaries of today are largely set up to fight the 'last war' and hence have huge armoured and conventionally configured infantry formations backed up by airforces and navies designed to support or prepare for these forces. Many are today deployed against guerrillastyle opponents where their strengths cannot be used to effect. The mass formations of Industrial War are often seen as much less effective than the unconventional forces that these organisations also possess. The new opponents operate at a local level whereas Industrial armed forces work at a much higher 'theatre' level.

The nervous system of these new opponents is largely political rather than military hierarchical and adapted to the local supporting populace who hide them. The centre provides the political idea and driving logic perhaps with overall direction and some funding. Local groups decide their own plans, raise much of their own funds and may be more or less aligned to the centre's aims. Defeat of forces when revealed does not disable this type of organisation, many modern attack strategies will tend to increase the power of the group they are intended to weaken. A new more political strategy is perhaps more appropriate here with military backing. Such a strategy has been illustrated in the war between the IRA an adoption and codification is unclear.

11

GEOSTRATEGIC ENVIRONMENT AND THE INDIAN ARMY

DOCTRINE, CONCEPT AND STRATEGY

Military doctrines have provided the basic approach to all important aspects related to war for armies of most nations over the past few centuries. Prevailing strategic realities, threats, challenges, visualised opportunities and national aspirations are the major factors which have a strong influence on the formulation of military doctrines. A doctrine is generally a written document; it could also be a widely accepted understanding without being specifically enunciated.

In the Indian context the need for formulating and enunciating a comprehensive military doctrine has gained momentum with advancements in military technologies and the changing nature of war in our times. Military doctrine is neither dogma nor does it replace or take away the authority and obligation of the commander on the spot to determine a proper course of action under the circumstances prevailing at the time of decision.

In simple words, military doctrine is a particular policy taught or advocated; a set of principles by which military forces guide their actions in support of national objectives. Military doctrine can be defined as 'a formal expression of military knowledge and thought that an army accepts as being relevant at a given time, which covers the nature of current and future conflicts, the preparation of the army for such conflicts and the methods of engaging in them to achieve success'. It is authoritative but requires judgement in application. The illustration below depicts the inputs that traditionally contribute to the formulation of a military doctrine and outputs that flow from its enunciation.

Concept

A concept is defined as 'a general notion or statement of an idea, expressing how something might be done or accomplished, that may lead to an accepted procedure'. In the nascent stage a concept may be nebulous; however, it crystallises as it develops. In the Indian military context a concept is generally enunciated at the strategic and operational levels. It articulates, in very broad terms, a visualisation of the manner in which operations are to be conducted, and focuses on the principal elements which will drive them.

Strategy

Strategy is the art and science of developing and using elements of national power including political, economic, psychological, technological capabilities and military forces, as necessary, during peace and war to achieve national objectives. Military strategy is derived from the overall national or 'grand' strategy.

ENVIRONMENT AND THREAT

General

India is a country of continental size with land borders shared with a large number of countries, 1197 islands and a coastline of 7516 kilometres with a vast Exclusive Economic Zone. Despite her historically developed racial, cultural, linguistic and religious diversity, India is a nation with an innately allembracing, secular polity that has welcomed and assimilated various cultures into her existing milieu. Her modern values are rooted in democratic governance and profound respect for human life. We remain peaceful without being pacifists and have a vision for the future with a measure of confidence in ourselves as we strive for economic progress and integration in the global environment. Defending India calls for defending her physical, economic and cultural identity in the prevalent geopolitical milieu.

The Geopolitical Environment

The geopolitical scenario is fast changing and is likely to continue to do so in the coming decades. Although the USA remains the only super power today, the world is witnessing the emergence of various centres of power, with India emerging as one of the leading global players. Each centre of power is attempting to achieve a 'balance of interest' as opposed to the erstwhile 'balance of power'.

Greater reliance is being placed on democracy as a factor contributing to conflict prevention and increasing emphasis on bilateral or multilateral groupings as a means to deter aggression against weak nations. There is also a growing concern about the proliferation of weapons of mass destruction and the spread of terrorism. Energy security and control of scarce resources are assuming transnational proportions.

As part of the Southern Asian Region, India has considerable interests in the areas stretching from West Asia through Central Asia and South Asia to South East Asia. The Indian Ocean region is of great importance to India and it assumes strategic significance due to the high volume of Indian and international trade transiting through the Indian Ocean. Existing and emerging regional groupings give rise to competitiveness with the attendant possibility of increasing instability due to inter and intraregional conflicts.

The region also includes a number of nuclear weapon or nuclearcapable states. In addition, this region is witnessing an unprecedented proliferation in small arms and narcotics trafficking which, in turn, threaten the stability of states and societies. Transborder migration on economic grounds also raises serious security concerns.

India is a member of the South Asian Association for Regional Cooperation (SAARC), the Association for South East Asian Nations Regional Forum (ARF) and the Indian Ocean Rim Association for Regional Cooperation (IORARC). By virtue of her size and strategic location in the Indian Ocean region, India is expected to play her rightful role to ensure peace and stability in it.

The Economic Environment

With market forces playing an important role, economic strength is likely to become the currency of power. National economies are undergoing liberalisation to cater to globalisation. The dominance of the developed world over the global economy is, nonetheless, likely to continue. Even so, China and India have been acknowledged as emerging economic powers. Economic linkages and interdependence amongst countries are likely to result in mutual security becoming an important issue. Water, energy sources (mainly oil) and even environmental issues may emerge as causes of future conflict between states.

The Security Environment

The security challenges facing India are varied and complex. India has two unsettled borders. The country has experienced four major conventional border wars besides an undeclared war fought in Kargil in 1999. She is engaged in an externally abetted proxy war for the last several years in Jammu and Kashmir and has been combating terrorism perpetuated by militant and terrorist groups sponsored by a foreign State. At the same time, a number of insurgencies, spurred by tribal and ethnic aspirations in addition to left wing ideologies are being tackled in various parts of the country. A number of nuclear weapon states are in India's neighbourhood; hostile, radical or fundamentalist elements gaining access to and posing a threat with weapons of mass destruction (WMD) is also a possibility. It is in such an environment that the Indian Army is required to fulfil its roles in varied operating conditions across the entire spectrum of conflict.

Nature of Future Warfare

Like terrorism today, the likelihood of 'asymmetric wars' becoming the form of warfare of tomorrow is being discussed quite widely. Nonetheless, the fact that all countries continue to lay emphasis on preparedness for conventional war, underscores the predominant view that asymmetric wars cannot replace conventional wars, even though they can very much become an adjunct of and influence conventional wars themselves.

Future wars are likely to be characterised by:

- Emerging at short notice, being of short duration and being fought at high tempo and intensity.
- Nonlinear conduct of operations.
- Deeper and wider combat zones due to increased reach of integral firepower and surveillance resources, including spacebased systems.
- Added emphasis on the allarms concept and need for increased jointmanship between the land, naval and air forces.
- Enhanced reliance on a variety of surveillance systems and, resultantly, greater availability of information contributing to increased transparency of the battlefield.
- Improved accuracy, lethality and standoff capability of weapons leading to greater destructive capability.
- Ascendancy of Network Centric Warfare (NCW), Information Warfare (IW) and conduct of operations under the glare of the media.
- Threat from enemy special forces, insurgents and terrorists to rear areas which will necessitate earmarking of troops to provide security to lines of communication.

THE INDIAN ARMY

Role of the Indian Army: The Indian Army is the land component of the Indian Armed Forces which exist to uphold the ideals of the Constitution of India. As a major component of national power, along with the Indian Navy and the Indian Air Force, the roles of the Indian Army are as follows :

- *Primary Role*. Preserve national interests and safeguard sovereignty, territorial integrity and unity of India against any external threats by deterrence or by waging war.
- *Secondary Role*. Assist Government agencies to cope with 'proxy war' and other internal threats and provide aid to civil authority when requisitioned for the purpose.

Command and Control of the Indian Armed Forces: The President of India is the Supreme Commander of the Indian Armed Forces. As in all democracies, the Indian Armed Forces are controlled by the elected political leadership of the nation (Government of India). Executive control is exercised sequentially through the Union Cabinet, the Defence Minister, the Chiefs of Staff Committee (COSC) and the Chiefs of Army, Naval and Air Staff of their respective Services. The Ministry of Defence handles matters related to personnel, financial and resource management.

Tasks of the Indian Army: The Indian Army serves as the ultimate instrument for maintaining the unity and the integrity of the nation in the face of external threats and internal unrest and disturbances. The major tasks of the Indian Army are as follows:

- Effectively project deterrence and dissuasion through the medium of strong, wellstructured combat capability.
- Be prepared to engage in and conduct all types of military operations, singly or jointly, in the entire spectrum of conflict.
- Provide the requisite land forces component of the Strategic Forces Command.
- Provide aid to civil authority when called upon to do so for maintenance of law and order, humanitarian aid and assistance during disasters and calamities or any other circumstances including maintenance of essential services.
- Participate in United Nations peacekeeping operations in consonance with India's commitment to the United Nations Charter. Be prepared to render military assistance to friendly countries when required to do so.

PEACE, CONFLICT AND WAR

The States of Peace, Conflict and War

At any given point in time, a country will be in a state of peace, conflict or war or a combination of these. Nations act in their own selfinterest which includes the pursuit of political, economic, ideological or cultural objectives. When the interests of nations or a group of nations are in harmony, or at least pose no real or perceived threat to each other, there is peace. However, when the actions or policies of one nation are viewed as a threat to the vital interests of another, a condition of conflict arises. Conflict may escalate to war. The illustration below depicts the entire spectrum of peace, conflict and war.

Peace: Peace is defined as the absence of violencedirect or indirect, manifest or posed as a threat. Peace is often viewed as a temporary and fleeting condition. To be enduring and genuine, it must be based on mutual respect, shared interests and common values. Peace is most often the result of a balance of power and agreed political spheres of interest between nations or one nation manifesting a superior political will. This is invariably backed by preponderance of force which is militarily unchallenged by others. In either case, peace is ultimately sustained by, and is dependent upon, the willingness of states to use force to preserve it as well as restore it when lost.

Conflict: The essence of conflict is a clash, usually violent, between opposing human wills, each trying to impose itself on the other. In, both, interstate and intrastate conflicts, the means to impose one's will could include diplomatic, economic and political mechanisms as well as the application or threat of violence by military force. Military action is just one instrument, amongst several, which may be used to impose a nation's will. Armed conflict is synonymous with war. Today international mechanisms, including the influence exercised by major powers, are in place to resolve or limit conflicts because of their potential to lead to undesired war.

The State of War: War occurs when diplomatic and other negotiation mechanisms for resolving conflict or achieving desired political objectives either fail or are not operative. In such circumstances political aims and strategies are pursued by the use of armed force. War is prosecuted by the employment of strategy which aims at breaking the enemy's will to fight. Disengagement from war is difficult because it develops its own dynamics and pace, which in themselves are unpredictable and could spin out of control. While war is always to be avoided, democratic societies must, nonetheless, be prepared to engage in it to safeguard their national interests.

TYPES OF WARS

Conventional War

Conventional war conforms to the traditional image of war and is fought to achieve strategic and military objectives. It does not include the use of Nuclear, Biological and Chemical (NBC) weapons. It may be total or limited in terms of duration, the range of weapon systems employed, scope, objectives and its ultimate outcome. Given the prohibitive costs in terms of human lives and material, as well as the rising lethality of modern weapons, conventional war may be of short duration. Regional wars arise out of regional issues. The Gulf War (1991) and the Kosovo conflict (1995) are two such examples even though they had repercussions at the international level. A global or general war is a major unrestricted conflict fought between major powers involving some or all their allies. Initially it is likely to employ conventional weapons but may then escalate to the use of weapons of mass destruction to deny victory to the opponent(s). An extended global war of the Second World War pattern is highly unlikely.

Operations Other than War

Operations Other Than War (OOTW) encompass a wide range of activities where military power is used for purposes other than large scale combat operations normally associated with war. These include subconventional and noncombat operations; they usually involve the combined and coordinated effort of government (civil and military) and nongovernment agencies. In essence, OOTW activities assist to deter war, resolve conflict and promote peace and well being with use or demonstrated threat of use of force.

SubConventional War

Low Intensity Conflict (LIC): LIC is a generic term encompassing all kinds of armed conflicts that are above the level of peaceful coexistence amongst states and below the threshold of war. These include proxy war, terrorism and insurgencies; border skirmishes also fall within this category. It involves protracted struggle of competing principles and ideologies. Low Intensity Conflict Operations (LICO) figures at the lower end of the spectrum of conflict and is characterised by one or all of the following conditions :

- Asymmetry of force levels between the regular forces and the irregular opposition force.
- The force applied and the violence generated depends on the code of conduct and the capabilities of the weaker side.
- Laws of the land impose restrictions on the actions of security forces.

Proxy War: Proxy war is a war conducted between nations utilising nonstate players to fight on their behalf. At least one of them employs a third party to fight on its behalf. The extent and type of support provided by the states involved in proxy war will vary but financial and logistic support are normally always provided. An example of a proxy war is the foreign sponsored terrorism in Jammu & Kashmir.

Insurgency: Insurgency is an organised armed struggle by a section of the local population against the State, usually with foreign support. The many possible causes of an insurgency include nationalistic, ethnic, linguistic, religious or cultural separatism, poor governance, economic deprivation, corruption, discrimination and oppression. Its goals may be seizure of power and replacement of the existing regime or even liberation of a defined area. Employment of military force may not be able to stamp out an insurgency but may help to contain it. In most cases, it is a combination of military force backed by appropriate political and economic measures which can adequately resolve such situations. The latter part acquires even more importance than the use of force.

Irregular War: Irregular war may take many forms of which terrorism and guerrilla war are two important ones. Terrorism is the unlawful use or threatened use of force or violence against people or property to terrorise, coerce or intimidate governments or societies; this is most often resorted to with the aim of achieving political, religious, or ideological objectives. Terrorism thrives on a fear psychosis and could be achieved by arson, sabotage, hijacking, hoaxes, maiming bombing, seizure, kidnapping, assassination, taking hostages raids, ambushes and the threat to use or use of WMD. Guerrilla war is an irregular form of warfare which includes acts of subversion, assassination, attack on supply lines and terrorism Terrorism and guerrilla warfare can be employed across the entire spectrum of conflict.

NonCombat Operations and Aid to Civil Authorities

Noncombat operations are defined as military operations where the use of force may not be necessary but, at times, the most minimal use of force, or threat to use force, may be required. Noncombat operations include aid to civil authorities disaster relief, humanitarian assistance and peacekeeping operations.

Nuclear Chemical and Biological Warfare

Nuclear Warfare: A conventional war may escalate to a nuclear war when any of the belligerents decide to use nuclear weapons through any means of delivery to avoid defeat in the sphere of conventional warfare or to safeguard its vital national interests or even with the aim to bring the war to a decisive end. World opinion is against the use of such weapons. India is a nuclear weapon state and pursues a policy of 'Credible Minimum Deterrence' and 'No First Use'. India's nuclear policy clearly states that she will not use or use the threat of use of nuclear weapons against those states which do not posses nuclear weapons or are not aligned with nuclear weapon powers India reserves the right to retaliate with nuclear weapons in case of a strike against her by adversaries with nuclear, chemical or biological weapons.

Biological and Chemical Warfare: International conventions, to which India is a signatory, along with a large number of other countries, have banned the use of biological and chemical weapons. However, their use by adversaries and nonstate actors cannot be ruled out. Chemical weapons are relatively easy to produce without any elaborate infrastructure

As a consequence, our forces must be prepared for operations in a biological and chemical weapons environment. Both, active and passive defensive measures are being instituted to cater to this requirement.

Information Warfare

IW can be defined as actions taken to achieve 'information superiority by adversely affecting the adversary's information, informationbased processes, information systems, and computerbased networks whilst simultaneously protecting one's own information, informationbased processes, information systems and computerbased networks'. Correct and timely information made available to commanders at all levels contributes directly to effective Command and Control (C2) and helps in shortening the ObserveOrientDecideAct (OODA) Cycle (also known as the OODA Loop). IW has a vital impact upon the first three activities of the OODA Loop by disrupting the enemy's observation and surveillance systems, corrupting his orientation and misguiding his perception and thereby inducing him to arrive at wrong decisions.

Objectives of IW: The basic ingredients of IW are collection of data, sifting (to extract relevant information), analysis and assimilation of information to create intelligence which will help to achieve the objectives of IW. These objectives are:

- Develop and maintain a comprehensive information base of the capabilities of adversaries and forecast their likely actions.
- Deny information about own and friendly forces to adversaries.
- Influence perceptions, plans, actions and the will of adversaries to oppose own and friendly forces by offensive employment of IW techniques.
- Influence noncombatant and neutral organisations to support friendly missions or, at least, not to resist friendly activities.
- Protect friendly decisionmaking processes, information and information systems.
- Degrade the information systems of adversaries.

Forms of IW

The seven forms of IW are Command and Control Warfare (C2W), Intelligence Based Warfare (IBW), Electronic Warfare (EW), Psychological Warfare, Cyber Warfare, Economic Information Warfare and Network Centric Warfare (NCW). These are discussed in succeeding paragraphs.

Command and Control Warfare: The aim of C2W is to influence, deny information to, degrade or destroy enemy C2 capabilities while protecting own C2 systems against such actions. C2W is a dominant component of IW in the military arsenal. C2W operations integrate and synchronise the capabilities of EW, military deception, physical destruction, psychological operations and operational security.

Intelligence Based Warfare: IBW is a traditional component of IW and occurs when intelligence is directly fed into operations (notably targeting and battle damage assessment) to bring transparency to the battlefield rather than being used as an input for overall C2. IBW is the direct application of battlefield intelligence instantaneously into the battle and aims at creating an asymmetry in the level of transparency or situational awareness in relation to the enemy.

Electronic Warfare: EW is a set of military actions taken to deny the use of the electromagnetic spectrum to hostile forces while retaining the ability to use it oneself. This basically implies that the endeavour is to deny, degrade, delay or disrupt information in order to create a false picture so that the enemy is duped into making incorrect assessments and taking wrong actions. EW involves the use of electromagnetic and directed energy to control the electromagnetic spectrum or to attack the enemy. One of the most important developments in the field of EW has been the introduction of automated and integrated EW systems, which provide a high degree of information in addition to interception, directionfinding and jamming activities.

Psychological Warfare: Information is one of the several means to target the human mind. Psychological warfare is achieved through mass media such as newspapers, radio and television broadcasts and distribution of leaflets. The prevailing state of information technology allows effective psychological warfare to be conducted in a very subtle manner. In order to be effective,.psychological operations need to be conducted in conjunction with other operations. During peace time and in LIC operations, this effort can be termed as "psychological initiatives".

Cyber Warfare: This entails techniques to destroy, degrade, exploit or compromise the enemy's computerbased systems. Cyber warfare includes exclusive attacks, known as hacking, on enemy computer networks. Computer hacking has evolved to a stage wherein information stored or passing through computer networks is interfered with to degrade the adversary's C2 structure.

Economic Information Warfare: This form of warfare uses information as power to destabilise the economy of the adversary. Since all revenuegenerating industries of a country such as aviation, transport, power, banking and the like use computerbased systems, IW at the strategic level can play havoc with the national economy of the adversary.

Network Centric Warfare: NCW focuses on the combat power that can be generated by the effective linking or networking of the warfighting machinery and organisations. The basic elements necessary to generate the requisite shared battlespace awareness that can be exploited through selfsynchronisation to achieve the overall objective are given below:

- A virtual sensors grid that would provide a 'grid of capabilities' overlaying the battlespace instead of series of independent single sensors. This grid is termed as the Surveillance Grid.
- To leverage the strength of the worldwide telecommunications infrastructure, all communication networks could be viewed as virtual grids overlaying the tactical, operational and strategic areas. This grid is referred to as the Communications Grid.
- An abstract grid that comprises weapons available, sorted by suitability and availability against a hostile order of battle is termed as the Tactical Grid.

PRINCIPLES OF WAR

"There exists a small number of fundamental principles of war, which may not be deviated from without danger, and the application of which, on the contrary, has been in all times crowned with glory".Jomini, Precis de l' Art de la Guerre, 1838.

The Principles of War are broad guidelines which influence the conduct of war at every level of military operations. They are based on past experience wherein their application with judgement led to victory. They are not rules; yet disregarding them involves risk and could result in failure. These principles are outlined briefly in succeeding paragraphs.

Selection and Maintenance of Aim: The aim is expressed as an intention, purpose or end state. It should be selected carefully, defined clearly and stated simply and directly. Once selected, it must be maintained.

Maintenance of Morale: Morale is one of the more important elements of war. High morale fosters the offensive spirit and the will to win.

Offensive Action: Offensive action is the chief means of achieving victory. It results from offensive spirit and helps in the seizure and maintenance of initiative.

Surprise: Surprise implies catching the enemy off balance thereby forcing him to give battle in circumstances unfavourable to him.

Concentration of Force: Concentration of superior force at the chosen place and time ensures success in battle.

Security: Security relates to the physical protection of ground, troops, equipment, material and documents. It also involves denial of information.

Economy of Effort: Economy of effort connotes balanced deployment and judicious employment of forces to ensure success with minimum casualties.

Flexibility: Flexibility is the capability to react appropriately to changing situations.

Cooperation: All agencies involved have to work jointly

towards achievement of the overall aim to achieve success in war. Jointmanship leads to cooperation; cooperation produces synergy.

Administration: Placing the resources required at the right place and time to help commanders at all levels to achieve their respective objectives is the function of administration.

Intelligence: This is an addition to the widely accepted principles of war because of its preeminence in any future conflict. Military Intelligence involves acquisition and exploitation of information about the enemy. Informatics plays a major role in ensuring that intelligence is available in time and in the desired form.

> *"War should be made methodically for it should have a definite object; and it should be conducted according to the principles and rules of the art".Napoleon, Maxims of War, 1831*

OPERATIONAL PERSPECTIVES

Elements for Operational Success

> *"War is an art and as such is not susceptible of explanation by fixed formula."General George S. Patton, Jr, War As I Knew It, 1947.*

Operational Success: War is a national undertaking that is coordinated from the highest levels of policymaking to the basic levels of execution. The objective of military forces in war is to achieve early and decisive victory over the opposing forces with minimum casualties to own forces. The major aspects that contribute towards operational success are:

- Understanding the various perspectives of war.
- Employing operational art.
- Judicious application of combat power.
- Efficient exercise of C_2 in the battlefield.

Perspectives of War

The perspective of war varies based on which level it is viewed from even though the objectives to be achieved at strategic, operational and tactical levels would flow downwards from the top. For clarity of understanding of the complex nature of operational scenarios, it is imperative that the commanders at all levels recognize the fine differences between the three levels of perspective given in succeeding paragraphs. These perspectives are, however, not mutually exclusive and do tend to overlap at the fringes.

Strategic Perspective: Viewed from the strategic perspective, war is a continuum to secure national policy objectives in concert with defined or perceived national security goals. The end state of a war must provide the desired political advantage. Military activity at the strategic level will thus be clearly influenced by political and national considerations. At the strategic level, military power is one of the elements of national power available to a state to achieve its goals and enforce its policies. A military commander at the strategic level would be required to render advice to political leaders which should be in the form of strategic inputs through the established chain of command. Strategy itself has various levels. At the apex there is 'grand' or national strategy which coordinates the overall approach pertaining to each element of national power, such as national will, economic, political, geographic and military power. Whereas military strategy is only concerned with military operations, grand strategy must, of necessity, take a longterm view and therefore encompass all elements of national power. Military strategy has been defined as the art of distributing and applying military means to fulfil ends of national policy. A more modern definition could be 'the art and science of employing the armed forces of a nation to secure policy objectives by the application of force or threat of use of force'. In formulating military strategy it is important to note that it encompasses the following salient aspects:

- Identifying aims and objectives in a theatre of war.
- Outlining the general course of major operations and campaigns.
- Understanding the restrictions placed on military operations based on national policy.

- Allocating adequate resources for successful conduct of operations.

Operational Perspective: The operational perspective focuses on achieving military aims or objectives at the theatre level and coordinating the effort of the land, air and naval forces where and when applicable. The operational level uses tactical results to achieve strategic objectives. It involves planning of a campaign within the specified time and space to achieve desired strategic goals. Viewed in comparison to the tactical level, it covers larger areas of conflict, has a larger time and space horizon and has a more critical impact on theatre level operations. Major elements of the operational level of war are:

- Substantial combat power is kept out of contact till the opportune time. This is in sharp contrast to the tactical perspective wherein opposing forces actually see and engage each other and is thus more narrowly focused on specific military objectives.
- The operational perspective provides a wide enough view for the commander to enjoy independent command of military forces but is narrow enough to be relatively free of having to coordinate with the other elements of national strategy.
- Nonetheless, there is a need for a clear understanding of the strategic perspective.
- An operational perspective prevents a commander from overidentification with tactical battles. It is concerned with translation of abstract strategic aims to achievable tactical objectives through the design, organisation and conduct of major operations.

Tactical Perspective: The tactical perspective, having the narrowest view in the hierarchy of war, essentially concerns itself with optimising the application of military forces to achieve specified objectives. This level focuses on the application of combat power to defeat the enemy in combat at a particular time and place. It includes the employment of firepower and manoeuvre, the integration of different arms and the exploitation of success. Commanders at this level concern themselves with purely military objectives laid down for them, such as destroying enemy forces, seizing specific objectives or denying specific pieces of ground and so on. The means used in tactics are combinedarms formations and the ends are tactical victories. These engagements may be more than one, running concurrently in a theatre of operations spread over hundreds of kilometres. Seemingly disjointed in application of force, they are, nevertheless, bound to a common higher goal. A link is required to bring these various tactical pieces together to create the military conditions that can achieve strategic goals. That link is the operational level and it is for this reason that tactical battles are built and fought around an overarching operational design.

Level of Conduct: In our context, the operational level of war is generally at the Theatre or the Command level, while tactical level operations are conducted at Corps and lower levels. However, in certain cases where a Corps has been allocated an operationally strategic objective, it would be deemed to be conducting operations at the operational level. At times, depending upon the spectrum of conflict such as in LICO, there could be situations where even commanders subordinate to Theatre (Command) and Corps will have to work on an operational perspective as their activities may directly influence the achievement of strategic objectives in a theatre of operations.

Operational Art: In seeking to structure major operations, battles and engagements in pursuit of objectives, the operational level commander should design his campaign plans around a number of building blocks which help him to visualise as to how the operation would unfold. His skills at this stage form the essence of operational art. Based on the desired end state, he derives operational objectives, decides upon the 'centres of gravity', 'lines of operation' and 'decisive points' and analyses the options thrown up by the conclusions drawn from these. He must also keep in mind the importance of 'shaping the battlefield' by the employment of firepower and manoeuvre, maintaining the tempo and factoring in operational pauses when drawing up plans.

End States

Conflict Termination: Conflict is either resolved or terminated; military force contributes by the defeat of an opposing force. Defeat is defined as 'diminishing the effectiveness of the enemy to the extent that he is either unable to participate in combat or, at least, not being able to fulfil his intention'. Conflict termination describes the point at which the principal means of conflict shifts from the use of force to other means of persuasion. Conflict termination may take several forms; for example, the adversary may surrender, withdraw or negotiate an end to the conflict. Commanders and staff must plan for conflict termination requirements when developing campaign plans.

Exit Policy: Victory may not always be an appropriate term to describe the desired outcome of an operation; it may have to be defined in other terms such as reconciliation, stabilisation (acceptance of the status quo) or acceptance of an agreed peace plan. Where such acceptance is hesitant or reluctant, the prospect is of protracted involvement. While planning conflict termination it will be prudent to plan a suitable 'exit policy' which should cater to various contingencies related to politicomilitary aims.

Application of Combat Power

Combat Power: Combat power defines an army's ability to fight. It's three basic componentsconceptual, moral and physicalhave been dilated upon in Section 8. Overwhelming combat power is achieved when all combat elements are brought to bear simultaneously with violence, giving the enemy no opportunity to respond in a coordinated or cohesive manner, and thereby achieve victory at least cost.

Modes of Application of Combat Power: In combat the intention is to bring about strategic dislocation of the adversary by causing psychological paralysis amongst its decisionmakers. In the physical and logistical planes this is produced by a combination of IW, securing or isolation of critical objectives, threatening other objectives, capture of high value territory and selective destruction of the adversary's combat potential. The means to achieve such a state include the following:

- *Destruction.* Physical destruction of the enemy's capability to fight is but one of a number of means to defeat him. This would require focused and coordinated application of decisive combat power.
- *Attacking the Enemy's Will.* Conflict is subject to political, economic, ethical and moral constraints. These limit the freedom of military action. In this context, attempting to destroy the enemy's will solely by direct attack on his forces may be, both, costly and, at times, counterproductive. He must be made to feel constantly offbalance by one or more of the means enumerated below:
  - *Preemption.* To preempt the enemy is to seize an opportunity, often fleeting, before he does, in order to deny him an advantageous course of action. Its success lies in the speed with which the situation is subsequently exploited. Preemptive operations rely on rapid decisionmaking and surprise rather than ponderous preparation.
  - *Dislocation.* To dislocate the enemy is to deny him the ability to bring to bear his strengths. Unlike preemption, dislocation is a deliberate act, and is critically dependent on sound intelligence rather than intuition. Its purpose is much wider than the frustration of the enemy's plan; it is to render his strength irrelevant. It seeks to avoid fighting the enemy on his terms and can be achieved by either avoiding his strengths or by so fixing them that they cannot be used effectively. 'Posturing,' deep penetration thrusts and envelopment are classic forms of dislocation.
  - *Disruption.* To disrupt is to attack the enemy selectively, to break apart and throw into confusion the assets which are critical to the employment and coherence of his fighting power. Its purpose is to rupture the integrity of the enemy's fighting potential and to reduce it to less than the sum total

of its constituent parts. The enemy's moral and physical cohesion can be shattered by manoeuvring in a manner which surprises him, using firepower selectively to attack targets that contribute to his cohesion and by imposing on him the effects of tempo and simultaneity.

Command and Leadership

Command is the legal authority exercised by the commander over his troops to accomplish his mission. It carries with it the responsibility for planning, organising, training, directing, coordinating and controlling military forces to accomplish assigned, implied or inherent missions together with administrative responsibility for supply, health, welfare, morale, discipline, assignment and relief of personnel.

Exercise of Command in Battle: The art of command lies in conscious and skilful exercise of authority through visualisation, decisionmaking and leadership. Effective battle command demands timely and correct decisions based on the accurate and skilful judgement of battle situations. Effective decisionmaking combines judgement with information as an element of combat power. The commander must be able to perceive the plan being implemented and the critical junctures where his personal decisionmaking will facilitate success. Clear thinking and levelheadedness in trying situations greatly help in recognising the practicability of possible courses of action before embarking upon one of them.

Leadership in Battle: Yet another essential quality of a commander is effective and enlightened leadership. He should be fully cognizant of the strengths and vulnerabilities of the force that he commands. Closely overseeing and monitoring critical junctures in battle, being up forward to read the situations, offering encouragement and making onthespot decisions, particularly in adverse situations are the hallmarks of good leadership. Military history is replete with excellent instances of how great battles were won because of inspiring and decisive leadership.

Command and Control: Command has two componentsthe commander and the C_2 systems. Communication systems, surveillance systems and computer networks form the backbone of C_2 systems and enable commanders to lead from any point on the battlefield. Reliable communications are central to such systems. Sound C_2 should ensure unity of effort, provide for centralised direction and decentralised execution, provide an environment for applying common doctrine and ensure interoperability. Centralised direction and decentralised execution are two key prerequisites for successful C_2. Centralised direction is provided by the national leadership at the nationalstrategic level. This is then converted to a jointservices plan cojointly by the three Services and following which directives are transmitted to theatre commanders for execution. Informationgathering and decisionmaking must be centralised to enhance coordination and control over subordinate forces albeit with requisite freedom of action for subordinate commanders.

OPERATIONAL READINESS AND EFFECTIVENESS

Operational readiness is the state of preparedness of an organisation to perform the mission for which it is organised or designed. Military effectiveness is the standard by which the Army, from the platoon to the highest levels, is judged in peace and war. The efficiency with which operational readiness and effectiveness is achieved also needs to be optimised to ensure availability of maximum possible combat power when and where required. The level of operational readiness and effectiveness of a force has a major bearing on its ability to launch and successfully conduct operations. Ensuring operational readiness and effectiveness is a command responsibility.

Combat Power

The term 'combat power' defines an army's ability to fight. Combat power has three basic components and their interrelationship is shown in the figure below :

The Conceptual Component: This can be described as the thought process behind the ability to fight. It is a vital component in that, commanders at various levels have the benefit of the concepts and doctrines evolved over a period of time as well as the experience of their predecessors. It also helps commanders to imbibe a common understanding of principles and yet allows the freedom of exercising individual styles of command. The conceptual component comprises principles of war, military doctrine and development. The contribution of principles of war and military doctrine towards accomplishing operational readiness and effectiveness has already been amplified in earlier sections of this book. Development requires knowledge, an innovative approach and a mind open to all aspects of warfare; this includes force organisation, structuring and equipping of various types of units. Commanders also need to keep abreast of developments taking place in the environment and should have adequate knowledge of management of change so that they can work as facilitators. The higher the level of a commander, the wider should be his knowledge horizon so that he can understand the necessity to implement the desired change.

The Moral Component: The moral component concerns the ability to get people to fight. Maintenance of morale is a principle of war and, as such, embraces the moral and physical aspects of combat power. High morale stems from sound training, confidence in equipment and good administration as well as confidence in commanders, discipline, selfrespect and clear knowledge of what is going on and what is required. Yet the ability to get people to fight is not just a question of morale; it also involves the following aspects:

- *Basic Morality.* It is extremely important that the basic morality of individuals in the Indian Army is always above board. Professional honesty, courage of conviction, integrity, tolerance to accept reality and differing points of view are some of the essential qualities which should always be encouraged. The higher the position in the hierarchy, the greater should be the commitment to moral values. In addition, a commander should posses the courage to take hard decisions.
- *Motivation.* Soldiers who are well motivated, and well led work as a team. Teamwork breeds comradeship which, in turn, leads to pride in belonging to a team and fosters esprit de corps. Motivation thrives on a continuing

sense of purpose and it is the job of the commander to instil this purpose. Although national will, reflected in Government directives, serves to give the soldier this sense of purpose, it is the responsibility of the commander to make soldiers fully identify with these. It must be clearly understood that leading soldiers in pursuit of causes that they do not understand is a daunting task.

- *Leadership.* There are many definitions of military leadership. However, most simply defined, military leadership is the projection of personality and character by the leader to get soldiers to do what is required of them. Skill in the techniques of leadership is the foremost quality in the art of command and contributes very largely to success at all levels of war.
- *Management.* Good management can have considerable bearing upon morale and on military effectiveness. It involves making the best use of available resources in accomplishment of the mission. Management skills are essential elements of good and efficient military leadership.

The Physical Component: The physical component is the means to fight. It is defined as the total means of destructive or disruptive force which a military unit or formation can apply against the opponent at a given time. The 'total means' include the organising and provisioning of the main elements of combat power which are manpower, equipment, logistics, training and national assets.

Operational Readiness

Readiness of the Indian Armed Forces to meet national emergencies is a facet of national level endeavour. It calls for a synergised effort by all instruments of the Government to ensure that these forces are moved to their areas of operations, fullyequipped and within an acceptable timeframe. The Government, on its part, would indicate and maintain a clear and strong resolve to go to war when it orders a general mobilisation. There may also be other methods of preparation for war even without ordering general mobilisation. On the part of the Armed Forces, they are responsible for ensuring that they are operationally ready, troops are in a high state of morale and units are appropriately trained to execute the missions assigned to them.

Military mobilisation in the Indian context involves considerable effort because of the wide geographical spread of the peacetime locations of our units and formations, the considerable extent of our borders and the multiplicity of agencies that need to coordinate their actions in order to make it effective.

SURPRISE AND DECEPTION

Surprise

Surprise in war is a potent force multiplier. The payoffs of surprise are almost always in geometric proportions and it multiplies the chances of achieving quick and decisive military victory. As a decisive factor at all levels of warfare, and duly acknowledged as an autonomous principle of war, surprise allows the side that achieves it to concentrate superior forces unnoticed at the point of decision and to beat the opponent in terms of time, place, method or new technologies. The purpose of surprise, in essence, is to make the enemy react in an irrational and uncoordinated manner.

Strategic surprise can herald both the beginning and the end of a war. Considering the scope of its effects and the level at which it is planned, the phenomenon of military surprise can be classified as strategic, operational or tactical. However, in practice, the distinction between the strategic and operational and operational and tactical surprise is often hazy and they invariably tend to overlap. With battlefield transparency improving by the day, the ability to effect true surprise is progressively reducing. Military planners, therefore, need to concentrate more on deception, as a good and wellcoordinated deception plan would help to achieve surprise.

Deception

Deception needs to be developed as an integral component of peacetime and wartime national security policy. Deception is intentional, purposeful, calculated and deliberate. The target of deception should be the adversary's decisionmaking system. Deception should create perceptions and thereafter reinforce them. Deception should aim at misleading an adversary with regard to detectable information, whether actual or notional, by obscuring it. Often, the best and simplest deception is the presentation of the truth but in such a form that the adversary disbelieves it.

It must be clearly understood that given today's battlefield transparency, deception, in addition to surprise will be very difficult to achieve in the first instance; retaining the advantage that flows from it for an appreciable period of time will be even more difficult. For that reason alone this is one aspect which will require very thorough study, preparation and conceptualization.

Military deception operations are an inherent and expected responsibility of command at division level and above. It needs to be coordinated at the highest level to be effective and, should therefore, be indivisible from all other parts of the conception, planning and execution of military operations in peace and war. Deception ought to be intrinsic to and inseparable from all military thought and action, rather than a mere annexure, afterthought or an adjunct. The planning and practice of deception must be systematically integrated into devising a military strategy.

The process of deception is interactive and follows the sequential steps of planning, evaluation, coordination, integration, approval and execution. On completion of the last step of execution the situation needs to be reanalysed and process repeated, if required. The advent of IW offers unprecedented opportunities for deception operations in scope, effect and imagination. It is imperative that deception operations are planned as meticulously as actual operations, if not more. Deception plans may even be implemented by designated headquarters, supported by suitable allocation of resources. Nothing should be left to chance as an unfounded or unacknowledged assumption, supposition or assertion. Those charged with planning, approving, and executing deception operations, as well as the operators, must be absolutely adept in all the processes that these involve. Training and exercises should integrate the aspect of deception and appropriate resources should be instituted to develop and refine the art.

IMPACT OF TECHNOLOGY ON OPERATIONS AND THE REVOLUTION IN MILITARY AFFAIRS

Impact of Technology on Operations

Emphasis on IW: With the induction of better communication systems and the creation of a networked environment, our ability to collect, collate and analyse diverse inputs received from various agencies has been greatly enhanced. However, the vulnerabilities of such systems to disruption by the enemy have also increased and its resultant impact on conduct of operations would be magnified in proportion to the dependence on it. Due to the dependence of military forces on such systems, the role of technology in future warfare has expanded considerably, thereby enlarging our earlier concept of EW to C2W, which incorporates all functions of command dependent on communications and computers. Thus in a networkcentric environment, the emphasis will shift to IW and the various active and passive measures which form part of it.

Increased Battlefield Transparency and Situational Awareness: Today newer and better systems are available for the conduct of surveillance, identification and monitoring of the enemy and these have improved situational awareness. The nature of sensors and their platforms have extended the range of observation and enhanced the resolution thereby providing greater accuracy and detail in a shorter timeframes. The overall aim is to create a technological asymmetry so as to be in a better position to see, locate and monitor enemy forces and to plan for their destruction, degradation or disruption. In such an environment newer techniques or methods would be required to achieve surprise and deception. Increased reconnaissance and surveillance capability will enable manoeuvre force commanders to concentrate superior combat power at points of decision.

Enhancement in Degradation Capability: The range, precision and throwweight of weapon systems have increased substantially and have greatly enhanced the degradation capability of all forces. These weapon systems, coupled with air power, will be used in exploiting gains in battlefield transparency to shape the battlefield. Enhanced precision and standoff engagement capability, along with transparency sensors, will act as force multipliers.

Reduced Reaction Time: The time required for passage of information and orders will be reduced due to improved communications and networking. Accordingly, greater emphasis will have to be placed on directive style of command. The use of Command, Control, Communication, Computers, Intelligence, Information, Surveillance and Reconnaissance (C4I2SR) systems will result in expansion of the battlespace and compression of the time dimension. However, the adverse impacts of 'information overload' on the decisionmaking process of own forces need to be borne in mind and avoided.

Night Fighting: Technology has significantly improved night fighting capability. The ever increasing availability of new generation night vision devices will impact beneficially on tactical concepts.

Deception: Enhanced battlefield transparency will demand greater emphasis on deception so as to confuse or deceive the enemy about own movement, concentration, aim and intended area of operations. Management of the enemy's perceptions through C2W would become important in the future. This could well be achieved with modern technology by attempting to reinforce the enemy's beliefs and thereafter employ the tools of IW to blind or mislead enemy surveillance as part of a well coordinated plan.

Enhanced Mobility: Mobility of ground forces, especially in the plains and deserts has improved considerably. Enhanced battlefield transparency will facilitate and even require a shift from the existing attritionbased or positional concept of operations to that based predominantly on manoeuvre in offensive as well as defensive operations.

Enlarged Battle Area: Better surveillance capabilities, enhanced mobility of forces in the tactical battle area, longer ranges of weapon systems, stateofart communication systems, information technology enabling effective C_2 of forces over vastly extended areas have enlarged the battlespace. The ability to conduct nonlinear and simultaneous operations at greater depths adds to the battlespace over which a commander needs to exercise C_2.

Revolution in Military Affairs (RMA)

Recent conflicts have highlighted the dramatic impact of technology on warfare. This has caused a significant shift in the very nature of warfighting and is bringing about a RMA. Although we may not have the wherewithal to draw full benefits from it at present, the underlying message is unambiguoustechnology gives a clear edge and needs to be exploited to our advantage. We need to conceive and work towards a 'homespun' RMA that meets our needs and gives us an edge over our potential adversaries. Towards this end it will be essential to institutionalise methods for assimilating technology and adapting, and even anticipating, changes in doctrine, tactics and organisations. In so doing, special attention needs to be paid to the impact of RMA on LIC and asymmetric warfare waged by nonstate actors.

RMA is termed as 'a major change in the nature of warfare brought about by the innovative application of new technologies, which, combined with the dramatic changes in military doctrine, operational concepts and operations, fundamentally alters the character and conduct of military operations'.

The main constituents of RMA are doctrine, technology, tactics and training. Although the revolution is driven by technology, changes in doctrine, tactics and training are equally if not more important. Thus, the RMA, apart from the aspect of routine evolution that an Army undergoes in the process of modernisation, involves a transformation in the nature and conduct of military operations. It is the synergetic outcome of advances in technology suitably absorbed and applied by armed forces. There is a need, therefore, to focus on emerging technologies available to the armed forces to meet the strategic, operational and tactical requirements of the future and analyse the effect of cuttingedge technologies on future requirements. While doing so, aspects relating to orchestration of human resources and reorientation of training, which are imperative for unleashing the full potential of emerging technologies, must be factored in as technology alone can not influence the course of war unless there is a transformation in the manner armed forces think, train and fight.

The backbone of RMA is a C4I2SR system which facilitates dominant battlespace awareness and will therefore constitute a major thrust area. Five major components of RMA are IW, dominant manoeuvre, precision engagement, full dimensional protection and focused logistics. Advances in C4I2SR also make possible a new concept in war fighting viz NCW.

Analysis of major components of RMA indicates that they have great applicability in our context. We may however, have to follow an incremental approach in embracing these principles and acquiring the relevant technology. IW will form a key component of our war fighting doctrine. The excellent support base and infrastructure in information technology that is available in the country should be optimally exploited.

NCW has great potential in our context. We need to evolve our concept based on our security compulsions. Investment in 'infostructure' is an absolute imperative. This must be done jointly in conjunction with other Services so that seamless operations can be undertaken. As we progress to higher levels of technology, our ability to undertake NCW operations can be further refined. The advantages of operating with geographically dispersed forces must be fully exploited particularly in the backdrop of a nuclearised environment.

Meeting the challenge of RMA may demand substantial changes in our concepts, organisational philosophies and, most of all, attitudes. Concepts and organisational structures for exploitation of RMA would need to be evolved as the inevitable move towards greater use of high technology takes place.

RMA will have a dramatic effect on the Army and conduct of warfare through trends like lethality and dispersion, volume and precision of fires and their effects, processing and use of information, invisibility and detectability. Technologies that would need to be invested in are in the spheres of projecting and protecting the force, decisive operations, shaping of the battlefield and integrated logistics. Indigenous development of technologies to achieve self reliance will need sufficient investment to keep pace with RMA.

The impact of RMA on LIC is not as dramatic as in the field of conventional conflict. This does not imply that RMA has little to do in LIC; on the contrary, technology can play a significant role in LIC. We need to constantly refine our doctrines, concepts, organisations and tactics so as to optimise the effect of RMA in LIC.

CONDUCT OF OPERATIONS

Planning Considerations

Strategic Level.

- *International Environment.* There exists a strong international public opinion against war between nuclear weapon states on account of the attendant risk of triggering a nuclear weapons exchange. Hence, any intended military action requires careful calibration of international support. Proactive and aggressive diplomacy plays a pivotal role in preparing a suitable political environment prior to launching operations. Aspects such as economy, trade and commerce also come into play in such circumstances.

- *Synergy Between Diplomacy and Military Action.* Military conflict is usually the outcome of a diplomatic failure to ensure peaceful resolution of disputes. While coercive diplomacy may necessitate deployment of military forces as a prelude to offensive action, largescale mobilisation of forces would normally follow a firm decision at the highest level to adopt the military option with minimum loss of time.

- *Conflict Termination.* Conflict termination requirements and a viable exit policy should be incorporated at the national and appropriate military levels as part of overall campaign plans.

Operational Level.

- *Relation to Military Strategic Objectives.* Operational

level activity must directly contribute to achieving defined military strategic objectives.

- *Freedom of Action.* The operational level commander will dictate the nature of major operations, battles and engagements. Freedom of action to deploy reserves, assigning priorities and allocation of combat and logistic elements is, therefore, of critical importance. This freedom of action will, however, be within the confines of political and military constraints. While recognising these constraints, the commander will convey a clear statement of his intent which outlines his concept and establishes the objectives to be achieved by subordinate commanders within his theatre of operations.
- *Resources.* The resources made available to a commander to accomplish his operational objectives may be tangible (such as formations and units, combat and services support assets) or intangibles (such as delegated authority to achieve the given objectives). These give him freedom of action to exercise various options. Resources must be held at the level which ensures their most effective employment. Operational commanders must also utilise all civil infrastructure and resources available in their respective theatres to enhance their combat potential.
- *Civil Affairs.* The operational level commander will have certain explicit or implicit responsibilities for civil affairs within his theatre of operations. Movement of refugees and minimizing damage to civil infrastructure will have to be considered, in addition to his legal and moral obligations to minimize civilian casualties. Once operations have ended, initially the military may be the only organ available to exercise authority in the area and, therefore, responsibilities relating to civil affairs will assume greater importance. All formations entrusted with offensive operations in enemy territory will have an integral civil affairs element to handle tasks relating to control of the civilian population, management of resources and ensuring stability in captured territory.

However, aspects pertaining to the transition to civil control must be built into operational plans and be put into effect at the very earliest. This will ensure that fighting units are relieved at the earliest to carry out their primary roles.

Tactical Level.

- *Employment of Firepower and Mobility.* Commanders at the tactical level should ensure optimum employment of all the resources available to them and employ them effectively to fight decisive battles.
- *Earmarking Objectives.* All objectives at tactical level should lie well within the 'culmination point' of the forces earmarked to achieve such objectives. They should be in concert with, and part of the commander's overall operational design. Success should be achieved with overwhelming asymmetry and the use of firepower and force multipliers and with least cost to life and material.

Methodology of Conduct

Strategic Level.

- *Aim.* The military aim of war must be derived from the national aim and be clearly defined apart from being decisive and attainable. Each operation and battle must contribute to attainment of the overall military aim.
- *Terrain Considerations.* Since the Indian Army has to operate along vast borders of greatly varying terrain, it is important that planning for war, training and development of infrastructure is based on such terrain. Terrain is not neutral since it either helps or hinders the mobility of a force. The advantages and limitations of terrain should be identified and exploited for furthering own operations. 'Terrain appreciation' is, thus, a vital component in formulating plans. Military leaders must develop the ability to use terrain skilfully and should be able to visualise own and enemy forces on a given piece of terrain for maximizing own potential and degrading that of the enemy. Implications of terrain on different operations of war are available in various

General Staff publications.

- *Warning Period.* While it would be difficult to lay down any fixed warning period preceding a war, there will always be indicators and periods in which anticipatory action can be taken. All planning should aim to mobilise forces in the minimum possible time in order to take advantage of the many benefits that such a step offers.
- *Maximising Force Potential.* Ideally, this implies placing all available resources under one commander at each level. However, due to paucity, these may have to be placed under a commander only for particular phases of an operation or for a specified duration. Nevertheless, jointness is a prerequisite at the operational and theatre levels.
- *Balanced Force.* A force must be so composed and structured that its full combat power can be brought to bear in the most effective manner to achieve assigned objectives in the stipulated time.
- *Favourable Air Situation.* A favourable air situation over the tactical battle area, as well as the operational level battle area prior to launch of own operations is a decided advantage. Strategic constraints, however, may dictate the need for achieving objectives in a short timeframe, wherein both land and air campaigns may have to be fought concurrently. As a consequence a favourable air situation may not always be available.

Operational Level.

- *Force Projection.* This includes mobilisation, movement and deployment. Mobilisation encompasses marshalling of manpower, equipment, stores and training as also activating part or all reserve components as required. This involves preparation of welldesigned mobilisation schemes which should be frequently practiced and rehearsed. Anticipation of mobilisation helps the Army to be physically and mentally prepared. Flexible logistic support is a prerequisite for force projection and should be catered for accordingly.

- *Shaping the Battlefield.* The purpose of shaping the battlefield is to create conditions which will facilitate the success of own operations keeping the ultimate aim in view. In the human dimension, psychological operations serve to unbalance the enemy, create discord and weaken his will to fight.
- *Decisive Operations.* Military operations which force the enemy to submit to one's will are decisive operations. These are most effective when the application of combat power and force multipliers is wellorchestrated and fully integrated throughout the battlespace. Enemy vulnerabilities should be targeted to achieve a clearcut victory. Such operations will invariably be joint operations.
- *Protection.* This relates to the ability to conserve troops, information and equipment so that these can be utilised at the decisive time and place. It has relevance in both defensive and offensive operations.
- *Sustainment.* This is a continuous process which starts with mobilisation and continues till the end of hostilities. Towards this end there is a need for operational plans to be corelated to the available logistic support infrastructure.
- *Intelligence.* Sound and timely intelligence is critical for successful prosecution of war aims. It includes the entire gamut of obtaining information from various sources, converting it to intelligence by passing it through stages of synthesis and analysis, and the timely dissemination of processed intelligence to the user.

Offensive Operations

Offensive operations are a decisive form of winning a war. Their purpose is to attain the desired end state and achieve decisive victory. Offensive operations seek to seize the initiative from the enemy, retain it and exploit the dividends accruing from such actions. These operations end when the force either achieves the desired end state or reaches its culmination point.

Planning an Offensive.

- *Enemy Information.* Every possible means of acquiring intelligence and conducting surveillance must be employed to get accurate and timely information about the enemy. Of particular relevance will be his strategic thought process, intention, grouping of formations, deployment and location of reserves.
- *Joint Planning.* No operation launched in isolation can be expected to succeed in future offensive scenarios. Planning and coordination for operations should be undertaken jointly by all three Services and each should complement the strengths and offset the vulnerabilities of the other while formulating a joint plan.
- *Surprise and Deception.* With the availability of modern day hightechnology surveillance means, achieving complete surprise will be difficult. Accordingly, more than the element of surprise, it is deception at the strategic and operational levels which need to be given greater importance as this could, more easily, contribute to success.
- *Simplicity of Plans.* Even at the highest level, plans for offensive operations, must be simple. A common sense approach with minimum complexities will help in making the plan workable and thereby ensure better coordination and flexibility. This is especially relevant while planning joint operations.
- *Nuclear Factor.* Future operations will be conducted against a nuclear backdrop; all planning should take this important factor into account.
- *Terrorism and Insurgency.* Similar to the nuclear backdrop, a war in Jammu & Kashmir may have to be fought against the backdrop of terrorism and hence appropriate measures for rear area security will have to be inbuilt into operational plans.

Preparation for Offensive Operations.

- *Mobilisation.* Offensive forces should mobilise within

the shortest possible time in keeping with the prevailing operational environment.

- *Force Posturing*. 'Posturing' by offensive forces should be planned at the highest level to aid deception and preempt the enemy.
- *Reliable and Foolproof Communications*. Reliable and secure communications, with inbuilt redundancy, provides flexibility in employment of forces and assists the commander in influencing the outcome of battle.
- *Combined Arms Battle Concept*. The capabilities of all available forces must be understood and the cumulative strength of every Arm and Service must be exploited fully to achieve optimum results. Similarly, their weaknesses must also be known so that they can be mitigated through appropriate employment or deployment; this will obviate the possibility of the enemy taking advantage of weakness, if any.
- *Directive Style of Command*. Offensive operations throw up unexpected scenarios and fleeting opportunities which should be exploited to advantage. A directive style of command gives best results in offensive operations.

Conduct of Offensive Operations.

- *Shaping the Battlefield*. Adequate time and resources must be set apart for 'shaping the battlefield' before any offensive is launched. The results achieved will be dependent entirely upon the ingenuity with which firepower is delivered; this includes counter air operations and battlefield air interdiction, artillery engagements and strikes by surfacetosurface missiles. Offensive IW, including psychological operations, must be exploited optimally to demoralise and degrade the adversary.
- *Creation of Superiority at Points of Decision*. Absolute superiority across the board will be hard to achieve. Forces should, therefore, be deployed for the offensive in such a manner that they create force superiority at wellselected points of decision. Overwhelming combat

superiority or advantageous asymmetry reduces the time required for achieving success.

- *Indirect Approach.* The essence of operational art lies in planning an 'indirect approach' to the objective. Concepts such as the 'turning move', 'envelopment' and 'infiltration' provide dividends out of proportion to the force employed when seen in contrast to direct, frontal or head on operations.
- *Tempo of Operations.* An offensive should generate such a tempo that it should unbalance and paralyse the adversary. The design of operations should ensure that leading elements reach their objectives before the enemy reserves can be brought to effectively bear on them.
- *Employment of Forces.* Pivot or holding corps should be prepared to undertake offensive operations. Accordingly, only the minimum essential forces should be committed to holding vital areas and the remainder should be grouped, positioned and tasked to conduct offensive operations to improve the defensive posture and create 'windows of opportunity' for development of further operations. A few salient aspects are outlined below:
    * *Strike Corps.* Strike corps should be capable of being inserted into operational level battle, either as battle groups or as a whole, to capture or threaten strategic and operational objective(s) with a view to cause destruction of the enemy's reserves and capture sizeable portions of territory.
    * *Contingency Planning.* Formations should be prepared to switch from one theatre to another in the shortest possible time. Equipment commonality and preplanned, tailormade logistic support should be ensured to facilitate such switching.
    * *Employment of Heliborne, Airborne and Amphibious Forces.* These will primarily be employed to augment the offensive capability of conventional ground forces. They could also be employed for security of island territories, offshore resources and maritime trade routes.

Defensive Operations

Destruction of the enemy's armed forces and breaking his will to fight is the basic aim of war. This can be achieved by major offensive operations. Defensive operations are, nonetheless, necessary to ensure the security of own forces, provide the base for strike forces and to create a favourable situation for offensive operations to be undertaken. Defensive operations must, therefore, be basically aggressive in design and offensive in conduct.

Planning for Defence.

- *Importance of Intelligence.* Acquisition of intelligence about the enemy is as important for defensive operations as it is for offensive operations.
- *Offensive Defence.* Defensive plans at every level must be offensive in nature. This implies that the enemy should be engaged effectively from the earliest available opportunity with every possible means in a planned manner. It also implies taking offensive action at every level, as part of a coordinated plan, to wrest the initiative from the enemy at every stage during war. A preemptive strike on his likely launch pads would completely upset the enemy's strategic design, cause imbalance in the disposition of his forces and wrest the initiative from him right from the beginning of operations.
- *Pragmatic Appreciation for Defence.* Defensive plans must be made after a very detailed and deliberate appreciation of the enemy's capabilities, intentions and interests, starting from the strategic and operational levels and culminating in the identification of threat at the tactical level. The emphasis at operational and tactical levels should be on effective surveillance, gauging of enemy intentions and retaining strong reserves rather than holding every inch of ground.

Conduct of Defensive Operations.

- *Accurate Reading of Battle.* Accurate and continuous reading of battle by commanders at every level is a vital ingredient for fighting a successful defensive battle.

Availability of real time information at all levels is essential for this purpose.

- *Improvement of Defensive Posture.* Every formation must have wellcoordinated plans for improvement of its defensive posture. Depending on terrain conditions, these could range from expansion of its forward zone to capture of likely launch pads and dominating heights. Objectives for these offensive actions should be selected in a manner that ensures that these operations do not jeopardise and unbalance the subsequent defensive plans of the formation.
- *Heavy Attrition.* Once the enemy offensive has been discerned, all available firepower including air, armour, artillery and other weapon systems must be employed in a coordinated manner to cause heavy attrition and seriously degrade the enemy offensive.

Employment of Reserves: The key to conduct of a successful defensive battle is timely and skilful employment of reserves to thwart the enemy offensive at the critical juncture in battle.

SPECIAL FORCES OPERATIONS

Special Forces

Characteristics: The Special Forces are specially selected troops who are trained, equipped and organised to operate in hostile territory, isolated from the main combat forces. They may operate independently or in conjunction with other forces at the operational level. They are versatile, have a deep reach and can make precision strikes at targets of critical importance. They are particularly valuable in the early stages of a campaign when they can create conditions for decisive operations.

Concept of Employment: Allocation of tasks to Special Forces should be handled at the appropriate level. Special Forces will have access to the maximum possible intelligence inputs relevant to the task and absolute security will be maintained at all times relating to their intended employment. The principle of 'direct control and mission command' should be exercised. Special Forces units will be tasked to develop 'area specialisation' in their intended operational theatres to achieve optimum effect.

Missions: Missions that could be assigned to the Special Forces are given below:

- *Conventional War*. Strategic and tactical surveillance of vital targets, early warning of enemy activity in depth areas, denying strategic or operational assets and terminal targeting by precision munitions.
- *Low Intensity Conflicts*. 'Seek and Destroy' missions including transborder operations.
- *During Peace*. Hostage rescue, antiterrorist operations and assistance to friendly foreign governments.

Planning Special Operations: Keeping in mind the capabilities and farreaching consequences of Special Forces operations, it is imperative that planning is conducted meticulously in order to ensure success. Various aspects of planning include the following:

- *Purpose*. Commanders should specify the desired effect rather than courses of action.
- *Selection of Targets*. While the objectives are decided at the strategic level, commanders in the theatre of operations will evolve additional objectives for specific operational plans. Simultaneous assessment will be carried out by the air force and naval elements in case they too are involved.
- *Intelligence*. Intelligence agencies will be required to provide feasibility assessments prior to final acceptance of the task. Success will result from the precision with which Special Forces are employed against correctly identified enemy weaknesses.
- *Joint Planning*. Plans must be evolved jointly in conjunction with the Air Force and Navy where employment of their resources is involved.
- *Surprise*. In any operation, the force ratio would invariably be against the Special Forces; accordingly, achieving surprise will be essential for success.

- *Flexibility*. Special Forces operations are characterised by great flexibility. This is fostered and enhanced by improvisation, selfcontainment and detailed contingency planning.

Equipping: Because of the nature and gravity of their tasks with inherent risks, Special Forces need to be equipped with the very best of equipment and armament. The process of identifying needs and the pace of acquiring equipment for the Special Forces should, accordingly, be different from the rest of the Army in order to ensure that they are always suitably equipped.

Conduct of Operations

Security of plans, appropriate navigation aids and the support of air defence elements for aircrafts utilised to insert Special Forces into enemy territory should be ensured. Battlefield air strike and electronic support measures during landing will also form an important part of the conduct of operations.

Insertion, Extraction and Recovery: Special Forces will be trained for insertion by air, land, sea and inland waterways and detailed plans for extraction and recovery after accomplishment of missions are vital. Special Forces will be prepared and trained for exfiltration and extraction from the area of operations employing various means.

JOINT OPERATIONS

The nature of future warfare requires harmonious and synergetic application of land, sea and air forces. Joint operations are the most essential requirement of future wars and have to focus on the seamless application of all available resources to shock, dislocate and overwhelm the enemy. This necessitates an intimate understanding of the capabilities and limitations of each Service by the other two.

Optimal impact is achieved by evolving a joint operational plan which effectively integrates all designated resources. Joint operations encompass all actions required to successfully achieve a designated joint objective and involves activities relating to marshalling, deploying and employing the allotted forces. It also includes the intelligence, communication and logistic functions in support of such operations.

Principles of Joint Operations

Objectives: Joint operations will be planned and directed towards clearly defined, attainable and decisive objectives so that the combat potential of all components is exploited to obtain optimal effect.

Centralised Planning and Decentralised Execution: It is important to retain the freedom of action of own forces. Towards this end, while planning and coordination must be centralised, there should be adequate decentralisation of command and decisionmaking to the lowest practical level.

Unity of Effort: Planning for joint operations integrates the combat power of the three Services and their activities in time, space and purpose. Joint operations produce maximum application of the overall combat power at the decisive point towards attainment of common objectives.

Speed: Modern weapons, equipment and communications continue to accelerate the pace of warfare. The joint planning and execution process must facilitate rapid decision making and action.

Joint Focus: Jointness in training, intelligence, planning, execution and logistics foster interoperability and commonality of purpose in operations. Interoperability of equipment particularly that of communications needs special emphasis.

Planning for Joint Operations

Planning for joint operations commences at the level of the COSC and involves allocation of objectives and missions to designated successive levels of command of the Armed Forces.

Joint Planning Process: The COSC will nominate the Service Headquarters responsible for the overall conduct of joint operations and issue a directive defining the objectives, terms of reference and allocation of resources. An Overall Force Commander will also be nominated by the COSC. Thereafter, planning at various levels will be conducted as under:

- *Theatre Level.* A Joint Operations Centre at the

designated Command Headquarters will analyse the directive and will refer back unresolved issues, if any, to the COSC for a final decision. Thereafter, plans for surprise, deception and IW will be evolved and commanders in the theatre will issue their operational directives to subordinate formations.

- *Operational Level*. The directions of the Overall Force Commander will be analysed to decide on tactical objectives, lines of operations and decisive points. Joint staff at each successive level will facilitate optimisation and synergisation of joint resources.

LandAir Operations

Recent conflicts have demonstrated that spectacular successes can be achieved by wellcoordinated and integrated joint operations. Though the extent of involvement of each Service would depend on the missions assigned to it and the prevailing circumstances, the inherent speed and reach of combat air power allows rapid engagement of enemy ground targets within and outside the tactical battle area in conjunction with ground operations. Air operations in support of land forces will be planned jointly to obtain synergistic effect in the specified theatre or area of operations. However, all such air operations should contribute towards achievement of the overall military goal.

Land Operations: These will be undertaken with the aim of capturing designated objectives and destruction of enemy forces. Availability of intelligence, deception, attainment of surprise, speed of operations and concentration of combat power at the points of decision will be critical for success of land operations.

Air Operations: During joint operations, air power is employed for conduct of air operations in support of land forces operations. The objective of air operations will be to degrade the enemy's air power and reduce its capability to interfere with the operations of own land forces, deny enemy land forces the ability to move unhindered, create an imbalance in his force disposition and destroy or severely damage his surface communications and logistic means. Air operations will be the most effective means of disrupting the move of reserves and substantially reducing their potential before they arrive at their point of application. Air operations include tactical reconnaissance, counter air operations, battlefield air interdiction, counter surface force operations, air defence, air transport (including strategic and tactical airlifts), airborne and heliborne assault operations.

Joint Planning for Air Operations: All Army and Air Command Headquarters jointly set up Joint Army Air Operations Centres (JAAOC). Air support requirements of the land forces plan are intimated by JAAOC to the controlling Air Command in the form of targets to be engaged and degree of neutralisation required along with the timeframe in which to achieve these missions. Joint Operations Centre (JOC), at the level of Corps headquarters is the interface with designated air bases for providing air effort and liaison with JAAOC for allotment of air effort. Joint planning and execution facilitates quick response to air support demands of land forces to bring about synergised effect on the battlefield.

Airborne Operations

Characteristics: Airborne operations are conducted in hostile territory for executing an assault landing from the air. These may be conducted at the strategic or operational levels, either independently or in conjunction with other operations. With its inherent air mobility, an airborne force is an important means to achieve simultaneity of force application and gaining a foothold across obstacle systems in circumstances in which other forces would require considerably much more time to be effective. Airborne operations can be launched at any stage of a battle.

Missions: Due to their inherent flexibility, airborne forces are capable of being employed on various missions whether these are strategic or operational. Operational missions are generally in furtherance of land forces plans and involve close cooperation with them. Though launched independently into the depth areas of the enemy, a quick linkup by ground forces is essential for the success of an airborne operation.

Planning Airborne Operations: The sequence of planning of an airborne operation is illustrated below.

Conduct of Airborne Operations.

- Command and Control.
  - * *Army*. During flight, the air transport force commander will be the overall commander; after landing, the ground force commander will regain command of the land forces component.
  - * *Air Transport Force*. The overall control of the air transport force will be with Air Headquarters, represented by the Air Command in the theatre which, in turn, will nominate a task force commander.
- *Conduct*. During the execution phase, attention needs to be paid to creating a favourable air situation and taking appropriate air defence measures. Suitable deception measures and a rapid linkup are vital to the success of a mission.

Amphibious Operations

Bearing in mind India's extensive coastline and many island territories, an effective amphibious capability is essential for safeguarding national interests and creating deterrence so as to ensure peace and stability in the Indian Ocean.

Tasks and Employment Scenarios: Our amphibious forces have the capability to project a sustainable presence in coastal and offshore areas. Amphibious tasks are essentially categorised as assault, demonstration, raid and withdrawal operations. These tasks could be undertaken in various scenarios including conventional war, defence of island territories, assistance to friendly littoral states in the region, peacekeeping under the United Nations Charter and any other special operations necessitating employment of an amphibious force.

Command and Control: On the basis of the overall situation, content and objective of the operations the COSC will designate the Theatre Commander concerned who will be responsible for the overall campaign. He will function with an integrated staff from all component Services. The three Services will nominate their respective component force commanders, ie the Commander Amphibious Task Force (CATF), Land Force Commander (LFC) and Air Force Commander (AFC). Though the CATF will be the coordinator among the three Services during the planning phase, the CATF, LFC, and AFC will function with individual and independent access to the Overall Force Commander. However, during the embarkation, movement and assault phases, and until the ATF is dissolved, the CATF will exercise command authority over the ATF. Besides, the CATF will have command authority over all forces operating in the Amphibious Objective Area (AOA) including those that are not part of the ATF.

Planning: On receipt of the operational directive from the COSC, the Theatre Commander will issue an initiating directive to the CATF, LFC and AFC. This initiating directive is, in essence, an amplification of the operational directive and contains the information necessary to carry out the task. Thereafter the triService planning staff will prepare detailed plans based on which a formal operational order is issued; this constitutes the basis on which the three Services components would make their detailed plans.

Conduct: The assault phase encompasses the preparation of beaches for assault by naval guns, shiptoshore movement of the landing force, linkup between surface and airlanded assault forces and landing of the remaining elements of the landing force for accomplishment of the mission. Detailed planning, preponderance of firepower, and coordination for speedy landing of tanks, guns, vehicles and infantry in correct sequence are vitally important for success of amphibious assault. Air defence and maintenance of logistic support throughout the assault also need to be ensured.

12

OPERATIONS OTHER THAN WAR

Strategic Framework for LICO

Aim of Military Operations: When employing the Army in LICO, conflict management rather than conflict resolution will be the political objective. Therefore, operational objectives and intensity of operations should be oriented towards achieving a qualitative improvement in the situation which may not necessarily be possible in a short timeframe. It will be preferable to aim at low profile and peoplefriendly operations rather than high intensity operations related only to body and weapon counts.

Timeframe.

- *Precedence of Occurrence.* LICO may have to be undertaken prior to, simultaneously with or after the occurrence of a conventional war. In certain cases, these may be the initial step in the escalatory ladder of conflict that may have to be waged with an adversary bent on promoting and fuelling a proxy war. In other situations such operations may have to be undertaken after a conventional conflict while consolidating gains in captured territory.
- *Duration of Operations.* In order to ensure that the Army's efforts are effective and proportional to the task, LICO will generally be prolonged and will see a large number of changes in policy and directional imperatives. Commanders and troops executing the mandate will move on after completing their tours of duty during the conduct of such operations to be replaced by others. It

should be ensured that this should not result in an almost fresh start in any given area. Additionally, any tendency to resort to quick and seemingly efficient militarylike actions which may appear to resolve an immediate local issue but, in all probability, may seriously hurt longterm objectives and future stability should be curbed without exception.

Higher Direction: The apex body of the higher defence organisation will be responsible for conducting reviews of the military aspect of LIC and advise the Government on the application of the military instrument of power. It will lay down clearly stated objectives to Army theatre commanders, coordinate functioning with other government and nongovernmental agencies and monitor current and future changes in the nature of LIC with a view to recalibrate the nature and tempo of own operations. In addition, Theatre Commanders may also receive direct inputs from the local administration. As distinct from conventional war, clearcut directions in a LIC scenario may not always be available. Military commanders must, therefore, possess a high degree of tolerance for operating effectively in an environment of ambiguity.

Principles of LIC/CounterInsurgency (CI) Operations

The wellestablished principles of war are equally applicable to combat operations conducted within the overall ambit of LIC. Some other principles will need to be modified for the military environment. The commander on the spot will balance the application of each principle depending upon the nature of each specific operation. The commonly understood principles of CI and counterproxy war operations are given below:

- *Primacy of Overall Aim.* The scope and intensity of CI operations relate to the probability of finding political solutions. Therefore operational objectives will need to be oriented towards achieving a qualitative improvement in the situation. Clearly stated operational and tactical objectives should be directed towards an equally unambiguous overall strategic aim.
- *Unity of Effort.* This will be equally applicable to intraforce as well as interagency efforts. Apart from the

Army, a large number of police and paramilitary forces are often also committed in CI operations. As such, it will be essential to harmonise the efforts of each element and therein lies the importance of unity of command. Loosely defined, yet responsive, command arrangements may also need to be made within own forces.

- *Popular Support.* Popular support is the cornerstone of all CI operations. All actions, including military operations, should be undertaken to seek the voluntary and willing support of the people in the affected area. Winning the Hearts and Minds (WHAM) of the population through low profile and peoplefriendly operations is the most essential aspect of successful CI operations. In many a way they contribute even more than the actual operations.
- *Dynamic Conduct.* The conduct of military operations should break free from set patterns, stereotyped plans and rigid responses. The insurgents will invariably enjoy the support and sympathy of the local population and, thereby, remain ahead of the security forces in terms of information. As a consequence, security forces operations will generally be reactive. It is, therefore, of utmost importance that imaginative and innovative variations in time, scope and manner of force application forms the basis of all CI operations, to dominate the area, keep the insurgents on the run and gain physical and moral ascendancy.
- *Public Relations.* The broad spectrum of all military actions must be projected in a transparent, honest and positive manner for maximum psychological gains. The action of the Army should aim at respecting and protecting human rights, reducing the threat to the people and inspire a sense of security. Any excesses by the troops, provoked or otherwise, or errors of judgement of commanders, must be candidly and promptly admitted and swift corrective actions taken in a free and fair manner whilst guarding against any adverse effect on the morale of own troops. It needs to be noted that the

role of the media is critical in achieving a positive projection of military actions.

- *Code of Conduct*. The military code of conduct must be strictly observed by all ranks. Guidelines, issued by the Chief of the Army Staff, are given below:
  * Remember that the people you are dealing with are your own countrymen; your behaviour must be dictated by this single most consideration. Violation of Human Rights, therefore, must be avoided under all circumstances, even at the cost of operational success.
  * Be compassionate, help the people and win their hearts and minds.
  * Operations must be peoplefriendly and it should be ensured that least possible inconvenience and harassment is caused to the populace.
  * Minimum force should be used and collateral damage should be avoided.
  * Operations should not be undertaken without a police representative. All operations against women militants or terrorists should be conducted only in the presence of women police personnel.
  * Be truthful, honest and maintain the highest standards of integrity, honour, discipline, courage and sacrifice.
  * Sustain physical and moral strength, mental robustness and motivation.
  * Train hard, be vigilant and maintain high standards of military professionalism.
  * Synergise your actions with the civil administration and other security forces.
  * Uphold dharma and be proud of your country and the Army.
- Guidelines for Operating under Armed Forces Special Powers Act, 1958. Detailed instructions promulgated by

the Adjutant General Branch, Army Headquarters for conduct of operations under this Act, will be strictly adhered to. Salient aspects which need special attention are outlined below :

* Strictly adhere to the laid down rules, regulations and standard operating procedures when opening fire, conducting searches, arresting and seizing arms, ammunition, explosive and other incriminating material.
* Accounting and disposal of apprehended persons and material must also be conducted scrupulously as per prescribed rules.
* Provisions of procedure laid down in the Code of Criminal Procedure must be adhered to while effecting arrest, search of women and searching places occupied by women.
* Provide immediate medical aid to all persons injured during operations
* Maintain detailed records of all actions taken during operations.
* Promptly attend to the directions and instructions of civil courts. When summoned by a court, ensure dignified conduct and maintain decorum of the court.

Elements of CI Operations

Intelligence: Superior manpower and weapons have to be supported by efficient intelligence backup for success in CI operations. Concerted efforts are required to establish an intelligence grid; this is a longterm process and, hence, continuity must be maintained even if units rotate through turnovers.

Psychological Initiatives: Psychological initiatives play a major role in a CI environment. The planned management of information and other measures are important to influence the opinion, emotions, attitude and behaviour of hostile, neutral or friendly groups in support of current policies and aims. Themes for psychological initiatives should be chosen objectively taking into account the perceptions of the selected target audience.

Information Management.

- *Media*. Media caters to various needs of the people in society in peace and war. With its unlimited capabilities and reach, it is an effective force multiplier. Since insurgency is a battle for the hearts and minds of the people, media is the most potent weapon for conducting psychological initiatives.
- *Electronic Warfare*. EW plays a key role in supplementing intelligence. Timely and actionable intelligence is vital. This will go a long way in isolating scattered pockets of insurgents and depriving them of direction and coordination from their controllers and supporters.

Winning Hearts and Minds: Security forces must seek popular approval for their presence in insurgencyprone areas. WHAM involves actions to gain the confidence of uncommitted elements of the population in addition to obtaining, preserving and strengthening support from 'friendly' insurgents. WHAM focuses on undertaking civic action programmes to present the Army's human face.

These include providing education, creating medical facilities, construction and development projects in addition to social activities aimed at improving the quality of life and promoting better understanding and cooperation with local residents. Further, due consideration needs to be accorded to minimize inconvenience to the populace during conduct of operations apart from safeguarding human rights.

Human Rights and Legal Framework: With the Army's prolonged deployment in CI operations, there is a need to develop due respect for human rights, notwithstanding the tense, stressful and turbulent situations at the grass roots level. In this regard the Ten Commandments issued by the Chief of the Army Staff, as given earlier will be strictly followed.

Leadership: Good leadership is very important and will prove effective in ensuring that troops are convinced that the cause they are fighting for is just. Leaders need to display great tact and patience in coping with the difficulties in insurgency situations.

Conduct of Operations

CI operations need to be conducted in two different geographical contexts, more so in proxy war situations. The first is at the border or LC itself through which the insurgent cadre infiltrates. The second is in the hinterland, both urban and rural, wherein insurgents establish bases and hides from which strikes are launched. Therefore, it is essential that wellcoordinated operations need to be conducted to, first, check infiltration and then to deprive the freedom of action enjoyed by insurgents in the hinterland; this isolates them from their support base.

Checking Infiltration and Exfiltration: The porosity of our borders, difficult terrain and inclement weather conditions provide ideal conditions for infiltration. All possible measures must be undertaken to check infiltration and exfiltration. Incisive appreciation of terrain will help identify the likely infiltration and exfiltration routes, along which a multitiered surveillance grid should be established. Quick reaction teams should be based on surveillance centres to respond swiftly to any attempted infiltration and egress. In the long run, the success rate of infiltration attempts should be reduced so drastically that insurgents do not consider it costeffective. Whenever an obstacle, such as a fence, is created, it should be backed by surveillance equipment and troops physically guarding it from both sides. 'Jungle bashing' by large bodies, in the absence of intelligence, is the least effective method of operating in such conditions.

Operations in the Hinterland: These encompass the urban, rural and forest areas. Each of these has its own peculiarities which dictate the deployment pattern and density of troops in a given area. While inhabited urban areas will require firm but humane measures for population and access control and selective surgical operations based on specific inputs, more vigorous combat operations will be necessitated against wellestablished camps in rural areas and forests. The Army is more suited for the second category of operations. The deployment pattern and density of troops will be dictated by the overall number of insurgents operating in the area, their tactics and motivation, demographic realities, public attitude and terrain in addition to the prevailing political, economic and social conditions. It will be imperative to ensure own security and undertake measures to prevent the insurgents from exploiting vulnerabilities and, if they do so, to respond swiftly so that poststrike get away is prohibitively expensive for the insurgents.

Small Team Operations: Resources of the security forces will invariably be stretched over a large area of responsibility. In such an environment, operations based on small teams backed by good or specific intelligence increase the chances of contact with and success against insurgents. Helicopters can be very effectively employed for various tasks in CI operations. CI units ferried by helicopters should be employed for tasks of decisive nature where speed and surprise are of paramount importance particularly in remote or inaccessible areas.

Minimizing Casualties: Unlike conventional war, CI operations are seldom timebound. Casualties occur when operations are conducted without adequate intelligence, poor or inadequate standard of basic infantry skills and neglect of fundamentals. No effort should be spared to minimize casualties to own troops so as to maintain moral ascendancy over the insurgents.

NONCOMBAT OPERATIONS

Types of Operations

As mentioned earlier, noncombat operations are conducted primarily to assist the civil administration to meet sudden challenges to internal peace and tranquillity due to local disturbances initiated by a segment of the population or due to natural or manmade calamities. The suddenness and intensity of the event may catch the civil administration unprepared or unable to meet the immediate challenge, while the Army will be able to deploy speedily, provide relief and bring the situation to a state manageable by the civil administration. It must be noted that management of disasters is primarily a State subject.

Maintenance of Law and Order: Amongst all the duties generally performed by the Army in aid to civil authority, maintenance of law and order is the most important and sensitive. The lethality of weapons and the levels of violence encountered on such commitments have been progressively escalating with a corresponding increase in the frequency of the Army's deployment. Under such conditions, deployment and conduct of the Army has to be thought through and planned meticulously bearing in mind prevailing sensitivities. The Army should work on the well established principles of good faith, the use of minimum force and prior warning to the people when compelled to take action.

Disaster Relief: The Indian subcontinent is vulnerable to floods, droughts, cyclones, earthquakes and accidents. Disasters include earthquakes, landslides, floods, cyclones, wildfires, and epidemics on the one hand and accidents and manmade disasters on the other. The impact of these disasters is more predominant in underdeveloped and remote areas, where facilities to handle such calamities do not exist.

Humanitarian Assistance: These programmes consist of assistance provided in conjunction with military operations and training exercises. Humanitarian assistance should enhance national security interests and increase the operational readiness of units performing such missions. These may include provision of medical care, basic sanitation facilities, repair of public amenities and facilities, education, training and technical assistance.

Planning for NonCombat Operations

Levels of Planning: The Army carries out planning for disaster management at the national, state and field levels. The Ministry of Defence, including Headquarters Integrated Defence Staff and the three Service Headquarters are involved at the highest level. Command, Area or Sub Area Headquarters will interact with the civil administration, police and other organisations at the State level, through periodic `civilmilitary conferences'. Activities related to surveillance, preparedness and prevention should, nonetheless, continue even during normal conditions.

Full Utilisation of State Resources: All military commanders approached to provide aid must advise the civil administration to first fully utilise their own resources. They should synergise these with those of the Army once deployed. This is particularly applicable for duties involving maintenance of law and order particularly in circumstances when the State Government may be of the opinion that the task is beyond its capabilities. Though this may result in the Army having to step into an already deteriorated situation, it is necessary to maintain its longterm credibility and effectiveness and hence need to avoid highhandedness will be the key guiding principle.

Preparation: In order to be able to respond to any call in aid of civil authorities, it is important for all command echelons in the Army to be fully aware of the availability and deployment of State resources as also have complete understanding of the existing infrastructure in their areas of responsibility. Equally important is visualisation of the likely role that the Army may be assigned in a specific area, given its physical and social peculiarities. The capability of the Army to undertake various noncombat operations will require an indepth analysis and standard operating procedures should be worked out in consultation with civil administration. This will ensure that minimum time is lost in deployment of troops and that necessary training is imparted to own troops in advance for the purpose. The Army has charted out detailed allocation of responsibilities in all areas and all civil administrative officials are kept informed.

Requisitioning of Aid

PrePlanned Aid: In cases where rendition of aid can be planned, the civil authority will project its demands through the State Government and Ministry of Home Affairs to the Ministry of Defence which shall consider the demand. To enable local military authority to make necessary preparations, State Governments should keep the appropriate Army formation headquarters informed regarding ongoing developments and details of requests projected to the Ministry of Defence. Such formations or units will then carry out necessary preparations and make outline plans for the task, including allotment of troops, equipment and movement. Army Headquarters shall always be kept fully apprised of such details.

Aid in an Emergency: When time is short the designated civil authority may make a direct requisition to the nearest military authority for maintenance of law and order or for disaster relief. Local military authority will provide the necessary help without reference to the higher headquarters in exceptional cases where speed is essential to save human lives and property. However, in cases of a sensitive nature, prior clearance of the Army Headquarters will be obtained telephonically by the Command Headquarters concerned. The sanction of the Union Government will be obtained at the earliest even in such cases by the concerned State Governments. During natural calamities and other serious emergencies when time does not permit obtaining sanction of the Union Government, the local commander may, at his discretion, comply with the request of the civil authority to the best of his ability. In such circumstances, the civil and military authorities will immediately report their actions to the Union Government.

UNITED NATIONS (UN) PEACEKEEPING MISSIONS

India has an enviable record of participating in UN peacekeeping missions, having earned the respect and admiration of all parties for the impartial and professional manner in which our forces have discharged their duties. As a stable and mature democracy it is incumbent on India to continue contributing to peacekeeping efforts of the UN.

A UN peacekeeping mission is formally established after a resolution is adopted by the Security Council and a mandate to that effect is issued. Based on the mandate, missions can be classified as peacekeeping (Chapter VI) or peaceenforcement (Chapter VII) as spelt out in the UN Charter. Chapter VI deals with the settlement of disputes by the Security Council by negotiations, enquiry, mediation, conciliation, arbitration, judicial settlement, resorting to regional agencies or arrangements or other peaceful means. Chapter VII covers the actions to restore international peace and security with respect to threats to peace, breaches of peace and acts of aggression. These actions may include complete or partial interruption of economic relations or means of communications and severance of diplomatic relations, and if these fail, resorting to operations (demonstration, blockade and other operations) by air, sea or land force of member countries of the UN. When deciding to operate under Chapter VII, the consent of the parties involved need not be obtained.

Principles of PeaceKeeping: The basic principles of peacekeeping are consent of the parties involved, international support, unity of C_2, impartiality, mutual respect, legitimacy, credibility and coordination of effort.

UN Mandate: A mandate emerges from a Security Council resolution and will be the basic document for the mission and invariably include the following elements :

- Components of the mission and their tasks.
- Ceasefire or other agreements.
- Demobilisation and reintegration of the groups and forces involved in the conflict.
- Maintenance of forces during demobilisation.
- Final disposition of the forces and groups and disposal of their weapons and equipment.
- Discontinuation of foreign military aid to all parties.

Rules of Engagement: This is an important document which spells out the quantum and type of force that may be used and the circumstances in which it is to be used. Unit commanders of the mission must ensure that all ranks clearly understand these rules. When applying the rules of engagement the basic tenets of minimum force, proportionate action and minimum collateral damage must be ensured.

Mission Directives and Instructions: A military contingent operating under UN auspices is issued 'directives' by the Force Commander and 'instructions' by his staff. All ranks must understand these.

Functions of Military Personnel.

- *Under Chapter VI.* Military personnel may function as observers or as part of a contingent. The primary task of military observers is to collect and disseminate information in the mission area. A contingent should be prepared to perform tasks such as security, protection, civic action and logistics. The contingent could be called upon to carry out nonmilitary tasks also.

- *Under Chapter VII.* In such a situation the tasks (demonstrations, blockade or other operations) and functioning of the contingent would be similar to that while functioning as part of a multinational force.

Preparatory Activity: Once the decision to participate in a UN mission is taken by the Government, detailed planning and preparation of the contingent will be a prerequisite prior to deployment. This will include reconnaissance, equipping, assembly and staging forward of the force, induction, supply of the force in the mission area and deinduction. Various staff branches at Army Headquarters undertake these responsibilities and the overall effort necessitates a high degree of coordination and cooperation for smooth execution of the mission. Detailed guidelines and instructions will be laid down by the branches concerned.

Training: There are some differences in the methodologies of functioning, as compared to standard practices in the Indian Army, when operating under the UN flag and the earmarked contingent must train for these. The contingent will be briefed in detail regarding the nature of mission and envisaged tasks. Before induction, contingents will train for aspects such as peacekeeping operations and CI operations in addition to language training (if required). Other subjects to be covered are:

- Interpretation of directives such as Rules of Engagement.
- Contingent management at unit and sub unit levels.
- Public relations, media management and interaction with nongovernment organisations.
- Human rights, humanitarian affairs and legal matters.
- Logistic planning and contingent profiling under the new UN policies of wet and dry lease systems.
- Pay and allowances including method of reimbursement.

LOGISTICS

Functions, Principles and Logistic Support Systems

The territorial vastness and the geographical diversity of our country preclude application of a standard logistic template. The road and rail communications infrastructure in border areas is underdeveloped and availability of local resources is largely inadequate.

Thus, inter and intratheatre moves are timeconsuming and switching of logistic resources is difficult to execute. From the operational point of view, such conditions call for adequate stocks to be maintained at the theatre and sector levels to undertake operations at short notice.

Our logistic support system ensures that each theatre of operation is selfcontained and selfsustaining for the initial phases. In the long term there is a need to integrate the logistic resources of the three Services and utilise the existing national infrastructure more profitably to economise on overall effort.

Relationship between Strategy, Logistics and Operational Plans

Logistics is a command function and is the lifeline of an operational plan. No operational plan can succeed without a sound logistic plan and commanders must view operations and logistics as being interdependent. The three major responsibilities of a military high command are to create, support and employ combat forces. Therefore all major military decisions need a blend of strategy and logistics which are inseparable.

Logistics govern the fundamental relationship between strategy, military capability, scope and timing of operations. The composition, balance and deployment of forces, along with the rate of build up, are all determined by the complex interrelationship between strategic, logistic and technical considerations. In the course of an operation adequate logistic support must be ensured to sustain and regenerate combat power so that the assigned operational and strategic objectives are effectively accomplished in time.

The relationship between strategy, logistics and operational plans may be expressed as follows:

- Strategy determines the required level of military capability.
- Logistics sustain the military capability.
- Operational plans exploit military and logistic capability.

The relationship between the levels of war and logistic support is given below:

- *Strategic Level.* Involves national strategic security objectives and use of national resources to accomplish these objectives and encompasses the industrial base, mobilisation, strategic lift (air and sea), capabilities, procurement, material readiness, strategic stockpiles and regeneration.
- *Operational Level.* Links the employment of forces to strategic objectives and includes reception, staging, sustainment, redeployment, theatre distribution, intermediate intratheatre airlift and reconstitution.
- *Tactical Level.* Deals with the employment and manoeuvre of units in relation to the enemy in order to use their full potential and involves arming, manning, feeding, transporting and sustaining soldiers.

Principles of Logistics

Logistic planning must be simple and responsive to the needs of the operational situation. It should be based on the principles outlined below:

- *Foresight.* It is the ability to foresee operational requirements and involves identifying, stocking and maintaining the minimum resources and capabilities necessary to meet logistic requirements.
- *Simplicity.* Simplicity implies avoiding complexity in both planning and executing logistic operations.
- *Flexibility.* This is the ability to adapt logistic structures and procedures to changing situations and operational plans.
- *Economy.* Providing the most efficient support to accomplish the mission exemplifies economy.

Commanders must aim to achieve economy by prioritising and allocating resources.

- *Coordination*. This implies exploiting, synchronizing and coordinating logistic resources and infrastructure at the national and interService levels.
- *Protection*. Logistic installations are vulnerable to long range and precisionguided weapons. Survivability can be enhanced by decentralized logistics, limiting logistic assets in forward area and dispersing them widely.

Logistic Support System

The basic tenet of logistic philosophy is that the logistic support system must be responsive to the operational needs of the commander. As a philosophy, defence logistic development should be integrated with the national infrastructure and national development plans. It should determine the broad framework for the country's development of logistic infrastructure to meet national objectives. The basic aim should be to ensure optimum utilisation of national resources, industrial mobilisation and achieve costeffectiveness.

A joint approach in interService logistics is essential to ensure economy. A centralised agency is required for higher direction, control and coordination of the logistic effort amongst the three Services and to provide an interface between Service Headquarters and other government and nongovernment agencies. Concurrently there is a need to optimally utilise the considerable infrastructure of the private sector, trade and local resources to enhance the military logistic capability.

An efficient logistic structure contributes greatly towards meeting the requirements of the field force. This is particularly relevant in the context of the Indian Army which is deployed over a vast geographical spread in varied terrain and climatic conditions. Catering to its requirements in such an environment demands the following from the logistic infrastructure :

- A streamlined chain with lean organisations to eliminate multiplicity and repeated handling and thereby increase the velocity of logistic support.

- A 'sense and respond' system working on the 'push' model to increase user satisfaction.
- An efficient inventory management system to reduce excessive stocks. In this regard, procurement of commercially offtheshelf equipment is a viable alternative.
- Quick and effective casualty evacuation and management. In addition, existing civil medical facilities should be optimally utilised.
- Rapid recovery and redeployment of scarce logistic resources during various phases of operations.
- Specially tailored units for theatrespecific logistic requirements.

FUTURE TRENDS IN LOGISTICS

'Revolution in Military Logistics' is a concept being evolved to create a capabilitybased, modular and a flexible organisation capable of anticipating and predicting logistic requirements with the creation of matching infrastructure and facilities. It proposes a dynamic, distributionbased logistic system that could be projected rapidly and operated efficiently to provide widelydistributed combat forces with uninterrupted fuel and supplies.

With advancements in C4I2SR capabilities, along with automation providing total asset visibility of the logistic support system, it will be possible to introduce a major transformation in catering to user requirements as under:

- Logistic support for the complete spectrum of conflict from CI operations to an allout conventional war against a nuclear backdrop.
- Centralised logistic planning and execution at the highest level incorporating all available national resources and infrastructure and working towards synergy in the logistic support system of the three Services.
- Adopting a logistic support system that is geared to a limited preparatory period and high intensity, short

duration war. This calls for an efficient mobilisation plan which enables rapid move and deployment of formations to designated areas.

- Maintenance of a high state of logistic readiness by reduction in critical logistic voids, high state of equipment serviceability and adequate levels of stocks for selfcontained, theatrebased logistic support in the initial stages without dependence on intertheatre movement of resources.
- Maximum use of dualuse civil resources and infrastructure to enhance military logistic capabilities.
- Adoption of information technologies and decision support systems to improve inventory management and to maximize efficiency.
- Improved survivability of logistic echelons in a high technology weapon environment by dispersion and area air defence cover where possible.
- Adapting to a short duration conflict situation by greater emphasis on intratheatre regeneration and resupply of logistic resources and adoption of maintenance concept of replacement instead of repairs.
- Maximum reliance on aerial resupply for maintenance of momentum especially in mountain and desert terrains.
- Establishing modular and tailormade logistic arrangements for different types of terrain and operational contingencies.
- Retaining flexibility and redundancy in all theatres without resorting to crisis management.
- Redeployment of logistic resources in a balanced manner to permit synergized and wellorchestrated operations without any logistic pauses.

The diversity of terrain and the Indian Army's operational roles pose enormous logistic challenges; these require a dynamic, new approach to logistic support. The vision for the future is to develop a logistic system which is highly effective, responsive and provides the operational commander the freedom and ability to execute his mission successfully. The 'footprint' of logistics for the Army should ensure a seamless and fully networked system that provides information and situation awareness to enable asset visibility and enhanced velocity of logistic support. Concurrently, there is a need to reduce inventories significantly and rely on predictive and realtime information, coupled with rapid transportation, to meet user demands.

Harnessing advanced information technology, use of sensors and reliance on decision support systems will improve logistic efficiency and enhance operational readiness and, thus, reduce the number of personnel involved in the supply chain management. These advancements will significantly impact our operational and logistic philosophy for which future commanders must prepare and ensure a smooth change in logistic management.

PREPARING FOR WAR

Force Structuring

Apart from good training and high morale, the single most important factor which contributes to efficient conduct and success in war is wellstructured forces. Force structures need to be reviewed continually to keep pace with the dynamics of developing strategic scenarios. Advances in technology and shifts in operational concepts also impact significantly on force structures.

Basic Considerations

A very wide variety of factors determine the structures of armies. In the Indian context the following aspects have a major influence on the force structures :

- Prevailing threats and future challenges.
- Operating environments which encompass factors such as terrain and climate.
- Operational roles, tasks and missions allotted to different types of formations.
- Quantity and quality of various weapon systems and equipment available to the Army.

- Availability of funds to undertake changes and modernisation.

The Army will essentially be structured for its primary role. Nonetheless, it should be able to perform it's secondary roles equally well with no change in organisation except that temporary modifications in terms of equipping pattern may have to be resorted to for the purpose as is being done presently in Jammu & Kashmir and in the North Eastern states.

In addition to this, forces specially tailored to conduct CI operations such as Rashtriya Rifles and the Territorial Army units employed for such like tasks have to be suitably equipped.

Structure and Composition

The structure of the Army should ensure that it is capable of the following:

- Contributing to the overall strategic deterrence for preventing war.
- Engaging in all types of operations extending from one to the other end of the spectrum of conflict, by day and by night and in all weather conditions.
- Conducting offensive and defensive operations with the facility of interchanging the roles of various formations when required.
- Operating in all terrain and climatic conditions.
- Taking to battle at short notice for conducting sustained operations in highintensity scenarios against the backdrop of nuclear weapons and the prevailing terrorism and insurgencies.
- Operating jointly with the Indian Navy and Indian Air Force through appropriate structures and mechanisms.
- Ensuring rear area security built into all operational plans.
- Conducting CI operations employing specially designed forces in addition to other units, if required. Towards this end, it should be able to take under command and/

or operate in conjunction with state and central police forces.

- Ensuring a sound and effective logistic system at all times with adequate depth in all material stocks.
- Earmarking specially designated forces, with requisite strategic mobility, to assist friendly countries when such assistance is formally sought by them.

Future wars are likely to be short, highly intense and will involve the use of accurate and very lethal weapon systems. Battle will be fought in all the dimensions concurrently to achieve specified objectives as quickly as possible. Such a battlefield milieu will encompass large battlespaces, involve a variety of weapon and support systems and demand quick decisionmaking from military leaders. Systems and personnel will have to display stamina, robustness and staying power in trying conditions.

To be able to prosecute operations successfully, the Indian Army is gradually progressing towards widening the range of its arsenal. Thus, in addition to the traditional elements of armour, infantry, artillery, air defence, engineers and tactical communications, it is adding newer force multipliers such as wider surveillance, IW capabilities, decision support systems, target acquisition, precision strike and enlarged integral aviation.

The size, shape and composition of the field forces will be tailored to encompass the following types of forces and systems:

- Specially earmarked offensive strike formations, ranging from brigade to corps size, to secure objectives in varying depths in mountain, plains and desert terrains.
- Pivot formations capable of adopting a strong defensive posture and launching offensive operations to complement operations of strike formations.
- Airborne, heliborne, amphibious and Special Forces to operate either independently or in conjunction with other strike forces.
- A widespread grid to provide battlefield transparency

through the use of various types of surveillance and intelligencegathering systems during peace and in war.

- Extensive, secure and reliable communications with inbuilt redundancies, offensive EW systems and electronic counter measures systems.
- The ability to leverage the advantages of modern technologies in the spheres of informatics, communications, C_2.
- Assured and responsive logistic support in all operating environments.

TRAINING

Training Objectives

Training objectives must cater for 'management of change' as well as 'operational adaptation to change'. They must be focused towards achieving the following:

- Training in conventional operations against a nuclear backdrop at one end of the spectrum to fighting insurgency at the other end.
- Planning, training and validation of the conduct of war at operational and strategic levels with the focus on offensive operations in a joint Services environment.
- Implementation of a 'systems approach' to training to make training more focused, taskoriented, objective, costeffective and responsive to future requirements.
- Raising the technical threshold of all ranks to meet future challenges.

Organisation for Training

The conduct of training is a command responsibility. Organisation for training in the Indian Army envisages the control of all aspects of institutional training under Army Training Command with General Staff backup being provided by the Directorate General of Military Training at Army Headquarters. Issues pertaining to technical aspects of training are monitored by Line Directorates of various Arms and Services at Army Headquarters.

Approach to Training

Training in the Army should be based on a methodical and wellresearched scientific approach. A dynamic, comprehensive and operationallyfocused training philosophy is, therefore, a mandatory requirement for producing combatready troops and units.

Training Culture: The focus should be on creating a positive and supportive environment within which unit and subunit commanders can train their commands in a meaningful and realistic manner with minimum distraction and diversion of effort, personnel or resources. Superior commanders should clearly define the training objectives and then allow maximum freedom of action to subordinate commanders. Training must remain operationallyoriented, needbased, contemporary and structured towards practical applications.

Training of Contingency Forces: It is imperative that the forces earmarked for specified contingencies be suitably trained for the assigned operational role. These forces should exercise with and in the areas of their affiliated operational Commands. Training schedules, scope and location of training should be given out by the receiving Command Headquarters.

Training Infrastructure: We should progressively standardise the minimum level of training infrastructure required at unit and formation levels. In addition, the creation of training infrastructure in selected stations and training establishments must be accorded the highest priority. Efforts should continue to ensure increased use of simulators, computerbased training packages and promotion of self education and interactive elearning.

Focus of Training

Operational Level.

- *Joint Operations.* The planning and conduct of joint operations at the theatre level should be further finetuned. All issues related to joint training will conform to policies enunciated by the COSC.
- *Interoperability.* Interoperability between pivot and strike formations at the operational level and frequent

grouping and regrouping would be the norm in future operations. Complete synergy between the pivot and strike corps will be an operational imperative at the theatre level strike corps must develop and refine their capability to operate in varied operational scenarios.

- *Nonlinear Operations.* Increased ranges of weapon systems and improved mobility of all forces, coupled with high technology communications and battlefield surveillance systems, will result in a wider geographical spread over which the available combat power can be employed. Training for fighting an integrated and simultaneous battle across the entire battlespace in the form of close, deep and rear operations should therefore receive greater attention.
- *Manoeuvre Warfare.* As opposed to attrition warfare which focuses on physical destruction, manoeuvre warfare is an approach to battle which lays emphasis on disrupting the enemy commander's ability to make correct and timely decisions rather than attempting to inflict physical causalities. The need to lay greater stress on this approach during training requires no further emphasis.
- *Directive Style of Command.* Intrinsically linked to manoeuvre warfare is the centrality of the role of the leader and the philosophy of directive style of command. The directive style of command must be practised to enable commanders and leaders at appropriate levels to seize the initiative and generate action with maximum freedom in consonance with the higher commander's intent.
- *Training in Logistics.* Recent experiences during Operation Vijay (1999) and Operation Parakram (200102) have highlighted the importance of sound logistic planning and its execution at all levels. With the induction of high technology, sophisticated equipment into our Army, the management of equipment and engineering should receive added attention.
- *Professional Progression and Intellectual Development.*

Officers should be encouraged to develop critical thinking skills and continuously upgrade themselves and widen their horizon. Concurrently, there is a need to train and encourage officers who think 'outside the box' because tomorrow's war could be unconventional (not NBCW) and it is the thinking officer who will carry the day. Additionally, officers need to be formally trained in analysing information and optimising new technological developments that have military applications.

Tactical Level.

- *Basics*. This approach implies a high degree of physical fitness, skill at arms with enhanced emphasis on reflex shooting, fieldcraft, effective handling of equipment, small team operations and the regimental ethos. All training at small team level must be situationbased. Towards this end, possible battle situations must be visualised, analysed, rehearsed and mastered on ground by practical training.
- *Training of Young Officers*. Our young officers are highly motivated, exceptionally courageous and have always led from the front. There is a need to further build upon these sterling attributes through renewed focus on tactical and adventure training. Greater stress should be laid on developing the killer instinct, audacity, originality, innovative thinking, and the spirit of adventure. As leaders they should also be adept at imparting grassroots level tactical training .
- *Training of Junior Leaders and Personnel Below Officer Rank*. The role of junior leaders is to translate intentions of commanders into success. Renewed focus is being given on transforming regimental training centres into 'cradles of excellence'. Human resource development is an essential command function and, in this context, it needs to be understood that the soldier of tomorrow has to be an innovator who can combine imagination and knowledge with action. No amount of emphasis on Junior Commissioned Officers and Non Commissioned Officers training will be enough.

PROFESSIONALISM AND MILITARY ETHOS

The Profession of Arms

Nature and Legitimacy: The laws of armed conflict, encompassing the Geneva and Hague Conventions, set out the duties and responsibilities of commanders and soldiers and the legal parameters within which the military profession must operate. Governed by these longstanding moral and legal imperatives, the profession of arms is a calling established on the following principles:

- Service on behalf of a legitimate moral authority and being answerable to such authority.
- The conduct of military operations within prescribed norms such as the laws of armed conflict and the concept of military chivalry.
- The requirement for members of the profession to uphold a high standard of discipline to protect the weak and defenceless and to always act for the common good.

Function: The aspect of use and control of lethal force is what gives the military profession its unique standing and importance within the broader society that it serves. It must be emphasised that only a good citizen can become a good professional soldier. Having become a member of the armed forces, one must be an exemplary citizen.

Attributes: Responsibility, expertise and loyalty to the nation and the organisation are the hallmarks of the military profession. These are defined within the military context as follows:

- *Responsibility*. Responsibility is reflected in the oath of allegiance that the Indian officer and soldier take on joining the Army as well as the dedicated, apolitical and unbiased manner in which they must serve the nation. Responsibility further requires commanders to render objective professional advice to political leaders, to implement loyally and effectively decisions and policies of the Government, to be responsive to the needs and interests of the personnel under command and to be accountable for actions they take. However, the emphasis must be retained on the need to ensure that the Armed Forces, under no circumstances, are influenced by any sectarian or parochial considerations.

- *Knowledge and Expertise.* Knowledge and expertise are the cornerstones of professionalism. Application of knowledge and expertise to situations on ground with a view to resolve problems constitutes professionalism. This is reflected in the military professional's extensive and authoritative knowledge in all fields related to armed conflict including what constitutes appropriate military actions during peace and war. It encompasses leadership and management skills required for planning, preparing and executing complex military operations as well as a sound understanding of the capabilities of personnel, weapons and equipment. There is a requirement to put in concerted effort to enhance our knowledge and acquire expertise through formal education, selfstudy, training and application of the knowledge imbibed.
- *Loyalty to the Nation and Organisation.* Loyalty resides in the common military identity of members of the Indian Armed Forces and their shared commitment as volunteer citizens in serving the nation. It is derived from high standards of training, selfregulating discipline and strict adherence to the orders and directives of the Service. Loyalty to the organisation includes loyalty to seniors, colleagues and subordinates.

The Military Code

The military code by which we live is much the same as that which guides all honourable men. The major difference lies in the consequences of observing or violating it. For the officer, the consequences go beyond his person as it affects the lives of all the personnel that he commands.

Unlimited Responsibility: Under this unwritten clause of the military contract, members are obliged to carry out duties and tasks without regard to personal safety and, ultimately, be willing to risk and even give up their lives if the situation requires. While unlimited responsibility is generally associated with service in war, it is also present in military service during peace.

The Military Ethos: In the Army the concept of unlimited responsibility is inextricably linked to, and at the same time sustained by, a shared set of beliefs, values, and a moral code commonly known as the military ethos. Military ethos forms the basis of all aspects of service in the Indian Armed Forces, setting forth principles and ideals which men and women of the Army must subscribe to, both, collectively and as individuals. Its fundamental values are integrity, courage, loyalty, selflessness and selfdiscipline. This ethos further requires dedication to country, the upholding of Indian values and commitment to professional excellence. Maintaining the military ethos is critical to the Army's effectiveness in war and its readiness and preparedness in peace.

War and the Professional Soldier: A professional soldier is well aware of the horrors of war and of the need to be prepared for the worst. It is the preparation for war as an inherent part of his training, and the requirement to manage it within established constraints and moral boundaries, which necessitates the military ethos and justifies the profession of arms.

Regimental System: The regimental system is of critical importance to the Army as it is within the regiment or corps that the military ethos is most visibly embodied and practised. Its utility and value lie in the strong sense of comradeship that it fosters amongst members of a regiment or corps and which bonds soldiers together. The regimental system reflects Indian values, history, geography and the particular character of the Indian soldier. Regimental considerations must, however, never be allowed to impinge on professional or operational requirements. Nor should the regimental system be embraced in a way which might fragment or weaken the Army's need for institutional cohesion.

The Moral Contract: In a democracy the profession of arms implies the existence of a moral contract between the soldier and the broader society the soldier serves and is part of. This contract is one of mutual trust, confidence, support and reciprocity. It requires that members of the Indian Armed Forces be provided the tools and resources to do the job expected of them. In return, they are entitled to receive approbation and positive recognition from their fellow Indians. The families of the soldiers who die in battle must be looked after by the society as a part of this moral contract.

High morals and ethics in the Army are necessary for efficiency, effectiveness and maintenance of espritdecorps. Unless these aspects are nurtured throughout the career of the officer there may arise a serious deficiency in the application of our 'Honour Code'. Towards this end, formal instruction in this subject is considered essential.

NO MORE PRINCIPLES OF WAR

For the moment, America's Army has not one but two sets of principles for military operations. The first is the traditional list of nine, last examined in 1993. The second contains principles for operations other than war. The first formally appeared in US Army documents in 1921 (albeit in a slightly different form); the principles of operations other than war (OOTW) were introduced in the 1993 Operations manual. The principles of war have assumed a character of permanence, but soldiers and others have frequently challenged them, believing variously that nuclear weapons, improved understanding of irregular warfare, or the enhanced influence of public opinion and the media had made the list incomplete or no longer of value. The principles have nonetheless changed but slightly. In an army where change is the norm, the principles of war have remained largely unassailable.

Yet the sense of permanence is deceiving, for the history of the current principles of war is a volatile one. Even their presentation as a brief list with concise descriptions is a 20thcentury phenomenon. John I. Alger noted:

The term "principles of war" did not always connote the idea of a list of rules intended to facilitate the conduct of war. In fact, two distinct definitions of the term have been widely used. First, the principles of war represented a commonly accepted philosophy concerning the myriad of activities that collectively compose the conduct of war. In the present century, however, the idea that the principles of war are an enumerated list of considerations, few in number, capable of being simply expressed and essential to the successful conduct of war, has become increasingly accepted. The former definition was used by writers on war for centuries, but the latter, though it has become the standard in Englishspeaking nations, originated in the Napoleonic eraquite possibly with Napoleon himself.

Strategist Bernard Brodie was less reticent when he wrote,

> *Although Clausewitz himself speaks loosely of certain "principles" to be observed and followed,... he specifically rejected the notion that there could be any welldefined body of particular rules or principles that universally dictated one form of behavior rather than another.... It was not until the twentieth century that various army field manuals would attempt to encapsulate centuries of experience and volumes of reflection into a few tersely worded and usually numbered "principles of war." Clausewitz would have been appalled at such attempts, and not surprised at some of the terrible blunders that have been made in the name of those "principles."*

Perhaps Clausewitz would have been appalled; then again, he seems to have recognized that a few words are far easier to recall after fatigue and stress have blurred a leader's mind. "We must have recourse to the relevant principles established by theory," Clausewitz wrote. "These truths should always be allowed to become selfevident.... We will thus avoid using an arcane and obscure language, and express ourselves in plain speech, with a sequence of clear, lucid concepts." Clausewitz, it seems, would have had little problem with the tersely worded principle of "simplicity."

The Army is now revisingfor the second time since 1989its fundamental doctrine. FM 1005, Operations, will have been updated nine times since 1945on average every six yearswhen the 1998 version is published. Among the significant changes presented in the initial drafts of the 1998 edition were these: the "principles of operations other than war" were eliminated, two current principles were revised and two new ones added, and the resulting list was redesignated as "principles of operations." After vigorous debate in the field, with some soldiers strongly favoring the changes and others lending less support, the current draft of Operations leaves the "traditional" nine principles unaltered from their 1986 form.

The inquiring mind might wonder at this support for the status quo. Perhaps it was a reaction to seemingly uncontrollable change in the Army. Perhaps there is a belief within the service that the durability of the principles provides an anchor for Army doctrine. Conversely, the choice for constancy may have been made in ignorance of the origins of the principles and their historic mutability.

This article proceeds from the final proposition above. It has three objectives: first, to describe how the "traditional" principles assumed their current form, and second, to explain why eliminating "principles of operations other than war" is essential. Finally, the article suggests that the modifications and additions to the principles of war originally proposed for the next version of the Army's operational doctrine deserve one more look before we commit the Army's active and reserve components to a set of operational principles that may not yet be quite "all they can be."

THE ORIGINS OF THE PRINCIPLES

The US Army first provided its soldiers a list of principles in 1921. Training Regulation No. 105 listed nine principles of war identical to those in use today with the exception that "movement" and "cooperation" stood in the place of "maneuver" and "unity of command," respectively. This first appearance included no discussion of individual principles. The single paragraph that described their purpose and use also declared them to be "immutable." Charles A. Willoughby, who would later make his name as Douglas MacArthur's World War II Intelligence Chief in the Pacific, took the inviolate status of the principles a step further in his Maneuver in War. "These principles are basic and immutable," he wrote; "the great commanders have been guided by them, and success or failure has depended upon the extent and manner of their use. They are not subject to exception. Their proper execution constitutes the true measure of the military art." Willoughby published his work in 1939, the same year the principles reentered US Army doctrine. They had disappeared after 1928, only to reappear in the 1939 FM 1005, Tentative Field Service Regulations, Operations.

Willoughby traced the origins of these fundamentals, at the time new to the Army. He quoted Napoleon, who wrote that "Caesar's principles were the same as those of Alexander and Hannibal:

(a) to keep his forces in junction,

(b) not to be vulnerable in any direction, [and]

(c) to advance rapidly on important points."

From these, Willoughby believed, "One can hardly fail to recognize:

(a) the principle of concentration,

(b) the principle of security, and

(c) the principle of the objective."

Willoughby went on to extract what he thought was a comprehensive and concise list of Napoleon's principles by culling them from the emperor's writings, concluding that they included objective, offensive, mass, surprise, security, and movement. British military theorist J. F. C. Fuller did not concur with Willoughby's approach, believing that Napoleon laid "down no definite principles, yet he apparently worked by welldefined ones."

As Alger recognized, Napoleon and other pre20thcentury practitioners and theorists of war believed that war had fundamental rules, but they felt no compulsion to attempt their concise articulation.Nor did these earlier soldiers agree on the extent to which a commander was constrained by such rules. Writing in the first half of the 19th century, Jomini asserted that "the fundamental principles upon which rest all good combinations of war have always existed, and to them all others should be referred for the purpose of arriving at their respective merits. These principles are unchangeable; they are independent of the arms employed, of times, and of places." His contemporary Clausewitz did not share this sense of the principles' universality. Clausewitz concluded that the principles were important as guides rather than Jomini's rules "upon which rest all good combinations of war." Clausewitz continued:

Where the arch of truth culminates in such a keystone this tendency will be underlined. But this is simply in accordance with the scientific law of reason, to indicate the point at which all lines converge, but never to construct an algebraic formula for use on the battlefield. Even these principles and rules are intended to provide a thinking man with a frame of reference for the movements he has been trained to carry out, rather than to serve as a guide which at the moment of action lays down precisely the path he must take.

Both men agreed that principles of war existed; both discussed them at some length; neither provided the brief list that today's soldiers have come to expect.

Perhaps no Western military writer put more thought into the possibility that war's actions could be characterized by a single set of principles than J. F. C. Fuller. His lists evolved as he mulled over their nuances in many of his books and articles written before, during, and after the First World War. In his 1926 The Foundations of the Science of War, he listed three groups of principles, each of which itself contained three principles of war:

- *Principles of Control*: direction, determination, and mobility
- *Principles of Pressure*: concentration, surprise, and offensive action
- *Principles of Resistance*: distribution, endurance, and security

Fuller explained the relationship among the groups as follows: "We thus obtain a threefold order of control springing from a dual order of pressure and resistance, each of these dual forces being in itself a threefold one. Ultimately these three groups form one groupeconomy of force."

Fuller's contemporary B. H. Liddell Hart joined what was a growing fascination in Western armies with his discussion of maxims. Though Liddell Hart refused to call them principles in his 1932 The British Way in Warfare (for his were "practical guides, not abstract principles"), he nevertheless concluded that "the principles of war, not merely one principle, can be condensed into a single word`concentration.'

But for truth this needs to be amplified as the `concentration of strength against weakness.'... Here we have a fundamental principle whose understanding may prevent the fundamental error (and the most common) that of giving your opponent freedom and time to concentrate to meet your concentration." Liddell Hart went on to list his six maxims, saying "four are positive and two negative. They apply both to strategy and to tactics":

- Choose the line (or course) of least expectation.
- Exploit the line of least resistance.
- Take a line of operations which offers alternative objectives.
- Ensure that both plan and dispositions are elastic, or adaptable.
- Don't lunge whilst your opponent can parry.
- Don't renew an attack along the same line (or in the same form) after it has once failed.

With their reemergence in the US Army's 1939 Tentative FM 1005, the nine principles listed in the 1921 Training Regulation 105, Doctrine, Principles, and Methods, took the form of seven"General Principles" for use during the "conduct of war":

- Ultimate objective
- Concentration of superior forces, which required "strict economy in the strength of forces assigned to secondary missions"

- Offensive action, though "a defensive attitude may, however, be deliberately adopted as a temporary expedient"
- Unity of effort
- Surprise
- Security
- Simple and direct plans

There was no list of principles in the 1941 FM 1005. The reader was instead presented with several "doctrines of combat": ultimate objective, simple and direct plans and methods, unity of effort, offensive action, concentration of superior forces, surprise, and security. Only with the arrival of the 1949 FM 1005 did the principles of war match those in that manual's 1993 counterpart. The current, seemingly sacred, list of nine principles is therefore only 49 years old.

13

WAR AND THE MODERN ENVIRONMENT OF CONFLICT

Though the purpose and utility of principles of war were apparent to many military theorists in the first half of the 20th century, the introduction of nuclear weapons, increased influence of irregular warfare, and other changes caused some to question their value. Writing during the second decade of the Cold War, John Keegan concluded that "one of the purposes behind the principles has been to make new and strange circumstances comprehensible, to draw a thread from one war to another, to force events into a mold, and to make conflicts obey the dramatic unities....

A point is reached in the development of weapon systems beyond which one cannot compare the present and the past." Keegan went on to argue that the principles inherently implied "maximization of means," and therefore they were applicable to neither limited nuclear war nor modern conventional war.

The latter demanded "subtle response, patience, selfcontrol, firmness but not ruthlessness, and an ability to settle for something less than total victory," qualities Keegan implied were not supported by the nine principles of war.

That the application of those principles demanded adjustment of the means to the political objective, notably that all principles were ultimately subordinate to that of the "objective," did not enter into Keegan's argument. He seems to have had little faith that Western military leaders of the era could apply the principles with the skill Clausewitz, Fuller, and others required.

At the other extreme were arguments that the principles had universal application, that they were "a collection of concise rules for warfare intended to aid battle leaders from the lowranking officer to the general. Whether these rules are called principles, maxims, or axioms, they are independent of time, place, and situation." Such an argument was alluring on the surface; it would have been convenient if true, but the principles themselves had changed repeatedly both in appearance and substance since their 1921 introduction.

These changes were necessary to ensure that the principles maintained pace with doctrinal changes, changes themselves in part driven by advances in technology, adaptations by adversaries and potential adversaries, better understanding of military theory, and revisions in national strategy. The 1939 principle of "concentration," for example, was altered not only in form (later appearing as "mass"), but in substance over the ensuing decades. Limited ranges and the directfire nature of artillery in Napoleon's time meant that concentration required the bringing together of many soldiers and weapons at a given place and time on the battlefield. Later such concentration was not only unnecessarytechnology permitted massing effects while leaving the means dispersedit was potentially counterproductive. Rigid application of the principles, dictated rather than demonstrated by previous applications, was likely to promote failure rather than success.

Writing in Military Review in 1991, William C. Bennett understood the need for flexibility in applying the principles. He concluded that the principles of war in fact applied to actions that were outside the traditional scope of what was meant by war. Discussing Operation Just Cause in Panama (198990), he noted, "Certain events indicate that when the principles of war are applied to shortduration contingency operations in a [lowintensity conflict] environment, the interpretation of the principles must be viewed within a broader context than normal.

The forms that some of the principles may take are likely to be less traditional or `military' and more `police' or `political' in nature." The earliest introduction of the principles in the

1921 training regulations had shared this vision of greater scope during application: "Their application varies with the situation... not only in purely military work, but in administration and business operation.... All active military operations will be planned and executed in accordance with these principles."

Like those of the Army, the principles of war for other US armed services have changed over time. At one time the Air Force added "timing and tempo," "logistics," and "cohesion" to the list of nine it shared with the Army. The Navy and Air Force currently use the same nine principles of war listed in the Army's 1993 FM 1005 and Joint Pub 1, but unsurprisingly the definitions and applications vary somewhat. In Fleet Marine Force Manual (FMFM) 1, Warfighting, the Marine Corps speaks to "two concepts of such significance and universality that we can advance them as principles: concentration and speed." Otherwise the manual only alludes to the nine currently in use by the other services in their primary operational manuals. The Marine Corps also refers (in FMFM 13, Tactics) to "principles of tacticsgaining a decisive advantage, moving faster than the enemy, trapping the enemy, and the goal of all of them, achieving a decisive result." By implication, cooperation appears to be another element in this list.

US ARMY'S PRINCIPLES IN APPLICATION

Virtually all students of war have considered the principles and their applicability to combat operations sometime during their careers. The value of principles to such operations is readily apparent. It is less so, however, when the nature of the operations in question varies from those from which the principles evolved. This is the case when considering irregular warfare, space operations, weapons of mass destruction, or military activities that fall outside the range of those associated with traditional forms of conventional conflict. Many agreed with Keegan that the principles had little value when considering nuclear war. Others recognized tne need for adaptation rather than disposal; John O. Shoemaker concluded, "the principles of war have definite application to the Cold War.... In the military profession great stress is laid upon reducing problems to terms that can be easily understood. More important perhaps is the effort devoted to defining objectives, tasks, and desired goals in sufficient detail and clarity that they cannot be misunderstood."

Josiah A. Wallace similarly concluded that the principles were sufficiently robust to serve as guides to actions in counterinsurgencies, finding they were an "excellent device for the commander to use in analyzing all aspects of his counterinsurgency plans. If his plans conform to the principles of war, he is on firm ground." James H. Mueller likewise concluded that the principles of war were applicable to air, space, and aerospace doctrine and operations.

Although military requirements and political objectives might differ widely, conclusions that support application of the principles of war to nuclear scenarios, irregular warfare contingencies, and space applications are unlikely to surprise students of conflict. The capabilities needed and technologies applied may differ profoundly from case to case, but the fundamental subordinate relationship of military force to national objectives is still the same as that explained by Clausewitz: "The political objectthe original motive for the warwill thus determine both the military objective to be reached and the amount of effort it requires."

PRINCIPLES OF NOT ONLY WAR

Similar reasoning makes an apparent oxymoron logical: the application of the principles of war to military operations not involving war. Many, if not all, of the principles appear to be of value when executing nonwartime operations just as they have been during war.

Emory R. Helton concluded that six of the nine principles of warobjective, offensive, security, unity of command, economy of force, and simplicityapplied to Operation Provide Comfort in northern Iraq conducted after the 1991 Persian Gulf War, and that "five of these will probably apply to any future humanitarian operations." There is every reason to believe that mass, maneuver, and surprise would apply to operations that focused on stability or support requirements.

General Pershing perceived this wider application of the principles. There were considerable changes in the character of war over the span of his career, "but the principles of warfare as I learned them at West Point remain unchanged," he wrote. "They were verified by my experience in our Indian wars, and also during the campaign against the Spaniards in Cuba. I applied them in the Philippines and observed their application in Manchuria during the RussoJapanese War."

More recently, Richard Rinaldo argued that it was counterproductive to separate principles guiding war and operations other than war (OOTW): "This distinction seeks to create independence where there is interdependence, division where there is unity." Rinaldo went on to posit, much as did Pershing, that "the principles of war... are robust enough to withstand application across the full range of military operations.... OOTW is an unnecessary category for doctrinal treatment in terms of principles and fundamental guidelines." Brodie concurred in this regard, concluding that the principles were "essentially common sense propositions which are generally but by no means exclusively pertinent to the waging of war."

The principles of war have indeed been more robust than a narrow interpretation of their purpose would admit. Their application always demands careful consideration of the requirements unique to a given situation; with adaptation and exercise of the coup d'oeil so treasured by Clausewitz, however, this application is feasible even beyond the bounds of the battlefield.

Such adaptation implies flexibility not only in application, but in the definitions of the principles. Roger A. Beaumont believed "the list should be continually reviewed and updated, and used as a working tool for analysis.... New technologies of war may alter the balance and make new factors paramount. The military art, like any other, is continually in a state of evolution, with part of its nature formed by the past and the materials, and its essence deriving from the innovative genius of the artist."

Wellconsidered combinations of the principles have been the recipe for success whether applied to war or operations in other environments. At times one or several principles have dominated our thinking. In some instances a principle has been irrelevant or of greater value in its violation than in its observation. Again, however, more often than not the force that better applied the wisdom inherent in the principles was the victor:

Successful strategists never knowingly violate the principles of war unless they first evaluate the risks and estimate expenses.... Critics notwithstanding, the principles of war are utilitarian and they do make sense. The record shows that winners, by and large, took heed of the principles. The losers, discounting those who were overcome by sheer weight of manpower and material, by and large did not.

With the publication of its revised doctrine in the 1998 FM 1005, the Army plans to close the philosophical gap that has developed between combat operations and those not involving overt fighting. That is an essential outcome of this round of analysis of its warfighting doctrine. The first operation conducted by the fledgling US Army under the Constitution was not during wartime; it was an action to restore peace and stability to portions of Pennsylvania affected by the Whiskey Rebellion. Led by President Washington himself, the Army's threatened intervention ended the trouble in an operation that would today be considered a successful operation other than war. The preemptive character of the threat of force did not fundamentally alter the nature of the military action.

Similarly, soldiers preparing in 1998 for operations in Bosnia have had to undergo the same personal and unit readiness training required to prepare for armed conflict. Differences in rules of engagement altered neither the need for thorough preparation nor the utility of the principles during that preparation. Today's operational environment demands an expanded role for soldiers; being a warrior is still a necessary, but no longer a sufficient, qualification for service. The existing two lists of principles simply fail to emphasize what is common to any Army operation in the field.

These two lists imply difference where there is similarity. Simplicity is a principle of war, yet not of OOTW, to which it obviously applies in equal measure. Legitimacy is the reverse, cited as a principle of OOTW but not of war. It seems at first glance that legitimacy ought to be a principle of both war and OOTW, but one must again consider the role of principles. If they are in fact guides to action (rather than unquestioned truths with universal application to every military operation), then legitimacy is far better treated as an essential condition of any operation rather than as a principle. Unlike a principle that a commander can ignore (albeit at risk to success), no commander can reject legitimacy as the fundamental basis for a military operation.

War is one form of military operations, the most demanding, expensive, and traumatic of them all. But recent events reflect the historical experience of the US Army: combat is one of the least common of the kinds of operations conducted by the majority of those in the service. It is by no means the most frequent, and in some respects it can be less complicated than armed interventions in which the actions of a squad leader can have strategic implications. Consequently, one list of principlesand we should call them principles of operationsshould serve the full range of military operations. There would be no requirement for every principle to apply in equal measure to every activity, nor for some to apply to given contingencies at all. Yet each element on this established list would merit status as a principle in part because it requires consideration during planning and execution even if it is ultimately not applicable.

TOWARD CLARITY AND SYNTHESIS

Review of the longstanding principles of war was a natural starting point for developing a single list of principles of operations. But the recommendations from the field to retain the pre1993 set of principles of "war" and simply to dispose of the principles of operations other than war misses an opportunity. We have learned lessons in this postCold War era that deserve to be incorporated into the Army's next statement of land force doctrine. That we were coping with a flawed premise about the common features of any Army operation, combat or other, in no way invalidates those lessons. This section therefore provides the rationale for continuing on the course previously charted for the next version of FM 1005, Operations: take what's useful from our experiences in all recent operations, identify opportunities to adapt, and do so.

Table, below, lists the principles of war and operations other than war as they appear in Army doctrine in early 1998, and identifies the principles originally proposed for the next version. The discussion addresses principlesnew and modifiedthat ought to appear among those adopted by the Army in 1998.

Principles of War	Principles of Operations Other than War	Principles of Operations
Objective	Objective	Objective
Offensive	Perseverance	Offensive
Mass	Legitimacy	Massed Effects
Economy of Force	Restraint	Economy of Force
Maneuver		Maneuver
Unity of Command	Unity of Effort	Unity of Effort
Security	Security	Security
Surprise		Surprise
Simplicity		Simplicity
		Morale
		Exploitation

Principles of War and Operations Other than War (as in 1993 FM 1005, Operations) and Principles of Operations as proposed in Initial Draft, 1998 FM 1005, Operations.

Principle of Operations: Massed Effects (modified, previously "mass")

Though "mass" was one of the principles on the original 1921 Training Regulation 105 list, by the time FM 1005 was published in 1939 "concentration" appeared in its stead. The 1993 FM 1005 guidance regarding mass is clear and pertinent: "Mass the effects of overwhelming combat power at the decisive place and time." Unfortunately, "mass" is frequently neither understood nor applied in this manner. When Phillip Meilinger wrote that "precision air weapons have redefined the meaning of mass.... The result of the trend towards 'airshaft accuracy' in air war is a denigration in the importance of mass," he could not have been more incorrect. First, firepower is but one capability that a commander seeks to mass. Second, precision weapons are potentially a critical component of mass as it is construed today: the concentration of effects to accomplish the mission. If one missile, bomb, or artillery projectile can achieve a desired outcome, it is a supremely effective and efficient application of the principle of mass. The principle of "mass" no longer means what the concept seemed to mean in Napoleonic times: to bring together in time and space soldiers or supporting weapons. Such practices now and in the future could create conditions more likely to lead to disaster than to success by creating lucrative targets for an adversary's air and surface fire capabilities.

Nor is mass only the concentration of all fires in time and space. The concept implies the massing of the effects of all pertinent capabilities, military and other: Army assets (armor, artillery, and aviation); joint support (intelligence means, aviation, naval gunfire, and missiles); special forces; psychological operations; electronic warfare, and other means that could contribute to mission success. Whether it is steel, electrons, and convincing words applied to defeat an enemy, or the use of food and water, medical care, and engineering capabilities to aid refugees, the intent is to create and maintain success through the massing of the effects inherent in these capabilities. R. R. Battreall similarly misunderstood the application of the principle of mass when he wrote, "When a sufficient amount of armor is massed at one point, it becomes the critical point." "Mass" has too long been misunderstood; "massed effects" is the better term.

Principle of Operations: Unity of Effort (modified, previously "unity of command")

As has been noted, "cooperation" rather than "unity of command" was among the original principles of war in 1921. Unity of effort, with unity of command and cooperation as supporting concepts, first appeared in the 1939 manual as the preferred statement of this principle. Unity of effort remained the principle in the 1941 Operations manual, with subtle changes, but by 1949 the term was unity of command. This change occurred despite the fact that words used to describe it were identical to those used in the 1941 edition.

Consider how this principle (or doctrine of combat, in the case of the 1941 manual) was defined between 1939 and 1949 as successive authors struggled with the distinction between the desired form (unity of command) and function (unity of effort) over the 11year span (emphasis in the originals):

1939: "Unity of effort is necessary to apply effectively the full combat power of the available forces. It is obtained through unity of command. Where this is impracticable, dependence must be placed upon cooperation."

1941: "Unity of command obtains that unity of effort which is essential to the decisive application of full combat power of the available forces. Unity of effort is furthered by full cooperation between elements of the command."

1949: "Unity of command obtains that unity of effort which is essential to the decisive application of full combat power of the available forces. Unity of effort is furthered by full cooperation between elements of the command. Command of a force of joint or combined arms is vested in the senior officer present eligible to exercise command unless another is specifically designated to command."

The principle of unity of command that appeared in the 1993 FM 1005 stated that "for every effort," military leaders were to "seek unity of command and unity of effort." Unity of effort under the principles of operations other than war in the same manual directed soldiers to "seek unity of effort toward every objective."

Unity of command has historically been hard to attain. James Winnefeld called it "the single most difficult principle to gain in combined warfare.... Relinquishing national command and control of force is an act of trust and confidence that is unequaled in relations between nations. In a coalition it is achieved by constructing command arrangements and taskorganizing forces to ensure that responsibilities match contributions and efforts.... It is cardinal that compromises not be permitted to outweigh warfighting requirements."

Anthony Rice found unity of command "more honored in the breach than the observance" in recent American wars and joint doctrine. What he called "parallel command" has been far more common, a situation in which nations share common objectives but retain control of their forces.

Rice provided several examples, including Douglas Haig's World War I statement in 1915 that "I am not under General Joffre's orders, but that would make no difference, as my intention was to do my utmost to carry out General Joffre's wishes on strategic matters as if they were orders."

Haig made that decision following guidance from the British War Minister Lord Kitchener that his command "is an independent one and you will in any case not come under the orders of any allied general."

Rice concluded that unity of command "was never established among the forces arrayed initially against the Nazis." Further, although the United States was the "lead nation" during the Korean War, in Vietnam "the command structure seemed to take a step back in time.... A parallel command structure was adopted" instead.

During Operation Desert Storm, Rice observed, the coalition "achieved a marked improvement on the command arrangements for Vietnam, but still did not achieve unity of command." The US Army failed to establish local unity of command of even Army personnel in Somalia little more than two years later; the deaths of 18 soldiers in combat on 34 October 1993 was in no small part attributable to this failure.

Rice strongly endorsed unity of command despite the historical record and a joint doctrine that emphasized unity of effort. et he acknowledged that the emphasis in joint doctrine on unity of effort, despite ground truth that unity of command is the much preferred condition, reflected awareness that the latter has historically been difficult or impossible to achieve. This difficulty has been increased by the lack of clearly articulated national and international objectives during many operations. When military commanders must attempt to define and justify such objectives based on vague guidance or public statements, participants in operations may find it difficult to come to a consensus on end states, much less on the manner to achieve them.

Finally, there are organizations that may share general goals in a theater of operations but refuse to subordinate themselves to military authority. Some nongovernmental and private volunteer organizations (NGOs and PVOs) might respond to coercion or cajoling, but others will invariably remain autonomous.

A commander might consider withdrawing security or other support for these agencies in an attempt to compel compliance, but the strategic implications of casualties among NGO and PVO personnel makes such a policy infeasible.

Unity of command, then, is the preferred form of coordination and control. Unity of effort, the desired effects of which are achievement of a "common purpose and direction through unity of command, coordination, and cooperation," is the operational function that is the prerequisite to success.

Without unity of effort, any organization's work can negate the advances made by others. Unity of effort is the function we require for success in any operation; unity of command is the form we should seek to attain it. The operational principle is unity of effort.

PRINCIPLE OF OPERATIONS: MORALE (NEW)

In Ardant Du Picq's view, "Hannibal was the greatest general of antiquity by reason of his admirable comprehension of the morale of combat, of the morale of the soldier, whether his own or the enemy's."

A lengthy discussion of leadership in the 1939 FM 1005 asserted that "man is the fundamental instrument in war.... War places a severe test on the moral stamina... of the individual." John Baynes, in Morale, the classic study of the 2d Scottish Rifles in World War I, concluded that "the maintenance of morale is recognized in military circles as the most important single factor in war; outside these circles there is sometimes difficulty in appreciating why this is so."

Franklin D. Jones provided an explanation for both the soldier's recognition of the paramount importance of morale and his civilian counterpart's lack of appreciation of that importance: "Nowhere in civilian life is the social group of such major and crucial importance in the life of the individual as it is for the soldier in combat."

Maintenance of soldier and unit morale requires the building, maintaining, and restoration of fighting spirit. Morale includes the willingness to work together consistently for a common purpose, which in the Army is frequently the accomplishment of whatever tasks are assigned to the group of which the soldier is a member. Individuals and organizations have morale, and the good morale of both is essential to success in any military operation.

The difficulty in building and maintaining this most desirable quality is complicated by its multiple components. Selfconfidence is crucial, commitment to the unit essential, willingness to sacrifice for the whole a requirement. Field Marshal Sir William Slim provided additional fundamental elements that included those considered necessary by many others who have studied the subject:

Morale [has] certain foundations. These foundations are spiritual, intellectual, and material, and that is the order of their importance...

1. Spiritual

(a) There must be a great and noble object.

(b) Its achievement must be vital.

(c) The method of achievement must be active, aggressive.

2. Intellectual

(a) [The soldier] must be convinced that the object can be attained; that it is not out of reach.

(b) He must see, too, that the organization to which he belongs and which is striving to attain the object is an efficient one.

(c) He must have confidence in his leaders and know that whatever dangers and hardships he is called upon to suffer, his life will not be lightly flung away.

3. Material

(a) The man must feel that he will get a fair deal from his commanders and from the army generally.

(b) He must, as far as humanly possible, be given the best weapons and equipment for his task.

(c) His living and working conditions must be made as good as they can be.

Clausewitz considered victory in hand for the side that imposed its will on the other. That concept applies to the full range of military operations and to all parties who influenceor have the potential to influencethose operations.

The importance of robust morale to our own forces is apparent, but other groups have a say in whether American military undertakings will be successful. The first such group is the adversary. If operations truly involve a struggle of wills, then undermining an adversary's morale complements (and could be an alternative to) force destruction as a means of attaining one's political and military objectives.

The greater the success of psychological operations, continuous pressure, imposed confusion, maintenance of information dominance, and other assaults on his assurance, the less other means of influence will be needed and the sooner opposition will cease.

Successful attacks on morale are likely to prove far less costly than destruction of the personnel and equipment of an opposing force. In an era when even enemy casualties may be counterproductive in achieving a desired end state, undermining morale may be the only means of attaining or exploiting early successes.

Second, noncombatants in an area of operations can be ambivalent toward friendly military activities, can act in support of friendly force efforts, or can actively resist them. The presence of diverse groups of noncombatants means that all three conditions can occur simultaneously, and groups obviously can change behavior over time. History has demonstrated that failure to consider the effects of apparent noncombatants on military operations can prove costly.

Napoleon's forces in Spain and Germans in the Soviet Union during World War II paid the price of failing to win the support, or at a minimum the neutrality, of local citizens who later chose to become effective partisans.

The principle of morale, then, includes consideration of these noncombatants. Their disposition must be continuously monitored and shaped, if not to ensure support for friendly activities, then at a minimum to foster the ambivalence that denies an adversary their support.

Another essential component of noncombatant considerations is the American public. Clausewitz acknowledged the importance of a nation's populace; one part of his trinity was "primordial violence, hatred, and enmity," which he concluded "mainly concerns the people."

Thomas Vaughn wrote that "in a democracy such as ours, morale is also a function of national consensus." Donn A. Starry noted the dangers of an American tendency to call on the military in support of national objectives "without first having laid the requisite groundwork to attain and sustain strong public support for the policy course adopted." Herbert Wolff, writing in 1965, presciently declared "to win in Vietnam we require public support" and concluded such backing would prove to be so critical that public support should be "the tenth principle of war."

And while the armed forces cannot exert direct influence on the American public, US military leaders at the highest levels are in a position to suggest that political leaders recognize the need to maintain citizen support for their armed forces during an operation.

That morale was a necessary condition to success in military operations was evident to George C. Marshall, who described it as "a state of mind. It is steadfastness, courage and hope. It is confidence and zeal and loyalty. It is élan, esprit de corps, and determination. It is staying power, the spirit which endures to the endthe will to win. With it, all things are possible, without it everything else, planning, preparation, production, count for naught." Morale is a primary concern of commanders in peace and war. It deserves to be a principle of operations.

PRINCIPLE OF OPERATIONS

While US military forces have often demonstrated a superb ability to identify objectives and accomplish missions, often they have done less well at capitalizing on resultant successes. Success, be it in the form of military victory or mission accomplishment in a humanitarian operation, may prove transitory if not seized upon quickly.

The military must set the conditions for exploiting successes, whether the exploitation is to be completed through the execution of other American military actions or after a transfer of operational responsibility to others. The principle of exploitation, as it appeared in the initial draft of the 1998 FM 1005, advised soldiers to "take advantage of and make lasting the temporary effects of battlefield success."

Commenting on an earlier effort to add "exploitation" as a principle of war, Wolff wrote that it failed "to stand on [its] own merits.... Exploitation [is] subordinate to the principles of maneuver and objective." He was correct, for exploitation as a type of offensive operation is a function of other principles. However, the concept of exploitation presented here has a much broader scope.

It is by no means limited to combat operations, for it applies equally to any mission. It also pertains to capitalizing on all successes, and planning to do so even before achievement of success. Too often commanders and staffs develop plans for worstcase scenarios; they too rarely plan for greater success than might normally be expected.

The cumulative effects of multiple sequential or simultaneous successes are also seldom wargamed. In discussing exploitation as a potential principle of war, the authors of Military Strategy: Theory and Application supported a wider application for the concept: The principle of exploitation encourages momentum. It makes it possible for friendly elements to expand and consolidate gains, keeping the enemy off balance and on the defensive. Sage strategists follow the lines of least resistance that lead to vital objectives, pour on the pressure when opponents falter, reinforce successes, and abandon failures. Strategic exploitation involves far more than capitalizing on military advantage. It profits equally from political, economic, or psychological primacy and augments technological leads.

These observations apply with equal validity at the operational and tactical levels, in combat as well as noncombat operations. Exploitation, in its broadest strategic and operational context, should be added to the list of principles of operations.

CONCLUSION

The concept of adopting principles of operations as replacements for principles of war at first glance seems simple, but there is little simple about the conduct of war or any other aspect of the profession of arms.

Interventions in Haiti and Bosnia demonstrated that the absence of armed opposition in an operational area does not lessen the rigor of activities demanded of forces committed to such interventions.

Principles of operations assist in the study of the profession; understanding them and applying them wisely in the field is in turn possible only after repeated, careful analysis of their purpose and meaning. Experience may partially compensate for lack of study, but application of the principles will likely suffer from the unwilling student's inability to fully understand their value in establishing desired operational end states and achieving national strategic objectives. So too will soldiers suffer in executing the orders of those who have failed to educate themselves.

History reveals that the principles of war have frequently been the subject of long and often inspired debate; their character, number, and definition have changed repeatedly. They took their present form in US Army doctrine only 49 years ago. On the one hand, this span is but a fraction of the years spent in their study. On the other, much has transpired since 1949. One may legitimately ask whether the principles as they stand could meet the needs of US armed forces half a century from now.

The US Army has an unusual opportunity to expand and modify its list of principles of operations. The absence of a major threat to the United States and its allies makes such an effort both timely and feasible; it would complement efforts to determine requirements for force structure and weapon systems for the opening decades of the 21st century. This article restates the need for the synthesis of principles of war and of operations other than war in our operational doctrine, and demonstrates the benefits of acknowledging that the basic tenets of doctrine transcend conflict. As always, our doctrine must prepare us to prevail in war; the next version can and should, however, be expanded to reflect the lessons we have learned since the end of the Cold War.

BIBLIOGRAPHY

Alger, John I: *The Quest For Victory*, Westport, Greenwood Press, 1982.

Arend, A.: *International Law and the Use of Force,* London, Routledge, 1993.

Arrighi, G.: *The Long Twentieth Century: Money, Power and the Origins of Our Times,* N.Y., Verso Press, 1994.

Bellamy, C.: *Knights in White Armour: The New Art of War and Peace,* London, Random House, 1997.

Bellamy, Christopher: *The future of land warfare*, London, Croom Helm 1987.

Bond, B.: *The Pursuit of Victory: From Napoleon to Saddem Hussein,* Oxford, Oxford Univ. Press, 1996.

Campen, Allen D.: *The first information war*, Fairfax, AFCEA Press, 1992.

Chilcoat, Richard A: *Strategic art: the new discipline for 21st century leaders*, Carlisle Barracks, Strategic Studies Institute, 1995.

Collins, John M.: *Military space forces: the next 50 years*, Washington, Pergamon-Brassey's, 1989.

Damrosch, L.F.: *Law and Force in the New International Order,* Boulder, Westview Press, 1991.

Delanda, M.: *War in the Age of Intelligent Machines,* N.Y., M.I.T. Press, 1991.

DuBois, Edmund L., Wayne P. Hughes, and Lawrence J. Low: *A Concise Theory of Combat*, Institute for Joint Warfare Analysis, Monterey, 1997.

Fitzgerald, Mary C.: *The new revolution in Russian military affairs*, London, Royal United Services Institute for Defence Studies, 1994.

Friedman, G.: *The Future of War: Power, Technology and American World Dominance in the 21st Century*, N.Y., Random House, 1996.

Gray, C.H.: *Postmodern War: The New Politics of Conflict*, N.Y., The Guilford Press, 1997.

Gray, Colin S.: *The American revolution in military affairs : an interim assessment*, Camberley, Eng., Strategic and Combat Studies Institute, 1997.

Holsti, K.: *The State, War, and the State of War*, Cambridge, Cambridge Univ. Press, 1996.

Huntington, S.P.: *The Soldier and the State*, N.Y., Vintage Books, 1964.

Jablonsky, David: *The owl of Minerva flies at twilight : doctrinal change and continuity and the revolution in military affairs*, Carlisle Barracks, US Army War College, 1994.

Janowitz, M.: *The Professional Soldier: A Social and Political Portrait*, N.Y., The Free Press, 1960.

Kipp, Jacob W.: *The Russian military and the revolution in military affairs : a case of the oracle of Delphi or Cassandra?*, Fort Leavenworth, U.S. Army Foreign Military Studies Office, 1995.

Luttwak, E.N.: *Strategy: The Logic of War and Peace*, Cambridge, 1987, Harvard Univ. Press.

McInnes, Colin: *Hot war, Cold War: the British Army's way in warfare 1945-95*, London, Brassey's, 1996.

Metz, Steven and James Kievit: *The revolution in military affairs and conflict short of war*, Carlisle Barracks, U.S. Army War College, 1994.

Metz, Steven: *Armed Conflict in the 21st Century: The information revolution and Post-Modern Warfare*, Carlisle Barracks, Strategic Studies Institute, 2000.

Morton, D.: *A Military History of Canada*, Edmonton, 1985, Hurtig Publishers.

Murray, W.: *The Making of Strategy*, Cambridge, 1994, Cambridge Univ. Press.

O'Connell, Robert L.: *Of Arms and men: a history of war, weapons, and aggression*, New York, Oxford University Press, 1989.

Posen, B.R.: *The Sources of Military Doctrine,* Ithaca, 1984, Cornell Univ. Press.

Rodal, B.: *The Somalia Experience in Strategic Perspective,* Ottawa, 1997, Minister of Public Works.

Rosen, Stephen Peter: *Winning the next war : innovation and the modern military*, Ithaca, Cornell University Press, 1991.

Roseneau, J.: *Along The Domestic-Foreign Frontier,* Cambridge, 1997, Cambridge Univ Press.

Ruggie, J.G.: *Winning the Peace,* N.Y., 1996, Columbia Univ. Press.

Schneider, Barry and Lawrance Grinter: *Battlefield of the future : 21st century warfare issues*, Maxwell AFB, U.S. Air War College, 1995.

Simpkin, Richard E.: *Race to the swift: thoughts on twenty-first century warfare*, London, Brassey's Defence, 1986.

Sloan, Elinor C.: *The Revolution in Military Affairs : implications for Canada and NATO*, Montreal : McGill-Queen's University Press, 2002.

Sloan, Elinor C.: *The United States and the revolution in military affairs*, Ottawa, Directorate of Strategic Analysis, Dept. of National Defence, 1998.

Stanley, G.F.G.: *Canada's Soldiers,* Toronto, 1960, MacMillan Co. Ltd.

Tilford, Earl H.: *The Revolution in Military Affairs: prospects and cautions*, Carlisle Barracks, Strategic Studies Institute, 1995.

Van Creveld, M.: *Technology and War,* N.Y., 1991, The Free Press.

INDEX

A

B

C

D

□□□